SACRED SPACE

The Prayer Book 2019

from the website www.sacredspace.ie

Prayer from the Irish Jesuits

Messenger Publications,
37 Lower Leeson Street, Dublin D02 W938
www.messenger.ie

Published under arrangement with Loyola Press, Chicago, IL, USA.

Cover art credit: Liam O'Connell SJ

Printed by Hussar Books

ISBN: 978 1 788120 050

18 19 20 21 22 Versa 10 9 8 7 6 5 4 3 2 1

Contents

Sacred Space Prayer

Bless all who worship you, almighty God,
from the rising of the sun to its setting:
from your goodness enrich us,
by your love inspire us,
by your Spirit guide us,
by your power protect us,
in your mercy receive us,
now and always.

Preface

In 1999 an Irish Jesuit named Alan McGuckian had the simple—but at the time radical—idea of bringing daily prayer to the Internet. No one imagined that his experimental project would grow into a global community with volunteers translating the prayer experience into seventeen different languages.

Millions of people, from numerous Christian traditions, visit www.sacredspace.ie each year, and what they find is an invitation to step away from their busy routines for a few minutes each day to concentrate on what is really important in their lives. Sacred Space offers its visitors the opportunity to grow in prayerful awareness of their friendship with God.

Besides the daily prayer experience, Sacred Space also offers Living Space, with commentaries on the Scripture readings for each day's Catholic Mass. The Chapel of Intentions allows people to add their own prayers, while Pray with the Pope joins the community to the international Apostleship of Prayer. In addition, Sacred Space provides Lenten and Advent retreats, often in partnership with Pray as You Go, an audio prayer service from the British Jesuits.

The contents of this printed edition, first produced in 2004, are taken directly from our Internet site. Despite the increased use of Sacred Space on mobile devices, many people want a book they can hold and carry, and this book has proven especially helpful for prayer groups.

In 2014 the Irish Jesuits entered into an apostolic agreement with the Chicago-Detroit Jesuits, and Sacred Space now operates in partnership with Loyola Press.

I am delighted to bring you the *Sacred Space* book, and I pray that your prayer life will flourish with its help.

Yours in Christ,

Paul Brian Campbell, SJ

Introduction to *Sacred Space*, 2019

Saint Ignatius of Loyola, founder of the Society of Jesus, is famously known for wanting to find God in all things. *Is that even possible?* you might ask. He believed it was, but only as a gift from God and only as the fruit of our paying attention to our experience. Ignatius developed an optimistic spiritual practice that assumed the presence of God at every moment of our existence. While we tend to think of God's presence as a "sometimes thing," Ignatius came to believe that our perception of God's presence as a sometimes occurrence is a major spiritual hindrance. Ignatius believed that God is always creating this universe, always keeping it in existence, always working to bring about God's purpose in creation, and always trying to move us to join God in the great adventure of bringing about what Jesus called the kingdom of God.

In order to experience this ever-present God, we need to develop a regular spiritual practice, a practice Ignatius had learned from his experience as a relatively untutored layman. Ignatius began to teach people and to write down the spiritual practices that helped him move toward uniting himself with God's purposes and thus toward finding God in all things. *Spiritual Exercises* is Ignatius's manual for those who want to follow his example of helping others get in touch with our ever-present God. God wants a close personal relationship with each of us, and he wants each of us to join him in the great work of bringing about a world where peace and justice prevail. Over the almost five centuries since the time of Ignatius, Jesuits and many others have found through these spiritual practices the answer to their own deepest desires.

Over the centuries, the Spiritual Exercises have been adapted in many ways. Jesuits originally followed Ignatius's own practice of giving the Exercises to individuals for thirty days. But they also used the methods of prayer suggested in the Exercises in their preaching, missions, and talks to larger groups. Eventually, houses were set aside for the giving of the Exercises to individuals and large groups. One of the adaptations suggested by Ignatius himself was to make the Exercises in daily life under the direction of someone trained in giving them. In this format, an individual maintained his or her regular daily life and work but promised to devote time every day to the spiritual practices suggested by Ignatius and to see the spiritual director once a week. In the past fifty years, this adaptation has seen a worldwide resurgence and has touched many lives. It has also been used with groups to great advantage. In modern times, the giving of the Spiritual Exercises has become something of a cottage industry in many countries.

Enter the age of the Internet. Could this new tool be used to help large numbers of people move toward finding God in all things? The answer is a resounding *yes*! Many websites, in multiple languages, try to help people become more aware of God's presence in their lives, using practices stemming from the Spiritual Exercises. One example is the book you have in your hands. In 1999 the Irish Jesuits began offering daily prompts for prayer based on Ignatius's Exercises on the website Sacred Space (www.sacredspace.ie). The English edition was soon translated into other languages, and the site now features twenty-one languages that span the globe.

In my work as a spiritual director and in my travels, I have come across many, many people from various walks of life who use the daily prompts for prayer provided through Sacred Space. People find the site and the daily suggestions to be user-friendly, inviting, and—in keeping with Ignatian spirituality—optimistic. The suggestions help them pay attention to their experience, notice intimations of God's presence in that experience, and engage in honest conversations with God.

For each week, there is an overarching suggested theme and a method for spending time with God every day. One of the methods is to turn to the Scripture and reflections suggested for each day of the week. Each day's text is taken from the Gospel reading for Mass that day. Thus, someone who follows Sacred Space every day will, in the course of a year, work prayerfully through all four Gospels. No wonder that so many have been enthralled by this site!

In spite of the digital age, many of us still like the feel of a book in our hands. The book *Sacred Space*, which you now hold in your hands, was designed for the likes of us. I am very happy to introduce the book and even happier that Loyola Press, a Jesuit institution, is now the publisher. Ignatian spiritual practice has brought me closer to God, for which I am immensely grateful. Through Ignatius's spiritual practices I have experienced God's desire for my friendship, and I figure, if God wants *my* friendship, he wants *everyone's* friendship. If you take this book seriously and engage in the relationship with God that it suggests, you will, I'm sure, find as much joy in God's friendship as I have. Try it—you'll like it.

William A. Barry, SJ

How to Use This Book

During each week of the Liturgical year, begin by reading the section entitled "Something to think and pray about each day this week." Then proceed through "The Presence of God," "Freedom," and "Consciousness" steps to prepare yourself to hear the word of God in your heart. In the next step, "The Word," turn to the Scripture reading for each day of the week. Inspiration points are provided in case you need them. Then return to the "Conversation" and "Conclusion" steps. Use this process every day of the year.

December 2—December 8, 2018

Something to think and pray about each day this week:

What is a hero? A hero is a person who takes action to help people. That is what the Holy Spirit calls us to do. When the Spirit descended on Mary after the angel Gabriel told her she was to be the mother of Jesus, what did she do? She took action. She packed her things and journeyed to her cousin Elizabeth. To do what? To serve her. When the Holy Spirit descended on Jesus after his baptism by John, what did he do? He took action and did what? He began his ministry and began serving. When the Spirit descended on the apostles at Pentecost, what did they do? They relinquished fear and began serving the people. Not just one group of people but all people, of all nations.

We too are called to serve, to not be afraid. With the Holy Spirit already dwelling in us, there is no time to waste. We need to take action now and assist those around us, whether it's a family member, a friend, a coworker, a stranger on the street, our environment, our nation, or our world.

—Gary Jansen, *The 15-Minute Prayer Solution*

The Presence of God

As I sit here, the beating of my heart,
the ebb and flow of my breathing, the movements of my mind
are all signs of God's ongoing creation of me.
I pause for a moment and become aware
of this presence of God within me.

Freedom

Everything has the potential to draw from me a fuller love and life.
Yet my desires are often fixed, caught, on illusions of fulfillment.
I ask that God, through my freedom, may orchestrate my desires in a vibrant, loving melody rich in harmony.

Consciousness

I ask, how am I within myself today? Am I particularly tired, stressed, or off-form? If any of these characteristics apply, can I try to let go of the concerns that disturb me?

The Word

I read the word of God slowly, a few times over, and I listen to what God is saying to me. (Please turn to the Scripture on the following pages. Inspiration points are there, should you need them. When you are ready, return here to continue.)

Conversation

I begin to talk with Jesus about the Scripture I have just read. What part of it strikes a chord in me? Perhaps the words of a friend or a story I have heard recently will slowly rise to the surface of my consciousness. If so, does the story throw light on what the Scripture passage may be trying to say to me?

Conclusion

Glory be to the Father, and to the Son, and to the Holy Spirit,
As it was in the beginning, is now and ever shall be,
World without end. Amen.

Sunday 2nd December
First Sunday of Advent
Luke 21:25–28, 34–36

"There will be signs in the sun, the moon, and the stars, and on the earth distress among nations confused by the roaring of the sea and the waves. People will faint from fear and foreboding of what is coming upon the world, for the powers of the heavens will be shaken. Then they will see 'the Son of man coming in a cloud' with power and great glory. Now when these things begin to take place, stand up and raise your heads, because your redemption is drawing near. Be on guard that your hearts are not weighed down with dissipation and drunkenness and the worries of this life, and that day does not catch you unexpectedly, like a trap. For it will come upon all who live on the face of the whole earth. Be alert at all times, praying that you may have the strength to escape all these things that will take place, and to stand before the Son of man."

- Jesus is using traditional Jewish symbolism to describe what will happen when God's final judgment occurs. He says that people will see "the Son of Man coming in a cloud." The cloud is a symbol for God's presence. Jesus' message bursts with hope and confidence because, unlike those who have reason to fear his coming, Jesus' followers will be able to hold their heads high because their liberation is at hand.

- Jesus urges me to be on guard so that my heart is not weighed down by the worries of life. What are the worries and cares of life that weigh me down today? As I prepare for a conversation with Jesus, can I bring my worries and cares to him in prayer?

Monday 3rd December
Matthew 8:5–11

When [Jesus] entered Capernaum, a centurion came to him, appealing to him and saying, "Lord, my servant is lying at home paralyzed, in terrible distress." And he said to him, "I will come and cure him." The centurion answered, "Lord, I am not worthy to have you come under my roof; but only speak the word, and my servant will be healed. For I also am a man under authority, with soldiers under me; and I say to one, 'Go,' and he goes, and to another, 'Come,' and he comes, and to my slave, 'Do this,' and the slave does

- Jesus, true discipleship is as strong as the foundation on which it is built. You call me not merely to hear your word but to daily put it into action.

- Lord, when the rains fall and the floods come, threatening to overwhelm my faith in you, keep me firm, keep me rooted in you, my rock!

Friday 7th December
Matthew 9:27–31

As Jesus went on from there, two blind men followed him, crying loudly, "Have mercy on us, Son of David." When he entered the house, the blind men came to him; and Jesus said to them, "Do you believe that I am able to do this?" They said to him, "Yes, Lord." Then he touched their eyes and said, "According to your faith let it be done to you." And their eyes were opened. Then Jesus sternly ordered them, "See that no one knows of this." But they went away and spread the news about him throughout that district.

- The blind men follow you with persistence. They have one need, one prayer: "Have mercy on us."

- I too cry out to you for sight and insight. As I receive your healing touch of merciful love today, may I become an instrument of your mercy to all I encounter.

Saturday 8th December
The Immaculate Conception of the
Blessed Virgin Mary
Luke 1:26–38

In the sixth month the angel Gabriel was sent by God to a town in Galilee called Nazareth, to a virgin engaged to a man whose name was Joseph, of the house of David. The virgin's name was Mary. And he came to her and said, "Greetings, favored one! The Lord is with you." But she was much perplexed by his words and pondered what sort of greeting this might be. The angel said to her, "Do not be afraid, Mary, for you have found favor with God. And now, you will conceive in your womb and bear a son, and you will name him Jesus. He will be great, and will be called the Son of the Most High, and the Lord God will give to him the throne of his ancestor David. He will reign over the house of Jacob forever, and of his kingdom there will be no end." Mary said to the angel, "How can this be, since I am a virgin?"

The angel said to her, "The Holy Spirit will come upon you, and the power of the Most High will overshadow you; therefore the child to be born will be holy; he will be called Son of God. And now, your relative Elizabeth in her old age has also conceived a son; and this is the sixth month for her who was said to be barren. For nothing will be impossible with God." Then Mary said, "Here am I, the servant of the Lord; let it be with me according to your word." Then the angel departed from her.

• Years later, those surprised by the miracles of Jesus could only utter: "We have seen strange things today" (Luke 5:26). But for mother-to-be Mary, the news that the power of the Most High would cover her with its shadow was absolutely groundbreaking.

• Lord, may I grow each day in trusting your amazing annunciation to me: "You are my highly favoured one." I am not to be afraid. You rejoice in me! In the busyness of life, keep these thoughts before me. Like Mary, may I be ready to play my part in bringing you to birth.

December 9—December 15, 2018

Something to think and pray about each day this week:

Through concrete action, Jesus shows us how God loves. In the Gospels we see Jesus showing us how God loves through healing, forgiveness, mercy, and compassion. Jesus sees and responds to the deepest needs of human hearts. To a blind person he gives sight; to a paralyzed person he gives the ability to stand up and walk; to a leper and social outcast he gives cleansing and restoration to community; to a woman isolated by her illness he gives healing in both body and soul; to a person with a sinful history he gives mercy and hope for a better future.

Jesus shows us how God looks at us with eyes of compassion and love, accepting us where we are and loving us as we are. Jesus doesn't wait for people to be perfect or have their lives in order or for them to sin no more. Rather, Jesus enters the messiness of humanity and encounters people along the way in their brokenness, hurt, and mess.

—Becky Eldredge, *Busy Lives & Restless Souls*

The Presence of God

"Be still and know that I am God." Lord, your words lead us to the calmness and greatness of your presence.

Freedom

I am free. When I look at these words in writing, they seem to create in me a feeling of awe. Yes, a wonderful feeling of freedom. Thank you, God.

Consciousness

At this moment, Lord, I turn my thoughts to you.
I will leave aside my chores and preoccupations.
I will take rest and refreshment in your presence, Lord.

The Word

The word of God comes down to us through the Scriptures. May the Holy Spirit enlighten my mind and my heart to respond to the gospel teachings. (Please turn to the Scripture on the following pages. Inspiration points are there, should you need them. When you are ready, return here to continue.)

Conversation

Begin to talk with Jesus about the Scripture you have just read. What part of it strikes a chord in you? Perhaps the words of a friend—or some story you have heard recently—will slowly rise to the surface of your consciousness. If so, does the story throw light on what the Scripture passage may be trying to say to you?

Conclusion

Glory be to the Father, and to the Son, and to the Holy Spirit,
As it was in the beginning, is now and ever shall be,
World without end. Amen.

Sunday 9th December
Second Sunday of Advent
Luke 3:1–6

In the fifteenth year of the reign of Emperor Tiberius, when Pontius Pilate was governor of Judea, and Herod was ruler of Galilee, and his brother Philip ruler of the region of Ituraea and Trachonitis, and Lysanias ruler of Abilene, during the high priesthood of Annas and Caiaphas, the word of God came to John son of Zechariah in the wilderness. He went into all the region around the Jordan, proclaiming a baptism of repentance for the forgiveness of sins, as it is written in the book of the words of the prophet Isaiah,
"The voice of one crying out in the wilderness:

'Prepare the way of the Lord,
    make his paths straight.
Every valley shall be filled,
    and every mountain and hill shall be made low,
and the crooked shall be made straight,
    and the rough ways made smooth;
and all flesh shall see the salvation of God.'"

* John, the cousin of Jesus, is a challenging figure. He, the messenger of God, is the sharpened arrow whose words pierce to the heart's core. Some people listened to his uncompromising message and changed the direction of their lives. But others resisted.

* Lord, this Advent, give me a welcoming heart. Help me be open to the messengers of your word, especially to those whom, at first glance, I might resist, for they are your prophets today. They urge me to change my way of thinking and living.

Monday 10th December
Luke 5:17–26

One day, while he was teaching, Pharisees and teachers of the law were sitting near by (they had come from every village of Galilee and Judea and from Jerusalem); and the power of the Lord was with him to heal. Just then some men came, carrying a paralyzed man on a bed. They were trying to bring him in and lay him before Jesus; but finding no way to bring him in because of the crowd, they went up on the roof and let him down with his bed through the tiles into the middle of the crowd in front of Jesus. When he saw their faith, he said, "Friend, your sins are forgiven you." Then the scribes and the Pharisees began to question, "Who is this who is speaking blasphemies? Who can forgive sins but God alone?" When Jesus perceived their questionings, he answered them, "Why do you raise such questions in your hearts? Which is easier, to say, 'Your sins are forgiven you,' or to say, 'Stand up and walk'? But so that you may know that the Son of Man has authority on earth to forgive sins"—he said to the one who was paralyzed—"I say to you, stand up and take your bed and go to your home." Immediately he stood up before them, took what he had been lying on, and went to his home, glorifying God. Amazement seized all of them, and they glorified God and were filled with awe, saying, "We have seen strange things today."

- The lame will leap like deer, and the tongues of the dumb will sing for joy, prophesied Isaiah. Nature itself will be renewed, with water gushing in the desert. No less will the people be joyful of heart; the whole world is poised for a makeover.

- "We have seen strange things today," said the onlookers. May Advent renew in me the wonder of the first coming of the Savior. Am I open to seeing the world as strange because Jesus has come?

Tuesday 11th December
Matthew 18:12–14

"What do you think? If a man has a hundred sheep, and one of them has gone astray, does he not leave the ninety-nine on the mountains and go in search of the one that went astray? And if he finds it, truly I tell you, he rejoices over it more than over the ninety-nine that never went astray. So it is not the will of your Father in heaven that one of these little ones should be lost."

- The savior/shepherd king lives compassion and mercy. Not one of the persons in his care is a mere statistic—the shepherd's heart is wrung and totally preoccupied if even one individual goes missing. He is the shepherd who will not rest until he has found the stray.

- But he is also a shepherd with resources of strength and power. When I feel lost or that I've gone astray, may I remember that God loves me with compassion and mercy—but also with strength and power.

Wednesday 12th December
Luke 1:39–47

In those days Mary set out and went with haste to a Judean town in the hill country, where she entered the house of Zechariah and greeted Elizabeth. When Elizabeth heard Mary's greeting, the child leapt in her womb. And Elizabeth was filled with the Holy Spirit and exclaimed with a loud cry, "Blessed are you among women, and blessed is the fruit of your womb. And why has this happened to me, that the mother of my Lord comes to me? For as soon as I heard the sound of your greeting, the child in my womb leapt for joy. And blessed is she who believed that there would be a fulfillment of what was spoken to her by the Lord." And Mary said,

"My soul magnifies the Lord,
    and my spirit rejoices in God my Savior."

- Jesus, the child that Mary is carrying, is recognized by the child in Elizabeth's womb; John leaps in recognition of the one both mothers revere as "Lord," John himself being of miraculous origin from an elderly mother.

- When two people meet who have said yes to God in their lives, like Mary and her cousin Elizabeth in today's Scripture, the new life of God that is growing in one woman leaps for joy in recognition of the life of God growing in another. It is God in one greeting God in the other.

Thursday 13th December
Matthew 11:11–15

[Jesus said,] "Truly I tell you, among those born of women no one has arisen greater than John the Baptist; yet the least in the kingdom of heaven is greater than he. From the days of John the Baptist until now the kingdom of heaven has suffered violence, and the violent take it by force. For all the prophets and the law prophesied until John came; and if you are willing to accept it, he is Elijah who is to come. Let anyone with ears listen!"

- The people were looking for Elijah; Jesus says, "John is Elijah—pay attention!" Have I been looking for an answer or a blessing that has already arrived?
- "The kingdom of heaven has suffered violence." How does the kingdom suffer today? Where do I see the kingdom of heaven, and how do I participate in it?

Friday 14th December

Matthew 11:16–19

[Jesus spoke to the crowds,] "But to what will I compare this generation? It is like children sitting in the marketplaces and calling to one another,

> 'We played the flute for you, and you did not
> dance;
> we wailed, and you did not mourn.'

For John came neither eating nor drinking, and they say, 'He has a demon'; the Son of Man came eating and drinking, and they say, 'Look, a glutton and a drunkard, a friend of tax collectors and sinners!' Yet wisdom is vindicated by her deeds."

- What was on offer from the Lord had always been happiness deep as a river, children and descendants without number. But what the people chose to do was sulk. To Jesus, their objection was the company that he ate and drank with; to John, their objection had been that he neither ate nor drank but fasted.
- Lord, I recognize something of my own response to people here. I am not always open to listening and accepting those who are different. I can so easily judge, dismiss, and reject people. I need your help today.

Saturday 15th December

Matthew 17:9a, 10–13

As they were coming down the mountain, Jesus ordered them, "Tell no one about the vision until after the Son of Man has been raised from the dead." And the disciples asked him, "Why, then, do the scribes say that Elijah must come first?" He replied, "Elijah is indeed coming and will restore all things; but I tell you that Elijah has already come, and they did not recognize him, but they did to him whatever they pleased. So also the Son of Man is about to suffer at their hands." Then the disciples understood that he was speaking to them about John the Baptist.

- Shortly before this scene, Jesus' disciples saw Jesus transfigured in glory and flanked by Moses and Elijah. They ask Jesus for confirmation regarding the role of Elijah as forerunner of the end times. Jesus' reply was unexpected in more ways than one: the real forerunner is John the Baptist, who has been treated badly. This will also be Jesus' fate.

- The coming of Jesus was meant to bring about the kingdom of God on earth with the offer of salvation for all; but the people struck out against the bearer of the message. What is my response today, when I consider God's welcome to all people?

Third Week of Advent
December 16—December 22, 2018

Something to think and pray about each day this week:

Transition is the bridge that leads from the no longer to the not yet. Nobody can predict what that bridge is going to look like. It may be obvious and sturdy, and we may find it easily through the fogs of our bewilderment. Or it may be rickety and clearly unsafe, and we hardly dare entrust our weight to it. . . . The point is, however, that we have to cross the bridge, and as we risk that crossing, we will discover that the bridge itself is our guide and mentor, and it has everything to teach us about the path that lies ahead, beyond the transition. In fact, we will learn much more on that bridge, about ourselves, about life, and about God, in our transitions than on all the smoother pathways that we journey.

—Margaret Silf, *The Other Side of Chaos*

The Presence of God

"Come to me, all you who are weary and are carrying heavy burdens, and I will give you rest." Here I am, Lord. I come to seek your presence. I long for your healing power.

Freedom

"In these days, God taught me as a schoolteacher teaches a pupil" (Saint Ignatius).

I remind myself that there are things God has to teach me yet, and I ask for the grace to hear those things and let them change me.

Consciousness

Help me, Lord, to be more conscious of your presence. Teach me to recognize your presence in others.

Fill my heart with gratitude for the times your love has been shown to me through the care of others.

The Word

God speaks to each of us individually. I listen attentively to hear what he is saying to me. Read the text a few times; then listen. (Please turn to the Scripture on the following pages. Inspiration points are there, should you need them. When you are ready, return here to continue.)

Conversation

Conversation requires talking and listening.

As I talk to Jesus, may I also learn to be still and listen.

I picture the gentleness in his eyes and the smile full of love as he gazes on me.

I can be totally honest with Jesus as I tell him of my worries and my cares.

I will open my heart to him as I tell him of my fears and my doubts.

I will ask him to help me place myself fully in his care and to abandon myself to him, knowing that he always wants what is best for me.

Conclusion

I thank God for these moments we have spent together and for any insights I have been given concerning the text.

Sunday 16th December
Third Sunday of Advent
Luke 3:10–18

And the crowds asked him, "What then should we do?" In reply he said to them, "Whoever has two coats must share with anyone who has none; and whoever has food must do likewise." Even tax collectors came to be baptized, and they asked him, "Teacher, what should we do?" He said to them, "Collect no more than the amount prescribed for you." Soldiers also asked him, "And we, what should we do?" He said to them, "Do not extort money from anyone by threats or false accusation, and be satisfied with your wages." As the people were filled with expectation, and all were questioning in their hearts concerning John, whether he might be the Messiah, John answered all of them by saying, "I baptize you with water; but one who is more powerful than I is coming; I am not worthy to untie the thong of his sandals. He will baptize you with the Holy Spirit and fire. His winnowing fork is in his hand, to clear his threshing floor and to gather the wheat into his granary; but the chaff he will burn with unquenchable fire." So, with many other exhortations, he proclaimed the good news to the people.

- John proclaimed good news to the people, but he did it "with many other exhortations." We participate in the good news by living as God's people. Might I consider this today—that I can be part of the good news for others?

- The "people were filled with expectation." They knew that something worthwhile was coming. Do I go through a typical day expecting God to act—and expecting the Holy Spirit to show me what to do?

Monday 17th December
Matthew 1:1–17

An account of the genealogy of Jesus the Messiah, the son of David, the son of Abraham. Abraham was the father of Isaac, and Isaac the father of Jacob, and Jacob the father of Judah and his brothers, and Judah the father of Perez and Zerah by Tamar, and Perez the father of Hezron, and Hezron the father of Aram, and Aram the father of Aminadab, and Aminadab the father of Nahshon, and Nahshon the father of Salmon, and Salmon the father of Boaz by Rahab, and Boaz the father of Obed by Ruth, and Obed the father of Jesse, and Jesse the father of King David. And David was the father of Solomon by the wife of Uriah, and Solomon the father of Rehoboam, and Rehoboam the father of Abijah, and Abijah the father of Asaph, and Asaph the father of Jehoshaphat, and Jehoshaphat the father of Joram, and Joram the father of Uzziah, and Uzziah the father of Jotham, and Jotham the father of Ahaz, and Ahaz the father of Hezekiah, and Hezekiah the father of Manasseh, and Manasseh the father of Amos, and Amos the father of Josiah, and Josiah the father of Jechoniah and his brothers, at the time of the deportation to Babylon. And after the deportation to Babylon: Jechoniah was the father of Salathiel, and Salathiel the father of Zerubbabel, and Zerubbabel the father of Abiud, and Abiud the father of Eliakim, and Eliakim the father of Azor, and Azor the father of Zadok, and Zadok the father of Achim, and Achim the father of Eliud, and Eliud the father of Eleazar, and Eleazar the father of Matthan, and Matthan the father of Jacob, and Jacob the father of Joseph the husband of Mary, of whom Jesus was born, who is called the Messiah. So all the generations from Abraham to David are fourteen generations, and from David to the deportation to Babylon, fourteen generations; and from the deportation to Babylon to the Messiah, fourteen generations.

- This Gospel weaves the threads of the long history that eventually brings us to Jesus. His family tree is a mix of holy and unholy figures, public sinners and outcasts. Yet each played an important role, and no one's life was insignificant to God's plan. Jesus does own his family story. He does not airbrush out any one of his ancestors. Do I?

- Lord, I thank you for all who have been a carrier of your grace to me. Let not my limitations and inadequacy impede me from believing that I am important. Let me play my part in being a carrier of your love to the world.

Tuesday 18th December
Matthew 1:18–25

Now the birth of Jesus the Messiah took place in this way. When his mother Mary had been engaged to Joseph, but before they lived together, she was found to be with child from the Holy Spirit. Her husband Joseph, being a righteous man and unwilling to expose her to public disgrace, planned to dismiss her quietly. But just when he had resolved to do this, an angel of the Lord appeared to him in a dream and said, "Joseph, son of David, do not be afraid to take Mary as your wife, for the child conceived in her is from the Holy Spirit. She will bear a son, and you are to name him Jesus, for he will save his people from their sins." All this took place to fulfill what had been spoken by the Lord through the prophet:

"Look, the virgin shall conceive and bear a son,
    and they shall name him Emmanuel,"

which means, "God is with us." When Joseph awoke from sleep, he did as the angel of the Lord commanded him; he took her as his wife, but had no marital relations with her until she had borne a son; and he named him Jesus.

- His coming is nothing less than the inauguration of a whole new (although promised) "heaven and earth"-shaking epoch in the relationship between God and his people. Forgiveness of sin comes into the picture, so right away the child is accorded divine prerogative as Savior. The child's title, Emmanuel (God-with-us) designates him as the fulfillment of the promise: "I will be your God and you will be my people." His will be a leadership presence among his people.
- All these beautiful graces come together for me as I prepare to revere the newborn child.

Wednesday 19th December
Luke 1:5–25

In the days of King Herod of Judea, there was a priest named Zechariah, who belonged to the priestly order of Abijah. His wife was a descendant of Aaron, and her name was Elizabeth. Both of them were righteous before God, living blamelessly according to all the commandments and regulations of the Lord. But they had no children, because Elizabeth was barren, and both were getting on in years. Once when he was serving as priest before God and his section was on duty, he was chosen by lot, according to the custom of the priesthood, to enter the sanctuary of the Lord and offer incense. Now at the time of the incense offering, the whole assembly of the people was praying outside. Then there appeared to him an angel of the Lord, standing at the right side of the altar of incense. When Zechariah saw him, he was terrified; and fear overwhelmed him. But the angel said to him, "Do not be afraid, Zechariah, for your prayer has been heard. Your wife Elizabeth will bear you a son, and you will name him John. You will have joy and gladness, and many will rejoice at his birth, for he will be great in the sight of the Lord. He must never drink wine or strong drink; even before his birth he will be filled with the Holy Spirit. He will turn many of the people of Israel to the Lord their God. With the spirit and power of Elijah he will go before him, to turn the hearts of parents to their children, and the disobedient to the wisdom of the righteous, to make ready a people prepared for the Lord." Zechariah said to the angel, "How will I know that this is so? For I am an old man, and my wife is getting on in years." The angel replied, "I am Gabriel. I stand in the presence of God, and I have been sent to speak to you and to bring you this good news. But now, because you did not believe my words, which will be fulfilled in their time, you will become mute, unable to speak, until the day these things occur." Meanwhile the people were waiting for Zechariah, and wondered at his delay in the sanctuary. When he did come out, he could not speak to them, and they realized that he had seen a vision in the sanctuary. He kept motioning to them and remained unable to speak. When his time of service was ended, he went to his home. After those days his wife Elizabeth conceived, and for five months she remained in seclusion. She said, "This is what the Lord has done for me when he looked favorably on me and took away the disgrace I have endured among my people."

- The promised child did finally arrive, but not without some testing of faith, given the couple's stage in life. And Zechariah learned also that the child foretold had already been designed for God's final intervention in the last days of this age: the child was being sent to prepare the way, in a role akin to that expected of the prophet Elijah. Even the name being invoked for the child—"God has shown favor"—spoke of God's intention.

- Elizabeth proclaims that the Lord has taken away her disgrace of being childless. Yet she knows that her story fits into the larger one of God's salvation. How does my life fit into this story?

Thursday 20th December
Luke 1:26–38

In the sixth month the angel Gabriel was sent by God to a town in Galilee called Nazareth, to a virgin engaged to a man whose name was Joseph, of the house of David. The virgin's name was Mary. And he came to her and

said, "Greetings, favored one! The Lord is with you." But she was much perplexed by his words and pondered what sort of greeting this might be. The
angel said to her, "Do not be afraid, Mary, for you have found favor with
God. And now, you will conceive in your womb and bear a son, and you
will name him Jesus. He will be great, and will be called the Son of the Most
High, and the Lord God will give to him the throne of his ancestor David.
He will reign over the house of Jacob forever, and of his kingdom there will
be no end." Mary said to the angel, "How can this be, since I am a virgin?"
The angel said to her, "The Holy Spirit will come upon you, and the power
of the Most High will overshadow you; therefore the child to be born will be
holy; he will be called Son of God. And now, your relative Elizabeth in her
old age has also conceived a son; and this is the sixth month for her who was
said to be barren. For nothing will be impossible with God." Then Mary
said, "Here am I, the servant of the Lord; let it be with me according to your
word." Then the angel departed from her.

- "Greetings, favored one! The Lord is with you." Mary, the young girl of
  no status, from the village of Nazareth, an utterly insignificant place,
  is signaled out, called, chosen, and overshadowed with God's Spirit. A
  unique gift, a "cause of our joy."

- "Do not be afraid": these words are for me, too. There is much to make
  me afraid. But nothing is impossible with God.

Friday 21st December
Luke 1:39–45

In those days Mary set out and went with haste to a Judean town in the hill
country, where she entered the house of Zechariah and greeted Elizabeth.
When Elizabeth heard Mary's greeting, the child leaped in her womb. And
Elizabeth was filled with the Holy Spirit and exclaimed with a loud cry,
"Blessed are you among women, and blessed is the fruit of your womb. And
why has this happened to me, that the mother of my Lord comes to me? For
as soon as I heard the sound of your greeting, the child in my womb leaped
for joy. And blessed is she who believed that there would be a fulfillment of
what was spoken to her by the Lord."

- Mary was a woman of faith. Elizabeth praises her, not because she has
  conceived the Christ but because she believed the angel's words. Let us

pray to her for the strong faith we need in these troubled times. God can do what we think impossible.

- Try to imagine what it meant to Mary to find a companion in Elizabeth, an older relative who has also been blessed miraculously by God. Elizabeth understands the importance of what both of them are going through. Consider if there are any wise women in your life who can encourage your journey with God. Pray for them and thank God for them. And if there is none, ask God to send you an Elizabeth.

Saturday 22nd December
Luke 1:46–56
And Mary said,

"My soul magnifies the Lord,
    and my spirit rejoices in God my Savior,
for he has looked with favor on the lowliness of his
       servant.
    Surely, from now on all generations will call me
       blessed;
for the Mighty One has done great things for me,
    and holy is his name.
His mercy is for those who fear him
    from generation to generation.
He has shown strength with his arm;
    he has scattered the proud in the thoughts of
      their hearts.
He has brought down the powerful from their
      thrones,
    and lifted up the lowly;
he has filled the hungry with good things,
    and sent the rich away empty.
He has helped his servant Israel,
    in remembrance of his mercy,
according to the promise he made to our ancestors,
    to Abraham and to his descendants forever."

And Mary remained with [Elizabeth] about three months and then returned to her home.

- At so many points in their history, the people of Israel were tiny in the face of menacing enemies. And at the very coming of Jesus they seemed to be at the mercy of the occupying Romans. We have the tradition of the Lord stepping in to vindicate or champion his people.

- This note will often be struck in the preaching of Jesus: the humble will be exalted and the exalted will be humbled. May I endure trials with patience, knowing that God's justice and mercy have the last word.

Fourth Week of Advent/Christmas
December 23—December 29, 2018

Something to think and pray about each day this week:

As all parents must, the Lady Mary and Joseph of Nazareth watched their boy begin to make up his mind about what to do with his life. There were cultural pressures, of course, one of them being the question of whether he would marry or not. His cousin John was moving toward the life led by the ancient prophets. Jesus thought seriously about his cousin's way, as his fasting and prayer in the desert suggest. But he was deeply attracted by and attached to the revealed word of God—Jesus cites the Pentateuch, the prophets, and the Psalms a lot—and he came to appreciate his vocation to serve the Father by spreading the Good News among the people. . . .

Mature discernment draws us through the mystery of the universal Savior to encounter Jesus of Nazareth, the carpenter's son. What does his human life show us? To begin with, Jesus discerned the fullness of his vocation only slowly as his life unfolded. In his public life, he gathered seventy-two disciples who were willing to go to others and tell about the Good News. From among them, he chose twelve with whom he worked on "the challenge of finding and sharing a 'mystique' of living together, of mingling and encounter, of embracing and supporting one another."

—Joseph Tetlow, SJ, *Always Discerning*

The Presence of God

"I am standing at the door, knocking," says the Lord. What a wonderful privilege that the Lord of all creation desires to come to me. I welcome his presence.

Freedom

Leave me here freely all alone / In cell where never sunlight shone / should no one ever speak to me. / This golden silence makes me free.

—Part of a poem written by a prisoner at
Dachau concentration camp

Consciousness

How am I really feeling? Lighthearted? Heavyhearted? I may be very much at peace, happy to be here. Equally, I may be frustrated, worried, or angry. I acknowledge how I really am. It is the real me whom the Lord loves.

The Word

I take my time to read the word of God, slowly, a few times, allowing myself to dwell on anything that strikes me. (Please turn to the Scripture on the following pages. Inspiration points are there, should you need them. When you are ready, return here to continue.)

Conversation

Do I notice myself reacting as I pray with the word of God? Do I feel challenged, comforted, angry? Imagining Jesus sitting or standing by me, I speak out my feelings, as one trusted friend to another.

Conclusion

Glory be to the Father, and to the Son, and to the Holy Spirit,
As it was in the beginning, is now and ever shall be,
World without end. Amen.

Sunday 23rd December
Fourth Sunday of Advent
Luke 1:39–45

In those days Mary set out and went with haste to a Judean town in the hill country, where she entered the house of Zechariah and greeted Elizabeth. When Elizabeth heard Mary's greeting, the child leaped in her womb. And Elizabeth was filled with the Holy Spirit and exclaimed with a loud cry, "Blessed are you among women, and blessed is the fruit of your womb. And why has this happened to me, that the mother of my Lord comes to me? For as soon as I heard the sound of your greeting, the child in my womb leaped for joy. And blessed is she who believed that there would be a fulfillment of what was spoken to her by the Lord."

• Two women meet, and each has received special blessing and calling from God. Perhaps this is what drew them together, what made Mary feel an urgency about visiting her cousin. This is but one example of God showing us how his holy will is accomplished not by a single person but in the context of community.

• Have I recently spoken confirmation of another person's gift or role in a good endeavor? Whom have I called "blessed"?

Monday 24th December
Luke 1:67–79

Then his father Zechariah was filled with the Holy Spirit and spoke this prophecy:

"Blessed be the Lord God of Israel,
    for he has looked favorably on his people and
        redeemed them.
He has raised up a mighty savior for us
    in the house of his servant David,
as he spoke through the mouth of his holy prophets
        from of old,
    that we should be saved from our enemies and
        from the hand of all who hate us.
Thus he has shown the mercy promised to our
        ancestors,

and has remembered his holy covenant,
the oath that he swore to our ancestor Abraham,
    to grant us that we, being rescued from the
        hands of our enemies,
might serve him without fear, in holiness and
        righteousness before him all our days.
And you, child, will be called the prophet of the
        Most High;
    for you will go before the Lord to prepare his
        ways,
to give knowledge of salvation to his people
    by the forgiveness of their sins.
By the tender mercy of our God,
    the dawn from on high will break upon us,
to give light to those who sit in darkness and in the
        shadow of death,
    to guide our feet into the way of peace."

- Zechariah, released from his silence, bursts forth in profound praise, proclaiming the activity of God at work in our world's history. The Savior is coming! His own son will act as witness and light-bearer to the lovingkindness and mercy of the Great and Holy One.

- Lord, as I move into Christmas Eve, remind me again of how mercy is the dominant theme in your walk with me. You are forever tender toward me. Help me grow daily in the awareness of your mercy and tenderness, which are constantly at work in my life.

Tuesday 25th December
The Nativity of the Lord (Christmas)
John 1:1–18

In the beginning was the Word, and the Word was with God, and the Word was God. He was in the beginning with God. All things came into being through him, and without him not one thing came into being. What has come into being in him was life, and the life was the light of all people. The light shines in the darkness, and the darkness did not overcome it.

There was a man sent from God, whose name was John. He came as a witness to testify to the light, so that all might believe through him. He himself was not the light, but he came to testify to the light. The true light, which enlightens everyone, was coming into the world.

He was in the world, and the world came into being through him; yet the world did not know him. He came to what was his own, and his own people did not accept him. But to all who received him, who believed in his name, he gave power to become children of God, who were born, not of blood or of the will of the flesh or of the will of man, but of God.

And the Word became flesh and lived among us, and we have seen his glory, the glory as of a father's only son, full of grace and truth. (John testified to him and cried out, "This was he of whom I said, 'He who comes after me ranks ahead of me because he was before me.'") From his fullness we have all received, grace upon grace. The law indeed was given through Moses; grace and truth came through Jesus Christ. No one has ever seen God. It is God the only Son, who is close to the Father's heart, who has made him known.

- It had been said that nobody can look on the face of God and live. But now we can see his glory because, as Scripture assures us, Jesus is the perfect image of the unseen God.

- As I work my way through the Gospel episodes, may the realization remain ever in my mind: looking at the face of Christ, I am looking at the face of God.

Wednesday 26th December
Matthew 10:17–22

Beware of them, for they will hand you over to councils and flog you in their synagogues; and you will be dragged before governors and kings because of me, as a testimony to them and the Gentiles. When they hand you over, do not worry about how you are to speak or what you are to say; for what you are to say will be given to you at that time; for it is not you who speak, but the Spirit of your Father speaking through you. Brother will betray brother to death, and a father his child, and children will rise against parents and have them put to death; and you will be hated by all because of my name. But the one who endures to the end will be saved.

- Often we struggle with the opposition we face when trying to live an honest Christian life, and with the increasing duplicity that seems to surround us. Jesus knows this, yet he still sends us to take the Gospel to this difficult world. But he also promises us his assistance: he asks us not to worry!

- This makes sense only if we are doing it "because of him." We are being his disciples, following him along the path he has already trod. I ask for the grace of fortitude until the end, for myself and for those who suffer for being witnesses to Jesus. I think especially of the Christians in the Middle East.

Thursday 27th December
John 20:1–8

Early on the first day of the week, while it was still dark, Mary Magdalene came to the tomb and saw that the stone had been removed from the tomb. So she ran and went to Simon Peter and the other disciple, the one whom Jesus loved, and said to them, "They have taken the Lord out of the tomb, and we do not know where they have laid him." Then Peter and the other disciple set out and went towards the tomb. The two were running together, but the other disciple outran Peter and reached the tomb first. He bent down to look in and saw the linen wrappings lying there, but he did not go in. Then Simon Peter came, following him, and went into the tomb. He saw the linen wrappings lying there, and the cloth that had been on Jesus' head, not lying with the linen wrappings but rolled up in a place by itself. Then the other disciple, who reached the tomb first, also went in, and he saw and believed.

- As described by Benedict XVI, "The Resurrection was like an explosion of light," a "cosmic event" linking heaven and earth. But above all, it was "an explosion of love." "It ushered in a new dimension of being, . . . through which a new world emerges." It is a "leap in the history of 'evolution' and of life in general towards a new future life, towards a new world which, starting from Christ, already continuously permeates this world of ours, transforms it and draws it to itself." The Resurrection unites us with God and others. "If we live in this way, we transform the world."

- "We proclaim the Resurrection of Christ," says Pope Francis, "when his light illuminates the dark moments of our life and we can share that with others: when we know how to smile with those who smile and weep with those who weep; when we walk beside those who are sad and in danger of losing hope; when we recount our experience of faith with those who are searching for meaning and happiness. With our attitude, with our witness, with our life, we say: Jesus is risen! Let us say it with all our soul."

Friday 28th December
Matthew 2:13–18

Now after they had left, an angel of the Lord appeared to Joseph in a dream and said, "Get up, take the child and his mother, and flee to Egypt, and remain there until I tell you; for Herod is about to search for the child, to destroy him." Then Joseph got up, took the child and his mother by night, and went to Egypt, and remained there until the death of Herod. This was to fulfill what had been spoken by the Lord through the prophet, "Out of Egypt I have called my son."

When Herod saw that he had been tricked by the wise men, he was infuriated, and he sent and killed all the children in and around Bethlehem who were two years old or under, according to the time that he had learned from the wise men. Then was fulfilled what had been spoken through the prophet Jeremiah:

"A voice was heard in Ramah,
    wailing and loud lamentation,
Rachel weeping for her children;
    she refused to be consoled, because they are no more."

- Starting with the scene of the holy family forced to flee into Egypt, I reflect in my prayer on the Jewish people once finding themselves in captivity in Egypt, and on their eventual release being withheld by Pharaoh until first the blood of a child flowed in every house of his own population.

- The road to the fullness of freedom (for the people in the Promised Land) had tragic turns—as the road before him was to have for Jesus himself; as in one way or another, the road before each of us will always have.

Saturday 29th December

Luke 2:22–35

When the time came for their purification according to the law of Moses, they brought him up to Jerusalem to present him to the Lord (as it is written in the law of the Lord, "Every firstborn male shall be designated as holy to the Lord"), and they offered a sacrifice according to what is stated in the law of the Lord, "a pair of turtledoves or two young pigeons."

Now there was a man in Jerusalem whose name was Simeon; this man was righteous and devout, looking forward to the consolation of Israel, and the Holy Spirit rested on him. It had been revealed to him by the Holy Spirit that he would not see death before he had seen the Lord's Messiah. Guided by the Spirit, Simeon came into the temple; and when the parents brought in the child Jesus, to do for him what was customary under the law, Simeon took him in his arms and praised God, saying,

"Master, now you are dismissing your servant in peace,
    according to your word;
for my eyes have seen your salvation,
    which you have prepared in the presence of all peoples,
a light for revelation to the Gentiles
    and for glory to your people Israel."

And the child's father and mother were amazed at what was being said about him. Then Simeon blessed them and said to his mother Mary, "This child is destined for the falling and the rising of many in Israel, and to be a sign that will be opposed so that the inner thoughts of many will be revealed—and a sword will pierce your own soul too."

- That spirit of God who all along (according to Simeon) was master of events has finally in our own day been sent even more directly into the world by the ascended Jesus.

- Lord, may your Holy Spirit rest on me today. Like Simeon, may I too recognize that you have come in the form of a vulnerable child.

December 30, 2018—January 5, 2019

Something to think and pray about each day this week:

Last year during our Advent Lessons, Lights, and Carols service, the priest read the genealogy of Christ. You'd think a list of forty-one names would make for a pretty dull liturgy, but for me it was the highpoint. He read it in sections. At regular intervals, between prayers and songs, there'd come a timpani roll from the choir loft, and then a few generations of names, each one pronounced gravely, as if recognizing a death. It felt like that, like a funeral for everyone. And it would have felt hopeless, but at some point the last drum roll came, and with it the sudden, shocking appearance not of yet another who would die and be gone but of Jesus who is called the Christ.

—Amy Andrews, *2017: A Book of Grace-Filled Days*

The Presence of God

"Be still, and know that I am God!" Lord, may your spirit guide me to seek your loving presence more and more, for it is there I find rest and refreshment from this busy world.

Freedom

By God's grace I was born to live in freedom. Free to enjoy the pleasures he created for me. Dear Lord, grant that I may live as you intended, with complete confidence in your loving care.

Consciousness

How am I today?
Where am I with God? With others?
Do I have something to be grateful for? Then I give thanks.
Is there something I am sorry for? Then I ask forgiveness.

The Word

God speaks to each of us individually. I need to listen, to hear what he is saying to me. Read the text a few times; then listen. (Please turn to the Scripture on the following pages. Inspiration points are there, should you need them. When you are ready, return here to continue.)

Conversation

How has God's word moved me? Has it left me cold?
Has it consoled me or moved me to act in a new way?
I imagine Jesus standing or sitting beside me.
I turn and share my feelings with him.

Conclusion

I thank God for these moments we have spent together and for any insights I have been given concerning the text.

Sunday 30th December
The Holy Family of Jesus, Mary, and Joseph
Luke 2:41–52

Now every year his parents went to Jerusalem for the festival of the Passover. And when he was twelve years old, they went up as usual for the festival. When the festival was ended and they started to return, the boy Jesus stayed behind in Jerusalem, but his parents did not know it. Assuming that he was in the group of travelers, they went a day's journey. Then they started to look for him among their relatives and friends. When they did not find him, they returned to Jerusalem to search for him. After three days they found him in the temple, sitting among the teachers, listening to them and asking them questions. And all who heard him were amazed at his understanding and his answers. When his parents saw him they were astonished; and his mother said to him, "Child, why have you treated us like this? Look, your father and I have been searching for you in great anxiety." He said to them, "Why were you searching for me? Did you not know that I must be in my Father's house?" But they did not understand what he said to them. Then he went down with them and came to Nazareth, and was obedient to them. His mother treasured all these things in her heart. And Jesus increased in wisdom and in years, and in divine and human favor.

- "In my Father's house." Do I believe that the Father's house may be found within myself? If I do, I can perhaps open myself to an even greater wonder: "Those who love me will keep my word, and my Father will love them, and we will come to them and make our home with them" (John 14:23).

- Let me take in this scene slowly. Jesus is coming of age, entering his teens, and is an eager student questioning his teachers. To his mother's query—"your father and I"—he points gently to another paternity: "I must be in my Father's house." No Gospel scene shows more clearly the gradual process by which he grew into a sense of his mission. Let me savor it.

Monday 31st December
John 1:1–18

In the beginning was the Word, and the Word was with God, and the Word was God. He was in the beginning with God. All things came into being through him, and without him not one thing came into being. What has come into being in him was life, and the life was the light of all people. The light shines in the darkness, and the darkness did not overcome it. There was a man sent from God, whose name was John. He came as a witness to testify to the light, so that all might believe through him. He himself was not the light, but he came to testify to the light. The true light, which enlightens everyone, was coming into the world. He was in the world, and the world came into being through him; yet the world did not know him. He came to what was his own, and his own people did not accept him. But to all who received him, who believed in his name, he gave power to become children of God, who were born, not of blood or of the will of the flesh or of the will of man, but of God. And the Word became flesh and lived among us, and we have seen his glory, the glory as of a father's only son, full of grace and truth. (John testified to him and cried out, "This was he of whom I said, 'He who comes after me ranks ahead of me because he was before me.'") From his fullness have we all received, grace upon grace. The law indeed was given through Moses; grace and truth came through Jesus Christ. No one has ever seen God. It is God the only Son, who is close to the Father's heart, who has made him known.

- The Word of God is more than a mere communication or message coming from God; it is nothing less than God's self-communication (and at more than one level). The Word—or "Wisdom"—is a personification of God and of God the Creator ("the world came into being through him") and the source of all light and life.

- God's self-sharing extended even to his Word, Jesus, being made flesh. Jesus has joined our humanity. And our humanity is forever joined to his divinity and glory.

Tuesday 1st January
Solemnity of Mary, the Holy Mother of God
Luke 2:16–21

So they went with haste and found Mary and Joseph, and the child lying in the manger. When they saw this, they made known what had been told them about this child; and all who heard it were amazed at what the shepherds told them. But Mary treasured all these words and pondered them in her heart. The shepherds returned, glorifying and praising God for all they had heard and seen, as it had been told them. After eight days had passed, it was time to circumcise the child; and he was called Jesus, the name given by the angel before he was conceived in the womb.

- The wonderful thing revealed in this story is that God's self-revelation as love is not to the select few but to you and me. Mary's greatness is apparent in the fact that she took time to ponder this revelation not just in her mind but also in her heart.

- In your prayer you might ask Mary to tell you the story of what happened and then ponder this with her.

Wednesday 2nd January
John 1:19–28

This is the testimony given by John when the Jews sent priests and Levites from Jerusalem to ask him, "Who are you?" He confessed and did not deny it, but confessed, "I am not the Messiah." And they asked him, "What then? Are you Elijah?" He said, "I am not." "Are you the prophet?" He answered, "No." Then they said to him, "Who are you? Let us have an answer for those who sent us. What do you say about yourself?" He said,

"I am the voice of one crying out in the wilderness,
'Make straight the way of the Lord,'"
as the prophet Isaiah said.

Now they had been sent from the Pharisees. They asked him, "Why then are you baptizing if you are neither the Messiah, nor Elijah, nor the prophet?" John answered them, "I baptize with water. Among you stands one whom you do not know, the one who is coming after me; I am not worthy to untie the thong of his sandal." This took place in Bethany across the Jordan where John was baptizing.

- John the Baptist's mission was to emphasize the importance of Jesus over himself. This became a major characteristic of Jesus' teaching, too: humility. This means facing two realities about ourselves: that there is a very small part of us that is limited and sinful but that this must not prevent us from seeing the far greater part of ourselves that is gifted by nature and even more so by grace.

- For a few moments of prayer, be with John the Baptist and let him tell you how fortunate you are to have met Jesus. Let him tell you of his own enthusiasm about Jesus.

Thursday 3rd January
John 1:29–34

The next day he saw Jesus coming toward him and declared, "Here is the Lamb of God who takes away the sin of the world! This is he of whom I said, 'After me comes a man who ranks ahead of me because he was before me.' I myself did not know him; but I came baptizing with water for this reason, that he might be revealed to Israel." And John testified, "I saw the Spirit descending from heaven like a dove, and it remained on him. I myself did not know him, but the one who sent me to baptize with water said to me, 'He on whom you see the Spirit descend and remain is the one who baptizes with the Holy Spirit.' And I myself have seen and have testified that this is the Son of God."

- In today's Gospel reading, John the Baptist speaks of God as the one who sent him and the Spirit as the one who descends on Jesus and remains with him. As Karl Rahner expressed it, "What is central to all Theology and Spirituality is that the three persons of the Trinity want to reveal themselves to you."

- For some moments of prayer be with Mary and John as they experience the purpose of the Old Testament unfolding before their eyes. This is the plan of the three persons of the Trinity to reveal themselves to you.

Friday 4th January

John 1:35–42

The next day John again was standing with two of his disciples, and as he watched Jesus walk by, he exclaimed, "Look, here is the Lamb of God!" The two disciples heard him say this, and they followed Jesus. When Jesus turned and saw them following, he said to them, "What are you looking for?" They said to him, "Rabbi" (which translated means Teacher), "where are you staying?" He said to them, "Come and see." They came and saw where he was staying, and they remained with him that day. It was about four o'clock in the afternoon. One of the two who heard John speak and followed him was Andrew, Simon Peter's brother. He first found his brother Simon and said to him, "We have found the Messiah" (which is translated Anointed). He brought Simon to Jesus, who looked at him and said, "You are Simon son of John. You are to be called Cephas" (which is translated Peter).

• Matthew, Mark, and Luke see the Christian vocation to be expressed in the words, "repent, and believe in the good news" (Mark 1:14–15). John, however, sees our vocation to be an answer to Jesus' words, "Come and see." This is an invitation to come to know Jesus as God's love made visible that the Holy Spirit wants to lead you into (John 16:13–15).

• If you have time to pray with today's Gospel, you might quiet yourself for a short while by listening to the sounds around you. Then let Jesus say the words, "Come and see" to you several times, pausing so that you hear the tone of his voice and see the expression on his face.

Saturday 5th January

John 1:43–51

The next day Jesus decided to go to Galilee. He found Philip and said to him, "Follow me." Now Philip was from Bethsaida, the city of Andrew and Peter. Philip found Nathanael and said to him, "We have found him about whom Moses in the law and also the prophets wrote, Jesus son of Joseph from Nazareth." Nathanael said to him, "Can anything good come out of Nazareth?" Philip said to him, "Come and see." When Jesus saw Nathanael coming toward him, he said of him, "Here is truly an Israelite in whom there is no deceit!" Nathanael asked him, "Where did you get to know me?" Jesus answered, "I saw you under the fig tree before Philip called you." Nathanael replied, "Rabbi, you are the Son of God! You are the King of Israel!" Jesus answered, "Do you believe because I told you that I saw you under the fig tree? You will see greater things than these." And he said to him, "Very truly, I tell you, you will see heaven opened and the angels of God ascending and descending upon the Son of Man."

- Today's reading is all about the call of the Christian, about your call to be with Jesus as your friend. Reflect on what it means to be a Christian today by pondering on how the Gospels are all about Jesus as he went about making friends to lead us into his own relationship with his Father.

- In the light of this, be with Jesus in a quiet place and ask him about the dream he has for you as his friend.

The Epiphany of Our Lord / Second Week of Christmas
January 6, 2019—January 12, 2019

Something to think and pray about each day this week:

Would you have noticed the star in the sky? Or would you have been too busy and distracted? Would you have been quiet and still enough to look up, to contemplate the stars and the greatness of the universe? To stop and be in awe? To breathe in the cold night air? To notice that something was happening? Sometimes we wait for God to come, but what we really need to do is be quiet and attentive enough to notice and discern what he is already doing. And, more often than not, God is found where we least expect him.

—Karen Beattie, *2018: A Book of Grace-Filled Days*

The Presence of God
Dear Jesus, today I call on you, but not to ask for anything. I'd like only to dwell in your presence. May my heart respond to your love.

Freedom
God my creator, you gave me life and the gift of freedom. Through your love I exist in this world. May I never take the gift of life for granted. May I always respect others' right to life.

Consciousness
I ask how I am today. Am I particularly tired, stressed, or anxious? If any of these characteristics apply, can I try to let go of the concerns that disturb me?

The Word
The word of God comes down to us through the Scriptures. May the Holy Spirit enlighten my mind and my heart to respond to the gospel teachings. (Please turn to the Scripture on the following pages. Inspiration points are there, should you need them. When you are ready, return here to continue.)

Conversation
I begin to talk with Jesus about the Scripture I have just read. What part of it strikes a chord in me? Perhaps the words of a friend—or some story I have heard recently—will rise to the surface in my consciousness. If so, does the story throw light on what the Scripture passage may be saying to me?

Conclusion
Glory be to the Father, and to the Son, and to the Holy Spirit,
As it was in the beginning, is now and ever shall be,
World without end. Amen.

Sunday 6th January
The Epiphany of the Lord
Matthew 2:1–12

In the time of King Herod, after Jesus was born in Bethlehem of Judea, wise men from the East came to Jerusalem, asking, "Where is the child who has been born king of the Jews? For we observed his star at its rising, and have come to pay him homage." When King Herod heard this, he was frightened, and all Jerusalem with him; and calling together all the chief priests and scribes of the people, he inquired of them where the Messiah was to be born. They told him, "In Bethlehem of Judea; for so it has been written by the prophet:

'And you, Bethlehem, in the land of Judah,
    are by no means least among the rulers of Judah;
for from you shall come a ruler
    who is to shepherd my people Israel.'"

Then Herod secretly called for the wise men and learned from them the exact time when the star had appeared. Then he sent them to Bethlehem, saying, "Go and search diligently for the child; and when you have found him, bring me word so that I may also go and pay him homage." When they had heard the king, they set out; and there, ahead of them, went the star that they had seen at its rising, until it stopped over the place where the child was. When they saw that the star had stopped, they were overwhelmed with joy. On entering the house, they saw the child with Mary his mother; and they knelt down and paid him homage. Then, opening their treasure chests, they offered him gifts of gold, frankincense, and myrrh. And having been warned in a dream not to return to Herod, they left for their own country by another road.

- The story told in today's Gospel is about people being called to follow their stars to find the fullness of life only Jesus can give. "I came that they may have life, and have it abundantly" (John 10:10).

- You may not have thought much about the nature of the star you follow. With a view to clarifying this, it may be worthwhile to ask yourself what you want for your children, your family, or your friends. Having done this, you might talk to Jesus about whether this is what he wants for you—if this is the star he wishes you to follow.

Monday 7th January
Matthew 4:12–17, 23–25

Now when Jesus heard that John had been arrested, he withdrew to Galilee. He left Nazareth and made his home in Capernaum by the sea, in the territory of Zebulun and Naphtali, so that what had been spoken through the prophet Isaiah might be fulfilled:

"Land of Zebulun, the land of Naphtali,
    on the road by the sea, across the Jordan, Galilee of the Gentiles—
the people who sat in darkness
    have seen a great light,
and for those who sat in the region and shadow of death
    light has dawned."

From that time Jesus began to proclaim, "Repent, for the kingdom of heaven has come near."

- Now that John is in prison, Jesus begins to preach the same message John preached: "Repent, for the kingdom of heaven has come near." There is continuity among God's prophets and preachers; even his Son takes up the baton John has had to set down.

- Holy Spirit, show me how my own calling and ministry fit into the long story of your work in this world.

Tuesday 8th January
Mark 6:34–44

As he went ashore, he saw a great crowd; and he had compassion for them, because they were like sheep without a shepherd; and he began to teach them many things. When it grew late, his disciples came to him and said, "This is a deserted place, and the hour is now very late; send them away so that they may go into the surrounding country and villages and buy something for themselves to eat." But he answered them, "You give them something to eat." They said to him, "Are we to go and buy two hundred denarii worth of bread, and give it to them to eat?" And he said to them, "How many loaves have you? Go and see." When they had found out, they said, "Five, and two fish." Then he ordered them all to get all the people to sit down in groups on the green grass. So they sat down in groups of hundreds and of fifties.

Taking the five loaves and the two fish, he looked up to heaven, and blessed and broke the loaves, and gave them to his disciples to set before the people; and he divided the two fish among them all. And all ate and were filled; and they took up twelve baskets full of broken pieces and of the fish. Those who had eaten the loaves numbered five thousand men.

- Notice that Jesus allows the disciples to grow uncomfortable; he gives them time to assess the need of the crowd and bring it to him. A proper leader has a better plan, doesn't he—thinks through all the logistics ahead of time? Had you been a disciple in that situation, how would you have responded?

- Jesus began with the food that was already there. Help me, Lord, to be aware of what you have provided and, with gratitude, may I continue forward with faith.

Wednesday 9th January
Mark 6:45–52

Immediately he made his disciples get into the boat and go on ahead to the other side, to Bethsaida, while he dismissed the crowd. After saying farewell to them, he went up on the mountain to pray. When evening came, the boat was out on the sea, and he was alone on the land. When he saw that they were straining at the oars against an adverse wind, he came towards them early in the morning, walking on the sea. He intended to pass them by. But when they saw him walking on the sea, they thought it was a ghost and cried out; for they all saw him and were terrified. But immediately he spoke to them and said, "Take heart, it is I; do not be afraid." Then he got into the boat with them and the wind ceased. And they were utterly astounded, for they did not understand about the loaves, but their hearts were hardened.

- Imagine yourself in the boat with the disciples and listen to what they say as the storm develops. Listen to them as they observe the figure coming across the water!

- Jesus saw that they were straining at the oars—that they were in difficulty. Yet he intended to pass by them. He shows care for their well-being yet it seems that he waits for their response. Ponder what the scene may indicate about how God watches over us.

Thursday 10th January

Luke 4:14–22a

Then Jesus, filled with the power of the Spirit, returned to Galilee, and a report about him spread through all the surrounding country. He began to teach in their synagogues and was praised by everyone. When he came to Nazareth, where he had been brought up, he went to the synagogue on the sabbath day, as was his custom. He stood up to read, and the scroll of the prophet Isaiah was given to him. He unrolled the scroll and found the place where it was written:

"The Spirit of the Lord is upon me,
    because he has anointed me
        to bring good news to the poor.
He has sent me to proclaim release to the captives
    and recovery of sight to the blind,
        to let the oppressed go free,
to proclaim the year of the Lord's favor."

And he rolled up the scroll, gave it back to the attendant, and sat down. The eyes of all in the synagogue were fixed on him. Then he began to say to them, "Today this scripture has been fulfilled in your hearing." All spoke well of him and were amazed at the gracious words that came from his mouth.

- Of all the texts available to him, Jesus chose this ringing description of his mission from Isaiah: to bring good news to the poor, to give sight to the blind, to let the oppressed go free. As I reflect on Jesus' own understanding of his mission, I look at our world as we struggle with so many social issues: the welcome of refugees and migrants to our countries and communities, the growing inequality between those who have and those who have not, the destruction of the environment. What is the Spirit of the Lord sending me to do, as a follower of Jesus? I ask for the grace not to be deaf to his call, but to carry it out with great generosity.

- Jesus went to synagogue on the sabbath day, "which was his custom." We tend to forget that Jesus was a practicing Jew of his time. He began his ministry in the midst of the people of his community and faith. What are the advantages and disadvantages of this? Can I relate to Jesus' situation in this scene?

Friday 11th January
Luke 5:12–16

Once, when he was in one of the cities, there was a man covered with leprosy. When he saw Jesus, he bowed with his face to the ground and begged him, "Lord, if you choose, you can make me clean." Then Jesus stretched out his hand, touched him, and said, "I do choose. Be made clean." Immediately the leprosy left him. And he ordered him to tell no one. "Go," he said, "and show yourself to the priest, and, as Moses commanded, make an offering for your cleansing, for a testimony to them." But now more than ever the word about Jesus spread abroad; many crowds would gather to hear him and to be cured of their diseases. But he would withdraw to deserted places and pray.

- Jesus sent the leper to the priest because a priest had to verify that a person was clean and healed before admitting the person back into the community. Healing always involves more than physical health. Consider the areas of life affected by a prolonged illness.

- After such a miracle, Jesus might have remained to receive the awe and praise of the people and to keep working among them. But he recognized that his source was time with the Father. If Jesus needed prayer, can I neglect it for myself?

Saturday 12th January
John 3:22–30

After this Jesus and his disciples went into the Judean countryside, and he spent some time there with them and baptized. John also was baptizing at Aenon near Salim because water was abundant there; and people kept coming and were being baptized—John, of course, had not yet been thrown into prison. Now a discussion about purification arose between John's disciples and a Jew. They came to John and said to him, "Rabbi, the one who was with you across the Jordan, to whom you testified, here he is baptizing, and all are going to him." John answered, "No one can receive anything except what has been given from heaven. You yourselves are my witnesses that I said, 'I am not the Messiah, but I have been sent ahead of him.' He who has the bride is the bridegroom. The friend of the bridegroom, who stands and hears him, rejoices greatly at the bridegroom's voice. For this reason my joy has been fulfilled. He must increase, but I must decrease."

- In this situation we see the typical need people have of knowing who is "in" and who is "out." Their loyalty to John was commendable but misplaced. What gets in the way of my being open to God's graces coming through many people and in various ways?

- John knew that his role in the sacred drama would soon fade, and he accepted that. What would diminishment look like in my life? How will I know when it is my time to decrease, and how can I prepare my heart to respond graciously?

January 13—January 19

Something to think and pray about each day this week:

As the year turns, from old to new, everything is turned on its head. Yesterday's endings become tomorrow's beginnings. The birth of Jesus is pure paradox. The *eternal* reveals itself *in time*. Perfect *spirit* takes on *flesh and blood*. The source of our being becomes the one who leads us toward our destiny. It defies all our rationalizations. It happened two thousand years ago; it is happening here and now and always. We can't begin to understand it, and yet it penetrates our hearts deeper than mere understanding. The one who is born will turn all our assumptions and expectations upside down, if we will allow it. Lord, the Christ-child overturned everything. Help me to live with paradox and with the turbulent effect of your presence.

—Margaret Silf in *Daily Inspiration for Women*

The Presence of God

As I sit here, the beating of my heart,
the ebb and flow of my breathing, the movements of my mind
are all signs of God's ongoing creation of me.
I pause for a moment and become aware
of this presence of God within me.

Freedom

Everything has the potential to draw from me a fuller love and life.
Yet my desires are often fixed, caught, on illusions of fulfillment.
I ask that God, through my freedom, may orchestrate my desires in a vibrant, loving melody rich in harmony.

Consciousness

I ask, how am I within myself today? Am I particularly tired, stressed, or off-form? If any of these characteristics apply, can I try to let go of the concerns that disturb me?

The Word

I read the word of God slowly, a few times over, and I listen to what God is saying to me. (Please turn to the Scripture on the following pages. Inspiration points are there, should you need them. When you are ready, return here to continue.)

Conversation

I begin to talk with Jesus about the Scripture I have just read. What part of it strikes a chord in me? Perhaps the words of a friend or a story I have heard recently will slowly rise to the surface of my consciousness. If so, does the story throw light on what the Scripture passage may be trying to say to me?

Conclusion

Glory be to the Father, and to the Son, and to the Holy Spirit,
As it was in the beginning, is now and ever shall be,
World without end. Amen.

Sunday 13th January
The Baptism of the Lord
Luke 3:15–16, 21–22

As the people were filled with expectation, and all were questioning in their hearts concerning John, whether he might be the Messiah, John answered all of them by saying, "I baptize you with water; but one who is more powerful than I is coming; I am not worthy to untie the thong of his sandals. He will baptize you with the Holy Spirit and fire." . . . Now when all the people were baptized, and when Jesus also had been baptized and was praying, the heaven was opened, and the Holy Spirit descended upon him in bodily form like a dove. And a voice came from heaven, "You are my Son, the Beloved; with you I am well pleased."

• Over the ages, the people of God had been waiting for the one who was to come. They sensed that right now was the eve of the great Savior's dawn. And their anticipation was not disappointed. At the baptism of Jesus, the Father in heaven's voice was heard—and the Holy Spirit appeared, too, ready to be poured out into the hearts of all who approached for purification.

• A new force was at large in the world, changing our hearts and filling our spirits with the life of heaven. May I remember, Lord, that this life is in me right now.

Monday 14th January
Mark 1:14–20

Now after John was arrested, Jesus came to Galilee, proclaiming the good news of God, and saying, "The time is fulfilled, and the kingdom of God has come near; repent, and believe in the good news." As Jesus passed along the Sea of Galilee, he saw Simon and his brother Andrew casting a net into the lake—for they were fishermen. And Jesus said to them, "Follow me and I will make you fish for people." And immediately they left their nets and followed him. As he went a little farther, he saw James son of Zebedee and his brother John, who were in their boat mending the nets. Immediately he called them; and they left their father Zebedee in the boat with the hired men, and followed him.

- "Follow me." The ways of following Jesus are as varied as people themselves. But following always entails breaking free from what one was before. We are true disciples when we challenge ourselves with the question, "How would Jesus act in the situation I'm in right now?"

- Lord, you call the disciples to follow you and share in your mission. Their response is radical and immediate. May nothing hinder me from generously responding to your daily call to follow you.

Tuesday 15th January
Mark 1:21–28

They went to Capernaum; and when the sabbath came, he entered the synagogue and taught. They were astounded at his teaching, for he taught them as one having authority, and not as the scribes. Just then there was in their synagogue a man with an unclean spirit, and he cried out, "What have you to do with us, Jesus of Nazareth? Have you come to destroy us? I know who you are, the Holy One of God." But Jesus rebuked him, saying, "Be silent, and come out of him!" And the unclean spirit, convulsing him and crying with a loud voice, came out of him. They were all amazed, and they kept on asking one another, "What is this? A new teaching—with authority! He commands even the unclean spirits, and they obey him." At once his fame began to spread throughout the surrounding region of Galilee.

- Saint Mark depicts Jesus engaged in a war against the cosmic forces of evil. Jesus overcomes the world's enemy, though in ways different from what we would expect. Do we believe he can do this, when we pray, "Deliver us from evil"?

- The teaching of Jesus is straight from his heart, from his relationship with God. I ask God to bless me so that all my words and actions profess my faith.

Wednesday 16th January
Mark 1:29–39

As soon as they left the synagogue, they entered the house of Simon and Andrew, with James and John. Now Simon's mother-in-law was in bed with a fever, and they told him about her at once. He came and took her by the hand and lifted her up. Then the fever left her, and she began to serve them.

That evening, at sunset, they brought to him all who were sick or possessed with demons. And the whole city was gathered around the door. And he cured many who were sick with various diseases, and cast out many demons; and he would not permit the demons to speak, because they knew him. In the morning, while it was still very dark, he got up and went out to a deserted place, and there he prayed. And Simon and his companions hunted for him. When they found him, they said to him, "Everyone is searching for you." He answered, "Let us go on to the neighboring towns, so that I may proclaim the message there also; for that is what I came out to do." And he went throughout Galilee, proclaiming the message in their synagogues and casting out demons.

- The first recorded hours of Jesus' ministry are a whirlwind of activity. We are meant to catch on to the fact that when Jesus enters human lives, things change fast and for the better for those who are open. A new creation is here! Everyone is meant to get in on it.

- What do I need from Jesus? Am I just a spectator, or am I fighting to get close to him? His presence brings wholeness—do I need that? People become more alive—do I need that? Simon's mother-in-law gets the energy to serve—do I need that?

Thursday 17th January
Mark 1:40–45

A leper came to [Jesus] begging him, and kneeling he said to him, "If you choose, you can make me clean." Moved with pity, Jesus stretched out his hand and touched him, and said to him, "I do choose. Be made clean!" Immediately the leprosy left him, and he was made clean. After sternly warning him he sent him away at once, saying to him, "See that you say nothing to anyone; but go, show yourself to the priest, and offer for your cleansing what Moses commanded, as a testimony to them." But he went out and began to proclaim it freely, and to spread the word, so that Jesus could no longer go into a town openly, but stayed out in the country; and people came to him from every quarter.

- "Moved with pity, Jesus stretched out his hand and touched him." Leprosy in the Bible was not precisely what we mean by the term but was a general name for any repulsive, scaly skin disease. Touch me, Lord.

Touch the ugly parts of me that I do not like to look at. If you will, you
can make me clean.

- Jesus affirms the desire of the man with leprosy: "I do choose" is his response to our desire for what is truly for our growth and well-being. The
leper knew his need and trusted that Jesus could help him. I pray with the
same attitude, not hiding my neediness, not hesitating about bringing it
before Jesus. And I listen for Jesus' encouraging response.

Friday 18th January
Mark 2:1–12

When he returned to Capernaum after some days, it was reported that he was
at home. So many gathered around that there was no longer room for them,
not even in front of the door; and he was speaking the word to them. Then
some people came, bringing to him a paralyzed man, carried by four of them.
And when they could not bring him to Jesus because of the crowd, they removed the roof above him; and after having dug through it, they let down
the mat on which the paralytic lay. When Jesus saw their faith, he said to the
paralytic, "Son, your sins are forgiven." Now some of the scribes were sitting
there, questioning in their hearts, "Why does this fellow speak in this way? It
is blasphemy! Who can forgive sins but God alone?" At once Jesus perceived
in his spirit that they were discussing these questions among themselves; and
he said to them, "Why do you raise such questions in your hearts? Which is
easier, to say to the paralytic, 'Your sins are forgiven,' or to say, 'Stand up and
take your mat and walk'? But so that you may know that the Son of Man has
authority on earth to forgive sins"—he said to the paralytic—"I say to you,
stand up, take your mat and go to your home." And he stood up, and immediately took the mat and went out before all of them; so that they were all
amazed and glorified God, saying, "We have never seen anything like this!"

- Faith opens a door to a living relationship with God in Jesus. The faith of
others helped the sick man. Our faithful time of prayer may help people
we know or do not know.

- Lord, sometimes I don't have the courage to act because of some failure
or criticism that took the heart out of me. Then I rely on the help of good
friends, like the four stretcher bearers, to bring me to the point where I
can hear you say, "Get up and walk."

Saturday 19th January
Mark 2:13–17

Jesus went out again beside the sea; the whole crowd gathered around him, and he taught them. As he was walking along, he saw Levi son of Alphaeus sitting at the tax booth, and he said to him, "Follow me." And he got up and followed him. And as he sat at dinner in Levi's house, many tax collectors and sinners were also sitting with Jesus and his disciples—for there were many who followed him. When the scribes of the Pharisees saw that he was eating with sinners and tax collectors, they said to his disciples, "Why does he eat with tax collectors and sinners?" When Jesus heard this, he said to them, "Those who are well have no need of a physician, but those who are sick; I have come to call not the righteous but sinners."

- I wonder how Jesus said the words "Follow me." Like an order, an invitation, a whisper, a definite challenge? However it was said, it provoked a response.

- Allow Jesus to address you in your prayer. How do you hear his call to follow him—as a gentle invitation or an urgent word? No matter how it is said, it is always spoken into the space of each person's interior freedom and deepest generosity.

Second Week in Ordinary Time
January 20—January 26

Something to think and pray about each day this week:

We're always moving from old to new. Our God is a God of new beginnings and renewal. We tend to be more aware of it during those points in the year that mark transition, like New Year's or Lent. One way of looking at our inherent feeling of lack is what Jesus called poverty of spirit. It describes the reality that I especially recognize each new year: My lack, my emptiness can never be filled completely with resolutions and good choices; only God can fill that space and poverty of spirit gives God the space to fill us. St. Ignatius realized this when he prayed to God, "Give me only your love and your grace. That is enough for me." And so, we build new dreams from the ashes of lack. Yet like all things in this world, they're temporary. We need not lament about our lack. Indeed, we can embrace poverty of spirit as a reminder that only God can fill us completely with love and grace.

—Andy Otto on *dotMagis*, the blog of *IgnatianSpirituality.com*

The Presence of God
Dear Jesus, I come to you today longing for your presence. I desire to love you as you love me. May nothing ever separate me from you.

Freedom
Lord, grant me the grace to be free from the excesses of this life. Let me not get caught up with the desire for wealth. Keep my heart and mind free to love and serve you.

Consciousness
Where do I sense hope, encouragement, and growth in my life? By looking back over the past few months, I may be able to see which activities and occasions have produced rich fruit. If I do notice such areas, I will determine to give those areas both time and space in the future.

The Word
God speaks to each of us individually. I listen attentively to hear what he is saying to me. Read the text a few times; then listen. (Please turn to the Scripture on the following pages. Inspiration points are there, should you need them. When you are ready, return here to continue.)

Conversation
What is stirring in me as I pray? Am I consoled, troubled, left cold? I imagine Jesus standing or sitting at my side, and I share my feelings with him.

Conclusion
Glory be to the Father, and to the Son, and to the Holy Spirit,
As it was in the beginning, is now and ever shall be,
World without end. Amen.

Sunday 20th January

John 2:1–11

On the third day there was a wedding in Cana of Galilee, and the mother of Jesus was there. Jesus and his disciples had also been invited to the wedding. When the wine gave out, the mother of Jesus said to him, "They have no wine." And Jesus said to her, "Woman, what concern is that to you and to me? My hour has not yet come." His mother said to the servants, "Do whatever he tells you." Now standing there were six stone water jars for the Jewish rites of purification, each holding twenty or thirty gallons. Jesus said to them, "Fill the jars with water." And they filled them up to the brim. He said to them, "Now draw some out, and take it to the chief steward." So they took it. When the steward tasted the water that had become wine, and did not know where it came from (though the servants who had drawn the water knew), the steward called the bridegroom and said to him, "Everyone serves the good wine first, and then the inferior wine after the guests have become drunk. But you have kept the good wine until now." Jesus did this, the first of his signs, in Cana of Galilee, and revealed his glory; and his disciples believed in him.

- In some incidents of the written narrative about Jesus we find signals and unmistakable gestures that indicate who he really is. We see magi and shepherds recognizing his lordship at his birth. We see the heavenly manifestations at his baptism in the Jordan. And here in John's Gospel we see a signal from Jesus himself: the replenishment of the wine for the large crowd of wedding guests.

- A banquet—including the free flow of wine—was always, for the people of God, a figure of the total fulfillment and happiness that would mark the Lord's final future coming. His overflowing generosity is always available to us. Can I image myself at the Lord's banquet feast?

Monday 21st January

Mark 2:18–22

Now John's disciples and the Pharisees were fasting; and people came and said to Jesus, "Why do John's disciples and the disciples of the Pharisees fast, but your disciples do not fast?" Jesus said to them, "The wedding guests cannot fast while the bridegroom is with them, can they? As long as they have the bridegroom with them, they cannot fast. The days will come when the bridegroom is taken away from them, and then they will fast on that day. No one sews a piece of unshrunk cloth on an old cloak; otherwise, the patch pulls away from it, the new from the old, and a worse tear is made. And no one puts new wine into old wineskins; otherwise, the wine will burst the skins, and the wine is lost, and so are the skins; but one puts new wine into fresh wineskins."

- People noticed the contrast between the Pharisees' preoccupation with laws and regulations and Jesus' love of celebrations and feasts. They saw Jesus as someone who was always ready for a party, who enjoyed life. In Jesus' parables, the kingdom of heaven is often a banquet, a wedding, a party. Am I more likely to cling to a set of standards I know well or to join a celebration I don't quite yet understand?

- "New wine, new wineskins." Lord, you caution me against having a closed mind. You challenge me not to cling to old ways and to be receptive to the new. Grant me openness of heart and mind. Let me trust in the depths of your creative Spirit, who is making all things new.

Tuesday 22nd January
Mark 2:23–28

One sabbath Jesus was going through the cornfields; and as they made their way his disciples began to pluck heads of grain. The Pharisees said to him, "Look, why are they doing what is not lawful on the sabbath?" And he said to them, "Have you never read what David did when he and his companions were hungry and in need of food? He entered the house of God, when Abiathar was high priest, and ate the bread of the Presence, which it is not lawful for any but the priests to eat, and he gave some to his companions." Then he said to them, "The sabbath was made for humankind, and not humankind for the sabbath; so the Son of Man is lord even of the sabbath."

- The Pharisees were skillful at pointing out deficiencies in others. Before God I review my thoughts and words to take care that I do not measure the world by my own small scale.

- Forgiveness, mercy, and compassion are at the heart of true religion. Without these, only heartlessness and empty performance remain. Lord, would others see me as a truly religious person?

Wednesday 23rd January
Mark 3:1–6

Jesus entered the synagogue, and a man was there who had a withered hand. They watched him to see whether he would cure him on the sabbath, so that they might accuse him. And he said to the man who had the withered hand, "Come forward." Then he said to them, "Is it lawful to do good or to do harm on the sabbath, to save life or to kill?" But they were silent. He looked around at them with anger; he was grieved at their hardness of heart and said to the man, "Stretch out your hand." He stretched it out, and his hand was restored. The Pharisees went out and immediately conspired with the Herodians against him, how to destroy him.

- Jesus was being watched to see what he might do, yet it did not stop him from doing good, from bringing life. I ask God for the courage I need to do what I know to be the right thing. The anger of Jesus is passion for life. I let myself imagine how Jesus wants to brush away whatever it is that holds me back from living fully.

- Lord, when you celebrated the Sabbath by healing a person, the Pharisees responded by plotting to kill you. You were stressing that God does not want to make our lives more difficult and does not impose arbitrary rules on us. The great commandment is the law of love. Would people who know me be able to say that I follow the law of love?

Thursday 24th January
Mark 3:7–12

Jesus departed with his disciples to the sea, and a great multitude from Galilee followed him; hearing all that he was doing, they came to him in great numbers from Judea, Jerusalem, Idumea, beyond the Jordan, and the region around Tyre and Sidon. He told his disciples to have a boat ready for him because of the crowd, so that they would not crush him; for he had cured many, so that all who had diseases pressed upon him to touch him. Whenever the unclean spirits saw him, they fell down before him and shouted, "You are the Son of God!" But he sternly ordered them not to make him known.

- Jesus is at ease in open spaces: near lakesides, hills, and the sky, unprotected by institutional walls. People converge on him from unexpected places, seeking healing and good news. Lord, I come to you seeking to be healed and to hear good news. No place is too far that we cannot come to you.

- The magnetism of Jesus is revealed here. Ordinary, unimportant people offer him an enthusiastic reception. They approach him with one desire: to touch him and be healed. Loving energy flows from Jesus. Am I easy about joining this enthusiastic crowd of poor people? Can I admit that I, too, need the healing touch of the Son of God? Do I radiate healing to others?

Friday 25th January
Mark 16:15–18

[Jesus said to the apostles], "Go into all the world and proclaim the good news to the whole creation. The one who believes and is baptized will be saved; but the one who does not believe will be condemned. And these signs will accompany those who believe: by using my name they will cast out demons; they will speak in new tongues; they will pick up snakes in their hands, and if they drink any deadly thing, it will not hurt them; they will lay their hands on the sick, and they will recover."

- Lord Jesus, we leave the frailty that is in us open to your touch. We commit to you the joys and the failures of our lives. Use them to bring good to others.

- I pray for healing for those parts of creation that are wounded and damaged, that have yet to experience the good news that Jesus sends us to proclaim. I proclaim this good news to the whole of creation by the way I live, by being a blessing to the world that God has made.

Saturday 26th January
Mark 3:20–21

[Then Jesus went home;] and the crowd came together again, so that they could not even eat. When his family heard it, they went out to restrain him, for people were saying, "He has gone out of his mind."

- Jesus' family considers him imbalanced. He has left the security and safety of Nazareth and his carpentry business. He is on course for a head-on collision with the orthodox leaders, and he has recently gathered a crowd of disciples who will do nothing for his career prospects. He has gone out of his mind!

- Lord, in choosing to live by the gospel, I, too, run the risk of being misunderstood and ridiculed. You faced opposition with determination and courage. Grant me your grace to follow you resolutely, especially when opposition comes from those near me.

January 27—February 2

Something to think and pray about each day this week:

Thanks to technology, we have a lot of individual control over what we hear. We have favorite songs on our phones, podcasts we can tune into whenever we drive, and headphones to block out the conversation around us on an airplane. We are increasingly able to skip anything we don't want to listen to, be it an uninspiring song or the flight attendant's safety spiel. We can spend much of our time in a little cocoon of our favorite sounds. This is nice, certainly, but perhaps it has a downside. It puts us at risk of insulating ourselves from the broader world. It can also prevent us from making happy discoveries of new songs or sounds we love. There's something to be said for periodically ditching the personal playlist and simply listening to the things that are going on around us. I tried this the other day, deciding not to put on my favorite songs as I worked on the computer. Instead, I tuned in to what I could hear through the open window. When I paid attention to what was out there, I realized that there was a great deal going on, even in my little corner of the neighborhood.

—Ginny Kubitz Moyer on *dotMagis*,
the blog of *IgnatianSpirituality.com*

The Presence of God

"I am standing at the door, knocking" says the Lord. What a wonderful privilege that the Lord of all creation desires to come to me. I welcome his presence.

Freedom

I will ask God's help
to be free from my own preoccupations,
to be open to God in this time of prayer,
to come to know, love, and serve God more.

Consciousness

In God's loving presence I unwind the past day,
starting from now and looking back, moment by moment.
I gather in all the goodness and light, in gratitude.
I attend to the shadows and what they say to me,
seeking healing, courage, forgiveness.

The Word

Now I turn to the Scripture set out for me this day. I read slowly over the words and see if any sentence or sentiment appeals to me. (Please turn to the Scripture on the following pages. Inspiration points are there, should you need them. When you are ready, return here to continue.)

Conversation

Sometimes I wonder what I might say if I were to meet you in person, Lord. I think I might say "Thank you" because you are always there for me.

Conclusion

I thank God for these moments we have spent together and for any insights I have been given concerning the text.

Sunday 27th January

Luke 1:1–4; 4:14–21

Since many have undertaken to set down an orderly account of the events that have been fulfilled among us, just as they were handed on to us by those who from the beginning were eyewitnesses and servants of the word, I too decided, after investigating everything carefully from the very first, to write an orderly account for you, most excellent Theophilus, so that you may know the truth concerning the things about which you have been instructed. . . . Then Jesus, filled with the power of the Spirit, returned to Galilee, and a report about him spread through all the surrounding country. He began to teach in their synagogues and was praised by everyone. When he came to Nazareth, where he had been brought up, he went to the synagogue on the sabbath day, as was his custom. He stood up to read, and the scroll of the prophet Isaiah was given to him. He unrolled the scroll and found the place where it was written: "The Spirit of the Lord is upon me, because he has anointed me to bring good news to the poor. He has sent me to proclaim release to the captives and recovery of sight to the blind, to let the oppressed go free, to proclaim the year of the Lord's favor." And he rolled up the scroll, gave it back to the attendant, and sat down. The eyes of all in the synagogue were fixed on him. Then he began to say to them, "Today this scripture has been fulfilled in your hearing."

• A "year of favor" was a season when God would visit his people; God would come and overturn a situation in which his people had been at the mercy of enemies. He would relieve the oppressed, set free the imprisoned, cure the disabled and those who had succumbed to illness. It would be a whole new age: God would lift his people out of their distress.

• Jesus tells his hearers that, with his own coming, God is visiting his people right now. And he's visiting every single one of his people, from that day to this.

Monday 28th January

Mark 3:22–30

And the scribes who came down from Jerusalem said, "He has Beelzebul, and by the ruler of the demons he casts out demons." And he called them to him, and spoke to them in parables, "How can Satan cast out Satan? If a kingdom is divided against itself, that kingdom cannot stand. And if a house is divided against itself, that house will not be able to stand. And if Satan has risen up against himself and is divided, he cannot stand, but his end has come. But no one can enter a strong man's house and plunder his property without first tying up the strong man; then indeed the house can be plundered. Truly I tell you, people will be forgiven for their sins and whatever blasphemies they utter; but whoever blasphemes against the Holy Spirit can never have forgiveness, but is guilty of an eternal sin"—for they had said, "He has an unclean spirit."

• Like his family, the authorities are alarmed at the radical nature of what Jesus is doing and the change of mind and heart that he requires. They believe he is under the influence of Satan. The wisdom of Jesus, his passion for the truth, and his courage radiate from the scene. Talk to Jesus about how you admire his wisdom and courage, contemplate this as it unfolds in the story, and share with him how you feel about him being like this.

• Let Jesus express his admiration of how you try to be true to yourself, to your convictions about what for you is true and worthwhile. Tell him how you feel about what he says to you.

Tuesday 29th January
Mark 3:31–35

Then his mother and his brothers came; and standing outside, they sent to him and called him. A crowd was sitting around him; and they said to him, "Your mother and your brothers and sisters are outside, asking for you." And he replied, "Who are my mother and my brothers?" And looking at those who sat around him, he said, "Here are my mother and my brothers! Whoever does the will of God is my brother and sister and mother."

• Lord, I hear a gentleness, not a sharpness, in your voice. You blessed Mary not for the bond of blood with you but because she was the handmaid of the Lord, the one whose response to God's messenger led to the Incarnation. In a culture where blood relationships counted heavily, you were pointing to deeper relationships, like the one that I have with you.

• Jesus highlights that the primary relationship in life is to God. Even the deepest and most natural bonds are created within this primary love.

Mother and family were important to Jesus in his life and at his death; but the real call was within this family relationship to hear and keep the word of God. Do I feel a similar strong pull toward God as much as toward my biological family?

Wednesday 30th January
Mark 4:1–20

Again he began to teach beside the sea. Such a very large crowd gathered around him that he got into a boat on the sea and sat there, while the whole crowd was beside the sea on the land. He began to teach them many things in parables, and in his teaching he said to them: "Listen! A sower went out to sow. And as he sowed, some seed fell on the path, and the birds came and ate it up. Other seed fell on rocky ground, where it did not have much soil, and it sprang up quickly, since it had no depth of soil. And when the sun rose, it was scorched; and since it had no root, it withered away. Other seed fell among thorns, and the thorns grew up and choked it, and it yielded no grain. Other seed fell into good soil and brought forth grain, growing up and increasing and yielding thirty and sixty and a hundredfold." And he said, "Let anyone with ears to hear listen!" When he was alone, those who were around him along with the twelve asked him about the parables. And he said to them, "To you has been given the secret of the kingdom of God, but for those outside, everything comes in parables; in order that 'they may indeed look, but not perceive, and may indeed listen, but not understand; so that they may not turn again and be forgiven.'" And he said to them, "Do you not understand this parable? Then how will you understand all the parables? The sower sows the word. These are the ones on the path where the word is sown: when they hear, Satan immediately comes and takes away the word that is sown in them. And these are the ones sown on rocky ground: when they hear the word, they immediately receive it with joy. But they have no root, and endure only for a while; then, when trouble or persecution arises on account of the word, immediately they fall away. And others are those sown among the thorns: these are the ones who hear the word, but the cares of the world, and the lure of wealth, and the desire for other things come in and choke the word, and it yields nothing. And these are the ones sown on the good soil: they hear the word and accept it and bear fruit, thirty and sixty and a hundredfold."

- If your word is like a seed, Lord, then it is an organism, with a life of its own. My part is to receive it, give it roots and depth so that it survives hardships, and protect it from the thorns of multiple cares and desires. If I allow your word some space in my life, there is no limit to the fruit it may bear.

- The sower knows that not all seed will flourish. I pray for forgiveness and healing for the rocky, bare places I observe in my life. I pray that I may not neglect where there is growth but that I may grow in gratitude and hope.

Thursday 31st January

Mark 4:21–25

[Jesus] said to them, "Is a lamp brought in to be put under the bushel basket, or under the bed, and not on the lampstand? For there is nothing hidden, except to be disclosed; nor is anything secret, except to come to light. Let anyone with ears to hear listen!" And he said to them, "Pay attention to what you hear; the measure you give will be the measure you get, and still more will be given you. For to those who have, more will be given; and from those who have nothing, even what they have will be taken away."

- When Jesus begins revealing the earth-changing coming of his kingdom, he doesn't want the teaching twisted to others' ends by political agitators or by sensationalists. So he sometimes makes his points in a veiled way—fully explaining them later to a circle of trusted followers.

- In listening, hearing, and following Jesus, I grow in familiarity with his voice and hear more—as to what I have, more is added. I give thanks and I pray for those who have nothing, that they might take time with God who has such time for them.

Friday 1st February

Mark 4:26–34

[Jesus said to the crowd,] "The kingdom of God is as if someone would scatter seed on the ground, and would sleep and rise night and day, and the seed would sprout and grow, he does not know how. The earth produces of itself, first the stalk, then the head, then the full grain in the head. But when the grain is ripe, at once he goes in with his sickle, because the harvest has come." He also said, "With what can we compare the kingdom of God, or what parable will we use for it? It is like a mustard seed, which, when sown upon the ground, is the smallest of all the seeds on earth; yet when it is sown it grows up and becomes the greatest of all shrubs, and puts forth large branches, so that the birds of the air can make nests in its shade." With many such parables he spoke the word to them, as they were able to hear it; he did not speak to them except in parables, but he explained everything in private to his disciples.

- Thank you, Lord, for this most consoling of images. I was not brought into this world to help you out of a mess. You above all are the one who is working. Your dynamism, active in nature from the beginning of time, should humble me. You are the force of growth, and if you privilege me with the chance to add incrementally to that growth, that is your gift to me, not mine to you.

- Remind me today, Lord, that a very small seed of action or thought or prayer can grow and become fruitful.

Saturday 2nd February
The Presentation of the Lord
Luke 2:22–40

When the time came for their purification according to the law of Moses, they brought him up to Jerusalem to present him to the Lord (as it is written in the law of the Lord, "Every firstborn male shall be designated as holy to the Lord"), and they offered a sacrifice according to what is stated in the law of the Lord, "a pair of turtledoves or two young pigeons." Now there was a man in Jerusalem whose name was Simeon; this man was righteous and devout, looking forward to the consolation of Israel, and the Holy Spirit rested on him. It had been revealed to him by the Holy Spirit that he would not see death before he had seen the Lord's Messiah. Guided by the Spirit, Simeon came into the temple; and when the parents brought in the child Jesus, to do for him what was customary under the law, Simeon took him in his arms and praised God, saying, "Master, now you are dismissing your servant in peace, according to your word; for my eyes have seen your salvation, which you have prepared in the presence of all peoples, a light for revelation to the Gentiles and for glory to your people Israel." And the child's father and

mother were amazed at what was being said about him. Then Simeon blessed them and said to his mother Mary, "This child is destined for the falling
and the rising of many in Israel, and to be a sign that will be opposed so that
the inner thoughts of many will be revealed—and a sword will pierce your
own soul too." There was also a prophet, Anna the daughter of Phanuel, of
the tribe of Asher. She was of a great age, having lived with her husband for
seven years after her marriage, then as a widow to the age of eighty-four. She
never left the temple but worshiped there with fasting and prayer night and
day. At that moment she came, and began to praise God and to speak about
the child to all who were looking for the redemption of Jerusalem. When
they had finished everything required by the law of the Lord, they returned
to Galilee, to their own town of Nazareth. The child grew and became
strong, filled with wisdom; and the favor of God was upon him.

- The Holy Spirit is very important for St. Luke, and that Spirit is never
  far away. This text links him closely to Simeon, helping the old man to
  recognize and praise God, and to bless the parents of Jesus. What about
  me? The Holy Spirit dwells in me, too: I am his temple! But is he perhaps
  only a quiet lodger whom I hardly notice? Have I locked him up? Can
  he become my mentor whom I look to for advice and support? Can the
  Spirit and I create life together?

- Simeon's prayer is repeated daily in the Night Prayer of the church. Can
  I make it my own and accept the prospect of my own death, however it
  may come, whether quietly or suddenly?

February 3—February 9

Something to think and pray about each day this week:

The busier seasons can leave us with little time to relax in the armchair, to enjoy the glow of the log fire, to engage in leisurely conversations, and to delight in a shared, unhurried meal. Now is the time for home. But what is home? Not everyone finds "home" where it should be. Not every child is cherished. Not every teenager is listened to. Not every couple makes it through life together. Many long for the touch of a friendly hand and a chance to talk. Inner homelessness has become an epidemic of our time. Just by listening to another's story, reaching out a hand in friendship, just by something as simple as a smile, each of us is able to say to another, "Come on home." Is there anyone near you who is longing for a taste of home? What can you do for him or her this week?

—Margaret Silf in *Daily Inspiration for Women*

The Presence of God
At any time of the day or night we can call on Jesus.
He is always waiting, listening for our call.
What a wonderful blessing.
No phone needed, no emails, just a whisper.

Freedom
If God were trying to tell me something, would I know?
If God were reassuring me or challenging me, would I notice?
I ask for the grace to be free of my own preoccupations
and open to what God may be saying to me.

Consciousness
Help me, Lord, become more conscious of your presence. Teach me to recognize your presence in others. Fill my heart with gratitude for the times your love has been shown to me through the care of others.

The Word
In this expectant state of mind, please read the text for the day with confidence. Believe that the Holy Spirit is present and may reveal whatever the passage has to say to you. Read reflectively, listening with a third ear to what may be going on in your heart. (Please turn to the Scripture on the following pages. Inspiration points are there, should you need them. When you are ready, return here to continue.)

Conversation
Conversation requires talking and listening.
As I talk to Jesus, may I also learn to pause and listen.
I picture the gentleness in his eyes and the love in his smile.
I can be totally honest with Jesus as I tell him my worries and cares.
I will open my heart to Jesus as I tell him my fears and doubts.
I will ask him to help me place myself fully in his care, knowing that he always desires good for me.

Conclusion
I thank God for these moments we have spent together and for any insights I have been given concerning the text.

Sunday 3rd February
Luke 4:21–30

Then he began to say to them, "Today this scripture has been fulfilled in your hearing." All spoke well of him and were amazed at the gracious words that came from his mouth. They said, "Is not this Joseph's son?" He said to them, "Doubtless you will quote to me this proverb, 'Doctor, cure yourself!' And you will say, 'Do here also in your home town the things that we have heard you did at Capernaum.'" And he said, "Truly I tell you, no prophet is accepted in the prophet's home town. But the truth is, there were many widows in Israel in the time of Elijah, when the heaven was shut up for three years and six months, and there was a severe famine over all the land; yet Elijah was sent to none of them except to a widow at Zarephath in Sidon. There were also many lepers in Israel in the time of the prophet Elisha, and none of them was cleansed except Naaman the Syrian." When they heard this, all in the synagogue were filled with rage. They got up, drove him out of the town, and led him to the brow of the hill on which their town was built, so that they might hurl him off the cliff. But he passed through the midst of them and went on his way.

• Coming as Savior to visit his people, Jesus intends to lift their troubles from their shoulders—but effort is needed on their part too. He tells the townspeople of Nazareth that it's not just a question of spectacle, of a show of miracles. A deep change of heart will be required.

• Jesus offers healing and help to me, but am I open to allow him to act in my life?

Monday 4th February
Mark 5:1–20

They came to the other side of the sea, to the country of the Gerasenes. And when he had stepped out of the boat, immediately a man out of the tombs with an unclean spirit met him. He lived among the tombs; and no one could restrain him any more, even with a chain; for he had often been restrained with shackles and chains, but the chains he wrenched apart, and the shackles he broke in pieces; and no one had the strength to subdue him. Night and day among the tombs and on the mountains he was always howling and bruising himself with stones. When he saw Jesus from a distance, he ran and bowed down before him; and he shouted at the top of his voice, "What have you to do with me, Jesus, Son of the Most High God? I adjure you by God, do not torment me." For he had said to him, "Come out of the man, you unclean spirit!" Then Jesus asked him, "What is your name?" He replied, "My name is Legion; for we are many." He begged him earnestly not to send them out of the country. Now there on the hillside a great herd of swine was feeding; and the unclean spirits begged him, "Send us into the swine; let us enter them." So he gave them permission. And the unclean spirits came out and entered the swine; and the herd, numbering about two thousand, rushed down the steep bank into the sea, and were drowned in the sea. The swineherds ran off and told it in the city and in the country. Then people came to see what it was that had happened. They came to Jesus and saw the demoniac sitting there, clothed and in his right mind, the very man who had had the legion; and they were afraid. Those who had seen what had happened to the demoniac and to the swine reported it. Then they began to beg Jesus to leave their neighborhood. As he was getting into the boat, the man who had been possessed by demons begged him that he might be with him. But Jesus refused, and said to him, "Go home to your friends, and tell them how much the Lord has done for you, and what mercy he has shown you." And he went away and began to proclaim in the Decapolis how much Jesus had done for him; and everyone was amazed.

- This scene portrays for us a very powerful example of Jesus setting someone free from the demons that possessed him. The story becomes more relevant when we acknowledge that we all are afflicted by evil in some way, and it affects our relationship with Jesus.

- John of the Cross gives us the example of the small bird that cannot fly because it is anchored to the ground by the thinnest of threads. What liberates us more than anything is to consider how intensely attractive the love of Jesus can become if we take time to notice and savor it.

Tuesday 5th February
Mark 5:21–43

When Jesus had crossed again in the boat to the other side, a great crowd gathered round him; and he was by the sea. Then one of the leaders of the synagogue named Jairus came and, when he saw him, fell at his feet and begged him repeatedly, "My little daughter is at the point of death. Come and lay your hands on her, so that she may be made well, and live." So he went with him. And a large crowd followed him and pressed in on him. Now there was a woman who had been suffering from hemorrhages for twelve years. She had endured much under many physicians, and had spent all that she had; and she was no better, but rather grew worse. She had heard about Jesus, and came up behind him in the crowd and touched his cloak, for she said, "If I but touch his clothes, I will be made well." Immediately her hemorrhage stopped; and she felt in her body that she was healed of her disease. Immediately aware that power had gone forth from him, Jesus turned about in the crowd and said, "Who touched my clothes?" And his disciples said to him, "You see the crowd pressing in on you; how can you say, 'Who touched me?'" He looked all around to see who had done it. But the woman, knowing what had happened to her, came in fear and trembling, fell down before him, and told him the whole truth. He said to her, "Daughter, your faith has made you well; go in peace, and be healed of your disease." While he was still speaking, some people came from the leader's house to say, "Your daughter is dead. Why trouble the teacher any further?" But overhearing what they said, Jesus said to the leader of the synagogue, "Do not fear, only believe." He allowed no one to follow him except Peter, James, and John, the brother of James. When they came to the house of the leader of the synagogue, he saw a commotion, people weeping and wailing loudly. When he had entered, he said to them, "Why do you make a commotion and weep? The child is not dead but sleeping." And they laughed at him. Then he put them all outside, and took the child's father and mother and those who were with him, and went in where the child was. He took her by the hand and said to her, "Talitha cum," which means, "Little girl, get up!" And immediately the girl got up and began to walk about (she was twelve years of age). At this they were overcome with amazement. He strictly ordered them that no one should know this, and told them to give her something to eat.

- This reading presents us with two stories about how Jesus healed people. At the end of the first of these stories Jesus gives us the key to his healing ministry when he says, "Daughter, your faith has made you well; go in peace, and be healed of your disease." The main sickness Jesus is intent on healing is that brought on by our sense of insignificance. The remedy Jesus says is faith in his love.

- In your prayer, perhaps spend time talking to Jesus about his work of healing. Focus on some aspect of your own sense of insignificance. When are you most vulnerable to it? What words or actions of Jesus can draw you out of this false sense of self?

Wednesday 6th February
Mark 6:1–6

[Jesus] left that place and came to his hometown, and his disciples followed him. On the sabbath he began to teach in the synagogue, and many who heard him were astounded. They said, "Where did this man get all this? What is this wisdom that has been given to him? What deeds of power are being done by his hands! Is not this the carpenter, the son of Mary and brother of James and Joses and Judas and Simon, and are not his sisters here with us?" And they took offense at him. Then Jesus said to them, "Prophets are not without honor, except in their hometown, and among their own kin, and in their own house." And he could do no deed of power there, except that he laid his hands on a few sick people and cured them. And he was amazed at their unbelief. Then he went about among the villages teaching.

- Even after all the miracles of healing Jesus had worked, he still was not accepted in his own town. As he taught in the synagogue there, his hearers were amazed that this ordinary man whom they knew as the carpenter could attain such wisdom, and they rejected him.

- Lord, help me see and feel your presence in the ordinary encounters of my day and notice the ways through which you desire to nourish me and give me life, because you are present in all things.

Thursday 7th February
Mark 6:7–13

Jesus called the twelve and began to send them out two by two, and gave them authority over the unclean spirits. He ordered them to take nothing for their journey except a staff; no bread, no bag, no money in their belts; but to wear sandals and not to put on two tunics. He said to them, "Wherever you enter a house, stay there until you leave the place. If any place will not welcome you and they refuse to hear you, as you leave, shake off the dust that is on your feet as a testimony against them." So they went out and proclaimed that all should repent. They cast out many demons, and anointed with oil many who were sick and cured them.

- Jesus calls the apostles and sends them on a mission to announce the message of repentance, cure the sick, and cast out demons. Notice how he sends them out in pairs, instructing them to trust in divine providence by taking nothing for their journey. They were to be dependent entirely on God—and on God's presence in one another.

- Jesus' trust in us is breathtaking. I too am being sent out each day to bring good news to those I engage with. Jesus, make me aware that you are with me wherever I go.

Friday 8th February
Mark 6:14–29

King Herod heard of it, for Jesus' name had become known. Some were saying, "John the baptizer has been raised from the dead; and for this reason these powers are at work in him." But others said, "It is Elijah." And others said, "It is a prophet, like one of the prophets of old." But when Herod heard of it, he said, "John, whom I beheaded, has been raised." For Herod himself had sent men who arrested John, bound him, and put him in prison on account of Herodias, his brother Philip's wife, because Herod had married her. For John had been telling Herod, "It is not lawful for you to have your brother's wife." And Herodias had a grudge against him, and wanted to kill him. But she could not, for Herod feared John, knowing that he was a righteous and holy man, and he protected him. When he heard him, he was greatly perplexed; and yet he liked to listen to him. But an opportunity came when Herod on his birthday gave a banquet for his courtiers and officers and for the leaders of Galilee. When his daughter Herodias came in and danced, she pleased Herod and his guests; and the king said to the girl, "Ask me for whatever you wish, and I will give it." And he solemnly swore to her, "Whatever you ask me, I will give you, even half of my kingdom." She went out and said to her mother, "What should I ask for?" She replied, "The head of John the baptizer." Immediately she rushed back to the king and requested, "I want you to give me at once the head of John the Baptist on a platter." The king was deeply grieved; yet out of regard for his oaths and for the guests, he did not want to refuse her. Immediately the king sent a soldier of the guard with orders to bring John's head. He went and beheaded him in the prison, brought his head on a platter, and gave it to the girl. Then the girl gave it to her mother. When his disciples heard about it, they came and took his body, and laid it in a tomb.

- Lord Jesus, you spent your last night before your crucifixion in prison. Bring comfort to the thousands of good people who are languishing behind bars. They are my sisters and brothers. There but for the grace of God I would be too.

- This is one of the most dramatic stories in world literature. John the baptizer is the helpless and innocent one, standing for the truth. He will suffer and die because of a weak ruler, Herod. He is laid in a tomb and disappears from human history. This all points to Jesus: he is also a great prophet, innocent, but doomed to suffer and die because of the weakness of Pontius Pilate. We are being warned not to lose faith in Jesus: he too will be laid in a tomb, but through his resurrection he will change the story of humankind.

Saturday 9th February
Mark 6:30–34

The apostles gathered around Jesus, and told him all that they had done and taught. He said to them, "Come away to a deserted place all by yourselves and rest a while." For many were coming and going, and they had no leisure even to eat. And they went away in the boat to a deserted place by themselves. Now many saw them going and recognized them, and they hurried there on foot from all the towns and arrived ahead of them. As he went ashore, he saw a great crowd; and he had compassion for them, because they were like sheep without a shepherd; and he began to teach them many things.

- This is the first encounter between the apostles and Jesus after he sends them out on mission. His fame had spread far and wide, and the apostles were so busy spreading the good news and giving witness to the glory of God that they didn't have time even to eat. Jesus extends his compassionate love to them, directing them to find refuge in a quiet, deserted place.

- Jesus invites me to come away from the busyness of my life and to go into that quiet space so that I can be with him. He always listens to my prayer and invites me to share with him my hopes, concerns, and dreams.

February 10—February 16

Something to think and pray about each day this week:

Nature's resilience to harsh conditions and extremes of weather is quite amazing. Different creatures adapt in different ways. Some dig themselves into burrows to ride out the winter storms, while those with wings take off to warmer climes, risking hazardous migratory journeys.
What about us? How do we react when things get tough? Perhaps nature's wintering can teach us something. Will we dig in and hide until the troubles have passed? Will we try to fly away in the hope of escaping them? Maybe wisdom invites us to do neither, and both. Not to hide away, but to go deeper into our hearts and draw on resources we perhaps never knew we possessed. Not to flee, but to rise above the immediate situation, and see it from a higher perspective. What difficulties or trouble do you face now? What's your instinct? Burrow? Fly? How might you modify your way of reacting?

—Margaret Silf in *Daily Inspiration for Women*

The Presence of God

As I sit here, the beating of my heart,
the ebb and flow of my breathing, the movements of my mind
are all signs of God's ongoing creation of me.
I pause for a moment and become aware
of this presence of God within me.

Freedom

It is so easy to get caught up
with the trappings of wealth in this life.
Grant, O Lord, that I may be free
from greed and selfishness.
Remind me that the best things in life are free:
Love, laughter, caring, and sharing.

Consciousness

Knowing that God loves me unconditionally, I can afford to be honest
about how I am.
How has the day been, and how do I feel now? I share my feelings openly
with the Lord.

The Word

Lord Jesus, you became human to communicate with me.
You walked and worked on this earth.
You endured the heat and struggled with the cold.
All your time on this earth was spent in caring for humanity.
You healed the sick, you raised the dead.
Most important of all, you saved me from death.
(Please turn to the Scripture on the following pages. Inspiration points are
there, should you need them. When you are ready, return here to continue.)

Conversation

Sometimes I wonder what I might say if I were to meet you in person, Lord.
I think I might say "Thank you" because you are always there for me.

Conclusion

I thank God for these moments we have spent together and for any insights
I have been given concerning the text.

Sunday 10th February

Luke 5:1–11

Once while Jesus was standing beside the lake of Gennesaret, and the crowd was pressing in on him to hear the word of God, he saw two boats there at the shore of the lake; the fishermen had gone out of them and were washing their nets. He got into one of the boats, the one belonging to Simon, and asked him to put out a little way from the shore. Then he sat down and taught the crowds from the boat. When he had finished speaking, he said to Simon, "Put out into the deep water and let down your nets for a catch." Simon answered, "Master, we have worked all night long but have caught nothing. Yet if you say so, I will let down the nets." When they had done this, they caught so many fish that their nets were beginning to break. So they signaled their partners in the other boat to come and help them. And they came and filled both boats, so that they began to sink. But when Simon Peter saw it, he fell down at Jesus' knees, saying, "Go away from me, Lord, for I am a sinful man!" For he and all who were with him were amazed at the catch of fish that they had taken; and so also were James and John, sons of Zebedee, who were partners with Simon. Then Jesus said to Simon, "Do not be afraid; from now on you will be catching people." When they had brought their boats to shore, they left everything and followed him.

• Lord, you tell me, as you told Simon, to "Put out into the deep water." You are ready to surprise me with the depths I can find in myself, with the work you can do through me. Save me from complacency, from settling for a routine existence. Open me to recognizing your hand in my daily encounters.

• God's grace comes to us tailor-made to fit our situation. Can I recall a moment when my efforts to do good were rewarded beyond my dreams? Did I see then that God was busily at work through me? Or do I tend to say, "This can't be done: it wouldn't work!" and then block God's action? May I allow God to be for me a God of surprises.

Monday 11th February

Mark 6:53–56

When [Jesus and the disciples] had crossed over, they came to land at Gennesaret and moored the boat. When they got out of the boat, people at once recognized him, and rushed about that whole region and began to bring the sick on mats to wherever they heard he was. And wherever he went, into villages or cities or farms, they laid the sick in the marketplaces, and begged him that they might touch even the fringe of his cloak; and all who touched it were healed.

- Do I catch the excitement of the people as Jesus, always so approachable, steps ashore from the boat? I bring my friends in need to him in prayer.

- Imagine that Jesus shows up in your marketplace! What would the reaction be? Does Mark intend us to see that the marketplaces of the world could be a center for divine power and healing, if the gospel were alive in them?

Tuesday 12th February
Mark 7:1–13

Now when the Pharisees and some of the scribes who had come from Jerusalem gathered around him, they noticed that some of his disciples were eating with defiled hands, that is, without washing them. (For the Pharisees, and all the Jews, do not eat unless they thoroughly wash their hands, thus observing the tradition of the elders; and they do not eat anything from the market unless they wash it; and there are also many other traditions that they observe, the washing of cups, pots, and bronze kettles.) So the Pharisees and the scribes asked him, "Why do your disciples not live according to the tradition of the elders, but eat with defiled hands?" He said to them, "Isaiah prophesied rightly about you hypocrites, as it is written, 'This people honors me with their lips, but their hearts are far from me; in vain do they worship me, teaching human precepts as doctrines.' You abandon the commandment of God and hold to human tradition." Then he said to them, "You have a fine way of rejecting the commandment of God in order to keep your tradition! For Moses said, 'Honor your father and your mother'; and, 'Whoever speaks evil of father or mother must surely die.' But you say that if anyone tells father or mother, 'Whatever support you might have had from me is Corban' (that is, an offering to God)—then you no longer permit doing anything for a father or mother, thus making void the word of God through your tradition that you have handed on. And you do many things like this."

- The storm clouds are gathering. Jesus' enemies come from Jerusalem, where he will be condemned and killed. The Pharisees and scribes are looking backward, not at the new world Jesus is opening up. They say, "This is what we have always done." God's dream upsets their cautious lives. Jesus puts God first, as always, whereas they are playing a role, inauthentic. When am I most tempted to act in inauthentic ways? In what situations am I afraid of change that would disturb my comfort?

- The command of God is to love as God loves. I must not let my practices and routines, my safe ways of doing things, interfere with the flow of divine love through me into the world.

Wednesday 13th February

Mark 7:14–23

Then he called the crowd again and said to them, "Listen to me, all of you, and understand: there is nothing outside a person that by going in can defile, but the things that come out are what defile." When he had left the crowd and entered the house, his disciples asked him about the parable. He said to them, "Then do you also fail to understand? Do you not see that whatever goes into a person from outside cannot defile, since it enters, not the heart but the stomach, and goes out into the sewer?" (Thus he declared all foods clean.) And he said, "It is what comes out of a person that defiles. For it is from within, from the human heart, that evil intentions come: fornication, theft, murder, adultery, avarice, wickedness, deceit, licentiousness, envy, slander, pride, folly. All these evil things come from within, and they defile a person."

- Mark is making clear to his gentile (non-Jewish) Christian community that to be a follower of Jesus Christ does not require the observance of a multiplicity of Jewish ritual ablutions. I am not defiled, separated from God, by externals, such as the kinds of food I eat, but by the sins of the heart, evil intentions, and sinful actions.

- Lord, you list twelve "evil intentions" that defile a person. Reveal to me the one I need to address right now!

Thursday 14th February

Mark 7:24–30

From there [Jesus] set out and went away to the region of Tyre. He entered a house and did not want anyone to know he was there. Yet he could not escape notice, but a woman whose little daughter had an unclean spirit immediately heard about him, and she came and bowed down at his feet. Now the woman was a Gentile, of Syrophoenician origin. She begged him to cast the demon out of her daughter. He said to her, "Let the children be fed first, for it is not fair to take the children's food and throw it to the dogs." But she answered him, "Sir, even the dogs under the table eat the children's crumbs." Then he said to her, "For saying that, you may go— the demon has left your daughter." So she went home, found the child lying on the bed, and the demon gone.

- Is Jesus being deliberately rude to this gentile (non-Jewish) woman? Her witty retort, however, delights him, breaks down his resistance, and shows he is open to persuasion. Is she teaching him a lesson?

- By writing about this delightful episode, Mark indicates that Jesus' message and mission go beyond the Jewish people. Who are my "people" today? What sort of person would I assume is not interested in what Jesus has to say? Today, I pray for anyone I meet today who appears to be an outsider.

Friday 15th February

Mark 7:31–37

Then he returned from the region of Tyre, and went by way of Sidon towards the Sea of Galilee, in the region of the Decapolis. They brought to him a deaf man who had an impediment in his speech; and they begged him to lay his hand on him. He took him aside in private, away from the crowd, and put his fingers into his ears, and he spat and touched his tongue. Then looking up to heaven, he sighed and said to him, "Ephphatha," that is, "Be opened." And immediately his ears were opened, his tongue was released, and he spoke plainly. Then Jesus ordered them to tell no one; but the more he ordered them, the more zealously they proclaimed it. They were astounded beyond measure, saying, "He has done everything well; he even makes the deaf to hear and the mute to speak."

- "He has done everything well." This recalls the Genesis creation story, in which God is pleased with his work and says it is good. Now the new creation is dawning in Jesus, and I am one who is being restored. If this does not bring me joy, what will?

- I imagine Jesus placing his hands upon me and praying that some space in my life will be opened. What space would that be? What area of my life has become closed off to hope or change?

Saturday 16th February

Mark 8:1–10

In those days when there was again a great crowd without anything to eat, he called his disciples and said to them, "I have compassion for the crowd, because they have been with me now for three days and have nothing to eat. If I send them away hungry to their homes, they will faint on the way—and some of them have come from a great distance." His disciples replied, "How can one feed these people with bread here in the desert?" He asked them, "How many loaves do you have?" They said, "Seven." Then he ordered the crowd to sit down on the ground; and he took the seven loaves, and after giving thanks he broke them and gave them to his disciples to distribute; and they distributed them to the crowd. They had also a few small fish; and after blessing them, he ordered that these too should be distributed. They ate and were filled; and they took up the broken pieces left over, seven baskets full. Now there were about four thousand people. And he sent them away. And immediately he got into the boat with his disciples and went to the district of Dalmanutha.

- Jesus requires the disciples to get involved before any miracle happens. And he begins with the situation at hand. What situation in my life or the life of a loved one needs God's help? Is God already showing me how to be involved?

- God is not stingy. After the people had eaten their fill, the leftovers filled seven baskets. Lord, may I remember, as I go through this day, that you are the God of abundance, not scarcity.

February 17—February 23

Something to think and pray about each day this week:

Jesus calls his disciples and sends them out, giving them clear and precise instructions. He challenges them to take on a whole range of attitudes and ways of acting. Sometimes these can strike us as exaggerated or even absurd. It would be easier to interpret these attitudes symbolically or "spiritually." But Jesus is quite precise, very clear. He doesn't tell them simply to do whatever they think they can.

Let us think about some of these attitudes: "Take nothing for the journey except a staff; no bread, no bag, no money." "When you enter a house, stay there until you leave the place" (cf. Mark 6:8–11). All this might seem quite unrealistic. We could concentrate on the words *bread, money, bag, staff, sandals,* and *tunic.* And this would be fine. But it strikes me that one key word can easily pass unnoticed among the challenging words I have just listed. It is a word at the heart of Christian spirituality, of our experience of discipleship: *welcome.* Jesus as the good master, the good teacher, sends them out to be welcomed, to experience hospitality. He says to them, "Where you enter a house, stay there." He sends them out to learn one of the hallmarks of the community of believers. We might say that a Christian is someone who has learned to welcome others, who has learned to show hospitality.

—Pope Francis, *Embracing the Way of Jesus*

The Presence of God

"Come to me, all you who are weary and are carrying heavy burdens, and I will give you rest." Here I am, Lord. I come to seek your presence. I long for your healing power.

Freedom

God is not foreign to my freedom. The Spirit breathes life into my most intimate desires, gently nudging me toward all that is good. I ask for the grace to let myself be enfolded by the Spirit.

Consciousness

I remind myself that I am in the presence of the Lord. I will take refuge in his loving heart. He is my strength in times of weakness. He is my comforter in times of sorrow.

The Word

I take my time to read the word of God slowly, a few times, allowing myself to dwell on anything that strikes me. (Please turn to the Scripture on the following pages. Inspiration points are there, should you need them. When you are ready, return here to continue.)

Conversation

Jesus, you always welcomed little children when you walked on this earth. Teach me to have a childlike trust in you. Teach me to live in the knowledge that you will never abandon me.

Conclusion

Glory be to the Father, and to the Son, and to the Holy Spirit,
As it was in the beginning, is now and ever shall be,
World without end. Amen.

Sunday 17th February

Luke 6:17, 20–26

He came down with them and stood on a level place, with a great crowd of his disciples and a great multitude of people from all Judea, Jerusalem, and the coast of Tyre and Sidon. . . . Then he looked up at his disciples and said: "Blessed are you who are poor, for yours is the kingdom of God. Blessed are you who are hungry now, for you will be filled. Blessed are you who weep now, for you will laugh. Blessed are you when people hate you, and when they exclude you, revile you, and defame you on account of the Son of Man. Rejoice in that day and leap for joy, for surely your reward is great in heaven; for that is what their ancestors did to the prophets. But woe to you who are rich, for you have received your consolation. Woe to you who are full now, for you will be hungry. Woe to you who are laughing now, for you will mourn and weep. Woe to you when all speak well of you, for that is what their ancestors did to the false prophets."

- I try to see which beatitude touches me today, whether because it helps me rejoice in God's gifts to me or because I feel a resistance in my heart. I pray for a listening heart.

- When my heart is breaking because of the misery of so many today, I must not think that God has forgotten them. Instead I thank God that for them the best is yet to come, and I ask to be included among them, at least as someone who cares about them.

Monday 18th February

Mark 8:11–13

The Pharisees came and began to argue with him, asking him for a sign from heaven, to test him. And he sighed deeply in his spirit and said, "Why does this generation ask for a sign? Truly I tell you, no sign will be given to this generation." And he left them, and getting into the boat again, he went across to the other side.

- Do I share the exasperation of Jesus at the stubborn obstinacy of the Pharisees, demanding a sign after he had first fed five thousand of his own Jewish people in Galilee (Mark 6:32–44) and then fed four thousand non-Jewish people on the eastern side of the Sea of Galilee (Mark 8:1–10)? At what situations today do I feel a similar frustration?

- By crossing and recrossing the sea from west to east and east to west, Jesus is reaching out to Jew and gentile alike—to all peoples. Am I a wavering disciple who cannot be depended on? I pray: "Jesus, don't leave me behind! Drag me along with you as you cross over to a place I cannot reach without you, the kingdom of God."

Tuesday 19th February
Mark 8:14–21

Now the disciples had forgotten to bring any bread; and they had only one loaf with them in the boat. And he cautioned them, saying, "Watch out— beware of the yeast of the Pharisees and the yeast of Herod." They said to one another, "It is because we have no bread." And becoming aware of it, Jesus said to them, "Why are you talking about having no bread? Do you still not perceive or understand? Are your hearts hardened? Do you have eyes, and fail to see? Do you have ears, and fail to hear? And do you not remember? When I broke the five loaves for the five thousand, how many baskets full of broken pieces did you collect?" They said to him, "Twelve." "And the seven for the four thousand, how many baskets full of broken pieces did you collect?" And they said to him, "Seven." Then he said to them, "Do you not yet understand?"

- Following on the feeding of the five thousand Jews and four thousand Gentiles (non-Jews), have I not yet understood that Jesus is the "one loaf," the Eucharistic bread of life, broken and shared, to achieve Christian fellowship for all people?

- Jesus' questions to the disciples lead them to see that God is working in their midst. To what evidence would Jesus direct me when I waver in my faith here and now?

Wednesday 20th February
Mark 8:22–26

They came to Bethsaida. Some people brought a blind man to him and begged him to touch him. He took the blind man by the hand and led him out of the village; and when he had put saliva on his eyes and laid his hands on him, he asked him, "Can you see anything?" And the man looked up and said, "I can see people, but they look like trees, walking." Then Jesus laid his hands on his eyes again; and he looked intently and his sight was restored, and he saw everything clearly. Then he sent him away to his home, saying, "Do not even go into the village."

- I put myself in the sandals of the blind man brought to Jesus, the healer everybody wanted to meet. He takes me gently by the hand, warm and reassuring. As he gives me his full attention, I grow in trust and confidence. Jesus opens my eyes, and I see what a good man he is.

- I cannot thank the Lord enough for his goodness and kindness. Every moment of my life is his gift to me. In fact, my prayer at this time becomes one of thanksgiving and remembrance of God's touch upon my life.

Thursday 21st February
Mark 8:27–33

Jesus went on with his disciples to the villages of Caesarea Philippi; and on the way he asked his disciples, "Who do people say that I am?" And they answered him, "John the Baptist; and others, Elijah; and still others, one of the prophets." He asked them, "But who do you say that I am?" Peter answered him, "You are the Messiah." And he sternly ordered them not to tell anyone about him. Then he began to teach them that the Son of Man must undergo great suffering, and be rejected by the elders, the chief priests, and the scribes, and be killed, and after three days rise again. He said all this quite openly. And Peter took him aside and began to rebuke him. But turning and looking at his disciples, he rebuked Peter and said, "Get behind me, Satan! For you are setting your mind not on divine things but on human things."

- This is a major turning point for Jesus and the disciples. It is also the most northerly point of his missionary journeys through the towns and villages of Galilee. More significantly, it is the point at which he is formally recognized by his disciples as the Messiah, the Christ. Try to identify the point in your own life when you understood who Jesus truly is for you.

- They turn south for Jerusalem. Jesus speaks plainly of the fate that awaits him there. Peter cannot cope with the idea of a Messiah who is to be killed. Jesus comes as a savior who walks our path with us and who triumphs by becoming a servant. Try to imagine how you would have responded to what Jesus is saying to the disciples in this conversation.

Friday 22nd February
Matthew 16:13–19

Now when Jesus came into the district of Caesarea Philippi, he asked his disciples, "Who do people say that the Son of Man is?" And they said, "Some say John the Baptist, but others Elijah, and still others Jeremiah or one of the prophets." He said to them, "But who do you say that I am?" Simon Peter answered, "You are the Messiah, the Son of the living God." And Jesus answered him, "Blessed are you, Simon son of Jonah! For flesh and blood has not revealed this to you, but my Father in heaven. And I tell you, you are Peter, and on this rock I will build my church, and the gates of Hades will not prevail against it. I will give you the keys of the kingdom of heaven, and whatever you bind on earth will be bound in heaven, and whatever you loose on earth will be loosed in heaven."

- Peter does well here: he has caught on to who Jesus is, and Jesus blesses him. But this is not the end of the journey, because when under pressure during the Passion, Peter will deny that he even knows Jesus. Reflect on how it is possible to be so full of faith one moment but severely lacking in faith when the situation changes. Why do you think Jesus calls Peter a rock, when he knows that Peter will not always be strong or faithful?

- Our faith requires that we give a personal answer to the question as to who Jesus (the Son of Man) is. It is not enough to quote the *Catechism of the Catholic Church* or the views of one or another theologian. "But who do *you* say that I am?" Try to answer not only from the head but from the heart. You might helpfully rephrase the question as: "Who is Jesus *for me?*" An answer can only be given in prayer.

Saturday 23rd February
Mark 9:2–13

Six days later, Jesus took with him Peter and James and John, and led them up a high mountain apart, by themselves. And he was transfigured before them, and his clothes became dazzling white, such as no one on earth could bleach them. And there appeared to them Elijah with Moses, who were talking with Jesus. Then Peter said to Jesus, "Rabbi, it is good for us to be here; let us make three dwellings, one for you, one for Moses, and one for Elijah." He did not know what to say, for they were terrified. Then a cloud overshadowed them, and from the cloud there came a voice, "This is my Son, the Beloved; listen to him!" Suddenly when they looked around, they saw no one with them any more, but only Jesus. As they were coming down the mountain, he ordered them to tell no one about what they had seen, until after the Son of Man had risen from the dead. So they kept the matter to themselves, questioning what this rising from the dead could mean. Then they asked him, "Why do the scribes say that Elijah must come first?" He said to them, "Elijah is indeed coming first to restore all things. How then is it written about the Son of Man, that he is to go through many sufferings and be treated with contempt? But I tell you that Elijah has come, and they did to him whatever they pleased, as it is written about him."

• I go up the mountain with Jesus and the three chosen apostles. We are dazzled as Jesus is transfigured before our eyes. I hear Elijah (the prophet/forerunner) and Moses (the lawgiver) talking to Jesus, confirming his decision to go to Jerusalem, where he will be crucified and then raised from the dead. Ultimately, it is in his resurrection from the dead that he will be proclaimed Son of God in all his power.

• What will I remember from this experience of seeing Jesus transfigured? Why do I think he allowed me to witness this?

February 24—March 2

Something to think and pray about each day this week:

Let yourselves be healed by Jesus. We all have wounds, everyone: spiritual wounds, sins, hostility, jealousy; perhaps we don't say hello to someone: "Ah, he did this to me, I won't acknowledge him anymore." But this needs to be healed! "How do I do it?" Pray and ask that Jesus heal it. It's sad in a family when siblings don't speak to each other over a small matter, because the devil takes a small matter and makes a world of it. Then hostilities go on, oftentimes for many years, and that family is destroyed. Parents suffer because their children don't speak to each other, or one son's wife doesn't speak to the other, and thus, with jealousy, envy. . . . The devil sows this. And the only One who casts out demons is Jesus. The only One who heals these matters is Jesus. For this reason I say to each one of you: let yourself be healed by Jesus. Each one knows where his wounds are. Each one of us has them; we don't have only one: two, three, four, twenty. Each one knows! May Jesus heal those wounds. But for this I must open my heart, in order that he may come. How do I open my heart? By praying. "But, Lord, I can't with those people over there. I hate them. They did this, this, and this . . ." "Heal this wound, Lord." If we ask Jesus for this grace, he will do it. Let yourself be healed by Jesus. Let Jesus heal you.

—Pope Francis, *Embracing the Way of Jesus*

The Presence of God
What is present to me is what has a hold on my becoming.
I reflect on the presence of God always there in love,
amid the many things that have a hold on me.
I pause and pray that I may let God
affect my becoming in this precise moment.

Freedom
By God's grace I was born to live in freedom. Free to enjoy the pleasures
he created for me. Dear Lord, grant that I may live as you intended, with
complete confidence in your loving care.

Consciousness
I exist in a web of relationships: links to nature, people, God.
I trace out these links, giving thanks for the life that flows through them.
Some links are twisted or broken; I may feel regret, anger, disappointment.
I pray for the gift of acceptance and forgiveness.

The Word
God speaks to each of us individually. I listen attentively to hear what he
is saying to me. Read the text a few times; then listen. (Please turn to the
Scripture on the following pages. Inspiration points are there, should you
need them. When you are ready, return here to continue.)

Conversation
I begin to talk with Jesus about the Scripture I have just read. What part of
it strikes a chord in me? Perhaps the words of a friend—or some story I have
heard recently—will rise to the surface in my consciousness. If so, does the
story throw light on what the Scripture passage may be saying to me?

Conclusion
Glory be to the Father, and to the Son, and to the Holy Spirit,
As it was in the beginning, is now and ever shall be,
World without end. Amen.

Sunday 24th February

Luke 6:27–38

[Jesus said,] "But I say to you that listen, Love your enemies, do good to those who hate you, bless those who curse you, pray for those who abuse you. If anyone strikes you on the cheek, offer the other also; and from anyone who takes away your coat do not withhold even your shirt. Give to everyone who begs from you; and if anyone takes away your goods, do not ask for them again. Do to others as you would have them do to you. If you love those who love you, what credit is that to you? For even sinners love those who love them. If you do good to those who do good to you, what credit is that to you? For even sinners do the same. If you lend to those from whom you hope to receive, what credit is that to you? Even sinners lend to sinners, to receive as much again. But love your enemies, do good, and lend, expecting nothing in return. Your reward will be great, and you will be children of the Most High; for he is kind to the ungrateful and the wicked. Be merciful, just as your Father is merciful. Do not judge, and you will not be judged; do not condemn, and you will not be condemned. Forgive, and you will be forgiven; give, and it will be given to you. A good measure, pressed down, shaken together, running over, will be put into your lap; for the measure you give will be the measure you get back."

- In a way, Jesus takes a lot of pressure off us. He says simply, "Don't judge." Think of all the time and energy I can save by following this one instruction! How much do I want to refrain from judging?
- God is "kind to the ungrateful and the wicked"; thus, if we act from God's heart, we will not pick and choose whom to love. In prayer now, I imagine walking through a typical day with the single agenda of loving without discrimination.

Monday 25th February

Mark 9:14–29

When they came to the disciples, they saw a great crowd around them, and some scribes arguing with them. When the whole crowd saw him, they were immediately overcome with awe, and they ran forward to greet him. He asked them, "What are you arguing about with them?" Someone from the crowd answered him, "Teacher, I brought you my son; he has a spirit that makes him unable to speak; and whenever it seizes him, it dashes him down; and he foams and grinds his teeth and becomes rigid; and I asked your disciples to cast it out, but they could not do so." He answered them, "You faithless generation, how much longer must I be among you? How much longer must I put up with you? Bring him to me." And they brought the boy to him. When the spirit saw him, immediately it convulsed the boy, and he fell on the ground and rolled about, foaming at the mouth. Jesus asked the father, "How long has this been happening to him?" And he said, "From childhood, but if you are able to do anything, have pity on us and help us." Jesus said to him, "If you are able!—All things can be done for the one who believes." Immediately the father of the child cried out, "I believe; help my unbelief!" When Jesus saw that a crowd came running together, he rebuked the unclean spirit, saying to it, "You spirit that keeps this boy from speaking and hearing, I command you, come out of him, and never enter him again!" After crying out and convulsing him terribly, it came out, and the boy was like a corpse, so that most of them said, "He is dead." But Jesus took him by the hand and lifted him up, and he was able to stand. When he had entered the house, his disciples asked him privately, "Why could we not cast it out?" And he answered, "This kind can come out only through prayer."

- I become part of the crowd involved in this disturbing incident, listening and watching. Jesus sees the disciples as faithless and stresses the need for faith and prayer. Given the failed attempts of the disciples, the father's faith was hesitant, but Jesus elicits a stronger affirmation of belief and responds to his faith-filled plea. What message is here for me?

- If Jesus were to ask me, "Do you believe?" what would I answer?

Tuesday 26th February
Mark 9:30–37

They went on from there and passed through Galilee. He did not want anyone to know it; for he was teaching his disciples, saying to them, "The Son of Man is to be betrayed into human hands, and they will kill him, and three days after being killed, he will rise again." But they did not understand what he was saying and were afraid to ask him. Then they came to Capernaum; and when he was in the house he asked them, "What were you arguing about on the way?" But they were silent, for on the way they had argued with one another about who was the greatest. He sat down, called the twelve, and said to them, "Whoever wants to be first must be last of all and servant of all." Then he took a little child and put it among them; and taking it in his arms, he said to them, "Whoever welcomes one such child in my name welcomes me, and whoever welcomes me welcomes not me but the one who sent me."

- Jesus never deceives. He tells his disciples the truth about his Passion. The mystery of the cross is set out starkly. He does not want them to get carried away by the image of a glorious messiah, a wonder-worker. Jesus works at a much deeper level: he identifies with all victims of injustice across human history, and he enters solidarity with them, even at the cost of his life. This is the love that will break the stranglehold of evil. God is with the outcasts of the earth and will give them first place in his kingdom.

- Lord, when suffering or betrayal come my way, let me offer them lovingly to you. Let me believe that my unavoidable sufferings, patiently and lovingly endured, play their part in the saving of the world.

Wednesday 27th February
Mark 9:38–40

John said to him, "Teacher, we saw someone casting out demons in your name, and we tried to stop him, because he was not following us." But Jesus said, "Do not stop him; for no one who does a deed of power in my name will be able soon afterward to speak evil of me. Whoever is not against us is for us."

- Jesus is not worried about competition. He knows who he is and what he is about. He is secure in his calling and purpose. How secure am I as I go through a day of work, relationships, ministry, and trying to do my best?

- "Whoever is not against us is for us." I cannot make this statement and remain suspicious of others and anxious about matters outside my control. In prayer, I ask Jesus to strengthen my sense of who I am in him. I tell him that I don't want to become easily threatened and defensive but to freely do the work he has given me to do.

Thursday 28th February
Mark 9:41–50

[Jesus said,] "For truly I tell you, whoever gives you a cup of water to drink because you bear the name of Christ will by no means lose the reward. If any of you put a stumbling block before one of these little ones who believe in me, it would be better for you if a great millstone were hung around your neck and you were thrown into the sea. If your hand causes you to stumble, cut it off; it is better for you to enter life maimed than to have two hands and to go to hell, to the unquenchable fire. And if your foot causes you to stumble, cut it off; it is better for you to enter life lame than to have two feet and to be thrown into hell. And if your eye causes you to stumble, tear it out; it is better for you to enter the kingdom of God with one eye than to have two eyes and to be thrown into hell, where their worm never dies, and the fire is never quenched. For everyone will be salted with fire. Salt is good; but if salt has lost its saltiness, how can you season it? Have salt in yourselves, and be at peace with one another."

- Do I hear in the harsh words of Jesus his concern for the "little ones"? To lead astray the needy, helpless, and defenseless ones is the blackest of sins. Lord, sharpen my sight and hearing to the needs of those who cannot speak for themselves.

- Jesus makes clear that it is better to lose a part of my life that leads me to sin than it is to keep everything but end up going the wrong way. What aspects of my life lead me away from your path, God? Show me where I am not free.

Friday 1st March
Mark 10:1–12

[Jesus] left that place and went to the region of Judea and beyond the Jordan. And crowds again gathered around him; and, as was his custom, he again taught them. Some Pharisees came, and to test him they asked, "Is it lawful for a man to divorce his wife?" He answered them, "What did Moses command you?" They said, "Moses allowed a man to write a certificate of dismissal and to divorce her." But Jesus said to them, "Because of your hardness of heart he wrote this commandment for you. But from the beginning of creation, 'God made them male and female.' 'For this reason a man shall leave his father and mother and be joined to his wife, and the two shall become one flesh.' So they are no longer two, but one flesh. Therefore what God has joined together, let no one separate." Then in the house the disciples asked him again about this matter. He said to them, "Whoever divorces his wife and marries another commits adultery against her; and if she divorces her husband and marries another, she commits adultery."

- Jesus stuns the Pharisees and his disciples by forbidding divorce. On what grounds? In words repeated in the marriage rite, he insists, "What God has joined together, let no one separate." Marriage creates a union between two people; in God's eyes, unions are to be nurtured, not ruptured. How do I respond to Jesus' strong statements here?

- In Jesus' day, women had few legal protections. A husband could divorce a wife through a simple procedure and did not require a good reason to do so. A woman divorced was put in a desperate position. Jesus no doubt had seen the sad results of cast-off wives, just as today, he sees the bitter fruit of broken families. I pray now for families I know that are struggling or that have already been through divorce or estrangement.

Saturday 2nd March
Mark 10:13–16

People were bringing little children to him in order that he might touch them; and the disciples spoke sternly to them. But when Jesus saw this, he was indignant and said to them, "Let the little children come to me; do not stop them; for it is to such as these that the kingdom of God belongs. Truly I tell you, whoever does not receive the kingdom of God as a little child will never enter it." And he took them up in his arms, laid his hands on them, and blessed them.

- I watch and listen as the mothers present their children to Jesus, the great prophet and teacher. For his time, Jesus' attitude to women and children was revolutionary.

- This is the only time Jesus is reported as being "indignant"! What angered him?

- Children love to hear about Jesus. Do I receive his teachings with the trustful simplicity of a child?

March 3—March 9

Something to think and pray about each day this week:

Every Christian can become a witness to the risen Jesus. And his or her witness is all the more credible, the more it shines through a life lived by the Gospel, a joyful, courageous, gentle, peaceful, merciful life. Instead, if a Christian gives in to ease, vanity, and selfishness, if he or she becomes deaf and blind to the question of "resurrection" of many brothers and sisters, how can [that person] communicate the living Jesus? How can the Christian communicate the freeing power of the living Jesus and his infinite tenderness?

Listen to Jesus. He is the Savior: follow him. To listen to Christ, in fact, entails *taking up the logic of his Pascal Mystery*, setting out on the journey with him to make of oneself a gift of love to others, in docile obedience to the will of God, with an attitude of interior freedom and of detachment from worldly things. One must, in other words, be willing to lose one's very life (cf. Mark 8:35), by giving it up so that all men might be saved; thus, we will meet in eternal happiness. The path to Jesus always leads us to happiness—don't forget it! Jesus' way always leads us to happiness. There will always be a cross, trials in the middle, but at the end we are always led to happiness. Jesus does not deceive us; he promised us happiness and will give it to us if we follow his ways.

—Pope Francis, *Embracing the Way of Jesus*

The Presence of God

"Be still and know that I am God!" Lord, your words lead us to the calmness and greatness of your presence.

Freedom

"In these days, God taught me as a schoolteacher teaches a pupil" (Saint Ignatius). I remind myself that there are things God has to teach me yet, and I ask for the grace to hear them and let them change me.

Consciousness

How am I really feeling? Lighthearted? Heavyhearted? I may be very much at peace, happy to be here.

Equally, I may be frustrated, worried, or angry.

I acknowledge how I really am. It is the real me whom the Lord loves.

The Word

God speaks to each of us individually. I listen attentively to hear what he is saying to me. Read the text a few times; then listen. (Please turn to the Scripture on the following pages. Inspiration points are there, should you need them. When you are ready, return here to continue.)

Conversation

Do I notice myself reacting as I pray with the word of God? Do I feel challenged, comforted, angry? Imagining Jesus sitting or standing by me, I speak out my feelings, as one trusted friend to another.

Conclusion

I thank God for these moments we have spent together and for any insights I have been given concerning the text.

Sunday 3rd March

Luke 6:39–45

He also told them a parable: "Can a blind person guide a blind person? Will not both fall into a pit? A disciple is not above the teacher, but everyone who is fully qualified will be like the teacher. Why do you see the speck in your neighbor's eye, but do not notice the log in your own eye? Or how can you say to your neighbor, 'Friend, let me take out the speck in your eye,' when you yourself do not see the log in your own eye? You hypocrite, first take the log out of your own eye, and then you will see clearly to take the speck out of your neighbor's eye. No good tree bears bad fruit, nor again does a bad tree bear good fruit; for each tree is known by its own fruit. Figs are not gathered from thorns, nor are grapes picked from a bramble bush. The good person out of the good treasure of the heart produces good, and the evil person out of evil treasure produces evil; for it is out of the abundance of the heart that the mouth speaks."

- It's a straightforward principle: I won't help others by pointing out their problems or sins while I am ignoring my own. In fact, my sins become obstacles to clear sight. May I use my irritation at others' sins as a prompt to search my own heart.

- Another simple idea: A good heart produces good actions. If I'm not happy with my actions, I tend to focus on the actions and feel guilty about them. Wouldn't it make more sense to explore what it is within me that has led to these actions? Help me, God—I need wisdom.

Monday 4th March

Mark 10:17–27

As he was setting out on a journey, a man ran up and knelt before him, and asked him, "Good Teacher, what must I do to inherit eternal life?" Jesus said to him, "Why do you call me good? No one is good but God alone. You know the commandments: 'You shall not murder; You shall not commit adultery; You shall not steal; You shall not bear false witness; You shall not defraud; Honor your father and mother.'" He said to him, "Teacher, I have kept all these since my youth." Jesus, looking at him, loved him and said, "You lack one thing; go, sell what you own, and give the money to the poor, and you will have treasure in heaven; then come, follow me." When he heard this, he was shocked and went away grieving, for he had many possessions. Then Jesus looked around and said to his disciples, "How hard it will be for those who have wealth to enter the kingdom of God!" And the disciples were perplexed at these words. But Jesus said to them again, "Children, how hard it is to enter the kingdom of God! It is easier for a camel to go through the eye of a needle than for someone who is rich to enter the kingdom of God." They were greatly astounded and said to one another, "Then who can be saved?" Jesus looked at them and said, "For mortals it is impossible, but not for God; for God all things are possible."

- An extraordinary meeting: Mark, the least poetical of the evangelists, throws in details that bring it to life. Why does Jesus take issue with the man calling him "good"? Then: "Jesus looking at him, loved him." Something in Jesus' gaze was unforgettable. Finally, Mark does not spare us the shock and grief of the man as he hears, and rejects, Jesus' invitation, or Jesus' calm acceptance of that refusal. He will not do violence to our freedom.

- I consider this scene and wonder what it was that Jesus loved about the young man. I allow myself time to think about what he loves about me— and I don't move on until I do! Jesus may show me the one thing that is holding me back from freedom. I can walk away, or I can ask for help to deal with it.

Tuesday 5th March
Mark 10:28–31

Peter began to say to Jesus, "Look, we have left everything and followed you." Jesus said, "Truly I tell you, there is no one who has left house or brothers or sisters or mother or father or children or fields, for my sake and for the sake of the good news, who will not receive a hundredfold now in this age—houses, brothers and sisters, mothers and children, and fields with persecutions—and in the age to come eternal life. But many who are first will be last, and the last will be first."

- The disciples have just been shocked by Jesus' stark observation, "How hard it will be for those who have wealth to enter the kingdom of God!" after a wealthy man had turned down the invitation to follow him. Peter, however, is assured of compensation in this world and the next. What is my response to this exchange?

- I reflect on this conversation as St. Peter might have done at the end of his life. What has it meant to me to follow Jesus? What have I given up? What was my hundredfold, in the way of joy, contentment, peace of soul?

Wednesday 6th March
Ash Wednesday
Matthew 6:1–6, 16–18

[Jesus said,] "Beware of practicing your piety before others in order to be seen by them; for then you have no reward from your Father in heaven. So whenever you give alms, do not sound a trumpet before you, as the hypocrites do in the synagogues and in the streets, so that they may be praised by others. Truly I tell you, they have received their reward. But when you give alms, do not let your left hand know what your right hand is doing, so that your alms may be done in secret; and your Father who sees in secret will reward you. And whenever you pray, do not be like the hypocrites; for they love to stand and pray in the synagogues and at the street corners, so that they may be seen by others. Truly I tell you, they have received their reward. But whenever you pray, go into your room and shut the door and pray to your Father who is in secret; and your Father who sees in secret will reward you. And whenever you fast, do not look dismal, like the hypocrites, for they disfigure their faces so as to show others that they are fasting. Truly I tell you, they have received their reward. But when you fast, put oil on your head and wash your face, so that your fasting may be seen not by others but by your Father who is in secret; and your Father who sees in secret will reward you."

- What motivates me, deepest down? Do I act solely to please God? Jesus gives hypocrites a hard time. They pretend to be what they are not; they are actors, performing behind their masks. When am I most likely to put up a pretense? Do I ever catch myself telling small lies to give others a better impression of myself?

- I must be content to be who I am. My deepest identity is not the one I create for myself but the identity given me by God. I am the beloved of God, and always will be. That is enough. The important person in my life must be not myself, nor others, but only God who sees in secret. God also knows my secret: when everything is said and done, I am infinitely loved!

Thursday 7th March
Luke 9:22–25

[Jesus said to his disciples:] "The Son of Man must undergo great suffering, and be rejected by the elders, chief priests, and scribes, and be killed, and on the third day be raised." Then he said to them all, "If any want to become my followers, let them deny themselves and take up their cross daily and follow me. For those who want to save their life will lose it, and those who lose their life for my sake will save it. What does it profit them if they gain the whole world, but lose or forfeit themselves?"

- At the start of Lent, Jesus puts before us the central events of his Passion, Death, and Resurrection. Jesus states clearly that his project to save the world will end in disaster for himself. I sit with him in silence and with gratitude that he does not simply give up and abandon humankind to its malice.

- Let me also chat with him about the things I endure. He is not saying that suffering is good, but that I can either accept it patiently or try to reject it. He looks hard at me and says, "You could spend your life just looking after yourself and trying to avoid pain and hurt. Or you can embrace the world with love and risk failure, betrayal, disappointment from those you try to serve. Of course you will get hurt, but an eternal blessing will be yours at the end." I respond: "Lord, let me live my life as you lived yours." He thanks me.

Friday 8th March
Matthew 9:14–15

Then the disciples of John came to Jesus, saying, "Why do we and the Pharisees fast often, but your disciples do not fast?" And Jesus said to them, "The wedding guests cannot mourn as long as the bridegroom is with them, can they? The days will come when the bridegroom is taken away from them, and then they will fast."

- John the Baptist and his disciples have their doubts about Jesus. Devout Jews observed regular obligatory fasts and would also undertake private fasting, by way of praying for God's salvation and hastening the coming of the kingdom. We can often feel like John's disciples, confused and unsure about what to do. The divisions in the Church upset us. But Jesus is saying: "With my coming, a wedding has started; a new creation is under way; be joyful!"

- Jesus wanted to celebrate and socialize with everybody, especially the outcasts, the prodigals, the sinners, to let them know that in him the joyful time of salvation had indeed come. I must stop living in no-man's-land. I must wake up—the Savior of the world has come, and I must join him.

Saturday 9th March
Luke 5:27–32

After this he went out and saw a tax collector named Levi, sitting at the tax booth; and he said to him, "Follow me." And he got up, left everything, and followed him. Then Levi gave a great banquet for him in his house; and there was a large crowd of tax collectors and others sitting at the table with them. The Pharisees and their scribes were complaining to his disciples, saying, "Why do you eat and drink with tax collectors and sinners?" Jesus answered, "Those who are well have no need of a physician, but those who are sick; I have come to call not the righteous but sinners to repentance."

- Tax collectors were despised: they were social and religious outcasts. Why then does Jesus choose Levi out of all possible candidates? Because he is determined to break down dramatically the barriers that fragment human community. Who are the tax collectors in my world?

- The banquet indicates table fellowship; eating and drinking together shows that the guests accept one another. Since Jesus is the main guest, we are shown that if we want to be with him at table, we must accept the companionship of people we have despised. At the Eucharist, Jesus invites everyone to participate, not simply as individuals but as fellow disciples who are both sinners and forgiven. Do I complain about this, in words, or silently in my heart?

March 10—March 16

Something to think and pray about each day this week:

God's world is a world in which everyone feels responsible for the other, for the good of the other. . . . [I]n reflection, fasting, and prayer, each of us deep down should ask ourselves, Is this really the world I desire? Is this really the world we all carry in our hearts? Is the world that we want really a world of harmony and peace, in ourselves, in our relations with others, in families, in cities, *in* and *between* nations? And does not true freedom mean choosing ways in this world that lead to the good of all and are guided by love? But then we wonder, Is this the world in which we are living? Creation retains its beauty, which fills us with awe, and it remains a good work. But there are also "violence, division, disagreement, war." These occur when man, the summit of creation, stops contemplating beauty and goodness, and withdraws into his own selfishness.

—Pope Francis, *Embracing the Way of Jesus*

The Presence of God
I remind myself that, as I sit here now,
God is gazing on me with love and holding me in being.
I pause for a moment and think of this.

Freedom
"There are very few people who realize what God would make of them
if they abandoned themselves into his hands, and let themselves be formed
by his grace" (Saint Ignatius). I ask for the grace to trust myself totally to
God's love.

Consciousness
Where do I sense hope, encouragement, and growth in my life? By looking
back over the past few months, I may be able to see which activities and occasions have produced rich fruit. If I do notice such areas, I will determine
to give those areas both time and space in the future.

The Word
Lord Jesus, you became human to communicate with me.
You walked and worked on this earth.
You endured the heat and struggled with the cold.
All your time on this earth was spent in caring for humanity.
You healed the sick, you raised the dead.
Most important of all, you saved me from death.
(Please turn to the Scripture on the following pages. Inspiration points are
there, should you need them. When you are ready, return here to continue.)

Conversation
What is stirring in me as I pray? Am I consoled, troubled, left cold? I imagine Jesus standing or sitting at my side, and I share my feelings with him.

Conclusion
Glory be to the Father, and to the Son, and to the Holy Spirit,
As it was in the beginning, is now and ever shall be,
World without end. Amen.

Sunday 10th March

Luke 4:1–13

Jesus, full of the Holy Spirit, returned from the Jordan and was led by the Spirit in the wilderness, where for forty days he was tempted by the devil. He ate nothing at all during those days, and when they were over, he was famished. The devil said to him, "If you are the Son of God, command this stone to become a loaf of bread." Jesus answered him, "It is written, 'One does not live by bread alone.'" Then the devil led him up and showed him in an instant all the kingdoms of the world. And the devil said to him, "To you I will give their glory and all this authority; for it has been given over to me, and I give it to anyone I please. If you, then, will worship me, it will all be yours." Jesus answered him, "It is written, 'Worship the Lord your God, and serve only him.'" Then the devil took him to Jerusalem, and placed him on the pinnacle of the temple, saying to him, "If you are the Son of God, throw yourself down from here, for it is written, 'He will command his angels concerning you, to protect you,' and 'On their hands they will bear you up, so that you will not dash your foot against a stone.'" Jesus answered him, "It is said, 'Do not put the Lord your God to the test.'" When the devil had finished every test, he departed from him until an opportune time.

• Lord, you told of these temptations to your disciples—how else would they have known? Can I put words on my own temptations, the weaknesses or wickedness that draw me in particular? Can I see my temptations as you did, against the backdrop of the vocation to which you call me?

• Jesus, like Moses before him, retreats into the wilderness where he fasts for forty days. Each temptation involves a seizure of power: power over the elements of creation by turning stones into bread; political and military power by gaining power over the kingdoms of the world; and the power to force God's protection in an inappropriate manner. That Jesus was tested throughout his ministry was widely held in early Christianity. The letter to the Hebrews tells us, "For do we not have a high priest [Jesus] who is unable to sympathize with our weaknesses, but we have one who in every respect has been tested as we are, yet without sin."

Monday 11th March
Matthew 25:31–46

[Jesus said,] "When the Son of Man comes in his glory, and all the angels with him, then he will sit on the throne of his glory. All the nations will be gathered before him, and he will separate people one from another as a shepherd separates the sheep from the goats, and he will put the sheep at his right hand and the goats at the left. Then the king will say to those at his right hand, 'Come, you that are blessed by my Father, inherit the kingdom prepared for you from the foundation of the world; for I was hungry and you gave me food, I was thirsty and you gave me something to drink, I was a stranger and you welcomed me, I was naked and you gave me clothing, I was sick and you took care of me, I was in prison and you visited me.' Then the righteous will answer him, 'Lord, when was it that we saw you hungry and gave you food, or thirsty and gave you something to drink? And when was it that we saw you a stranger and welcomed you, or naked and gave you clothing? And when was it that we saw you sick or in prison and visited you?' And the king will answer them, 'Truly I tell you, just as you did it to one of the least of these who are members of my family, you did it to me.' Then he will say to those at his left hand, 'You that are accursed, depart from me into the eternal fire prepared for the devil and his angels; for I was hungry and you gave me no food, I was thirsty and you gave me nothing to drink, I was a stranger and you did not welcome me, naked and you did not give me clothing, sick and in prison and you did not visit me.' Then they also will answer, 'Lord, when was it that we saw you hungry or thirsty or a stranger or naked or sick or in prison, and did not take care of you?' Then he will answer them, 'Truly I tell you, just as you did not do it to one of the least of these, you did not do it to me.' And these will go away into eternal punishment, but the righteous into eternal life."

- Each group goes to the place it has chosen. Those whose lives were oriented to love and mercy come to the love and mercy of God. Those who excluded people in need from their lives have excluded themselves from God's kingdom, where there is only acceptance and love. What place do I choose through my priorities and actions this day?

- This parable of the sheep and the goats is not about the future, but about opening my eyes here and now to the needs of my neighbor: the hungry, the homeless, the refugee, the isolated lonely ones. Jesus identifies with each one. If I turn away from my brothers and sisters in need, I am turning away from my brother Jesus.

Tuesday 12th March
Matthew 6:7–15

[Jesus said to his disciples,] "When you are praying, do not heap up empty phrases as the Gentiles do; for they think that they will be heard because of their many words. Do not be like them, for your Father knows what you need before you ask him. Pray then in this way:

"Our Father in heaven,
    hallowed be your name.
    Your kingdom come.
    Your will be done,
        on earth as it is in heaven.
    Give us this day our daily bread.
    And forgive us our debts,
        as we also have forgiven our debtors.
    And do not bring us to the time of trial,
        but rescue us from the evil one."

- God knows what I need before I ask. When, then, should I ask? Do you want me to hear for myself what I need, Lord? Do you long for conversation with me? Do you wait for me to rely on you and turn to you for what I need?

- When are my words "empty phrases"? How do I know when my prayer does not have meaningful content? How do I feel when prayer has become empty? I spend time recalling how I have experienced prayer at different times. Holy Spirit, show me what I need to see.

Wednesday 13th March
Luke 11:29–32

When the crowds were increasing, he began to say, "This generation is an evil generation; it asks for a sign, but no sign will be given to it except the sign of Jonah. For just as Jonah became a sign to the people of Nineveh, so the Son of Man will be to this generation. The queen of the South will rise at the judgment with the people of this generation and condemn them, because she came from the ends of the earth to listen to the wisdom of Solomon, and see, something greater than Solomon is here! The people of Nineveh will rise up at the judgment with this generation and condemn it, because they repented at the proclamation of Jonah, and see, something greater than Jonah is here!"

- The Ninevites were moved to repentance by the prophetic sign of Jonah, which they recognized as the authentic word of God. Later, God sends his Son into our world as the ultimate sign of his love for us. You, Lord Jesus, are the sign of signs. Those who go seeking further wonders have not truly seen you. In you I find all that I need to be fully human and to find my destiny with God.

- Jesus uses imagination trying to help his audience catch on to the mystery of who he is. So, he reminds them of famous characters in stories they already know well. He then tries to open their minds further by saying twice that "something greater" is here in his person. Do I cultivate my capacity for mystery, or do I live on the surface of life? Do I reduce the wonders of nature and of the cosmos to mere facts, or do I let myself be drawn to wonder what their author must be like? Everything is a divine mystery because all comes from God. Let me sit with Jesus and ask him to enliven the mystical dimension that may be dormant in me.

Thursday 14th March
Matthew 7:7–12

[Jesus said to his disciples,] "Ask, and it will be given to you; search, and you will find; knock, and the door will be opened for you. For everyone who asks receives, and everyone who searches finds, and for everyone who knocks, the door will be opened. Is there anyone among you who, if your child asks for bread, will give a stone? Or if the child asks for a fish, will give a snake? If you then, who are evil, know how to give good gifts to your children, how much more will your Father in heaven give good things to those who ask him!"

- In the very act of praying we receive something from God. As we open our hearts to God in prayer, God's hands are open to give us good gifts. We leave a time of prayer with an increase of faith, hope, and love, which is the consolation of God. No time of prayer is wasted; all prayer is in the service of love, and prayer increases within us our capacity to love.

- God welcomes me with a loving embrace, and desires to give me "good things" when I ask him with a sincere and open heart. Am I truly open with God in my prayer? Do I share with him all that I am living, my struggles and my joys, and the concrete situations for which I need his help?

Friday 15th March
Matthew 5:20–26

For I tell you, unless your righteousness exceeds that of the scribes and Pharisees, you will never enter the kingdom of heaven. You have heard that it was said to those of ancient times, "You shall not murder"; and "whoever murders shall be liable to judgment." But I say to you that if you are angry with a brother or sister, you will be liable to judgment; and if you insult a brother or sister, you will be liable to the council; and if you say, "You fool," you will be liable to the hell of fire. So when you are offering your gift at the altar, if you remember that your brother or sister has something against you, leave your gift there before the altar and go; first be reconciled to your brother or sister, and then come and offer your gift. Come to terms quickly with your accuser while you are on the way to court with him, or your accuser may hand you over to the judge, and the judge to the guard, and you will be thrown into prison. Truly I tell you, you will never get out until you have paid the last penny.

- The standards operating in the kingdom of heaven are high! Jesus does not dismiss Old Testament teaching but goes to the root of things. We can be smug and content with our conventional good behavior. However, Jesus says to us, "But what about your anger? What about insulting someone? Do you despise anyone, ever? Such behavior won't do anymore."

- Is there anybody I need to forgive? I pray for the grace to forgive that person in my heart and fully let go of any feelings of anger or resentment I may have toward him or her. I ask the Lord for the grace to go to that person and be reconciled with him or her and, if possible, restore the relationship to one of friendship and love.

Saturday 16th March

Matthew 5:43–48

[Jesus said,] "You have heard that it was said, 'You shall love your neighbor and hate your enemy.' But I say to you, Love your enemies and pray for those who persecute you, so that you may be children of your Father in heaven; for he makes his sun rise on the evil and on the good, and sends rain on the righteous and on the unrighteous. For if you love those who love you, what reward do you have? Do not even the tax collectors do the same? And if you greet only your brothers and sisters, what more are you doing than others? Do not even the Gentiles do the same? Be perfect, therefore, as your heavenly Father is perfect."

- Loving our enemies is among the most challenging precepts taught by Jesus. Notice how he finds motivation and a standard in the love shown by our Father in heaven: a love that is all-embracing, indiscriminate, inclusive. Modeling our love on that of the Father is the way to be perfect.

- Contemplate the wonder of God's unconditional love for you and ask for the grace to radiate that love in the different situations and activities of your day.

March 17—March 23

Something to think and pray about each day this week:

Something stirred from deep within. I felt it knocking, begging to be acknowledged and released. I could not put a name to it, but something felt awakened after a long period of dormancy. In truth, this gnawing sensation had been building for more than a year, but on the levee that day, I grappled with this powerful presence at work in me. I had no words for the hunger that was asking me for more. All I could do was attempt to be still and acknowledge its existence. I took a deep breath and looked to God above, begging for help with what felt like an insurmountable task: sitting still and being quiet. Slowly, as the deep breaths continued, inner stillness came. I began to notice my surroundings. In that moment, I saw everything as it was—beautiful, holy, God's gift. My heart welled to the point that I thought it would leap out of my chest. I realized that the hunger I felt was my desire for God. For one solid hour, I breathed deeply in the silence and in being with God. On that day, I touched something powerful: God within me, residing in the inner space that only God and I can access. I understood that holiness lived within me as much as it lived outside me in the beautiful surroundings of the retreat grounds.

—Becky Eldredge, *Busy Lives & Restless Souls*

The Presence of God

I pause for a moment
and reflect on God's life-giving presence
in every part of my body,
in everything around me,
in the whole of my life.

Freedom

Many countries are at this moment suffering the agonies of war. I bow my head in thanksgiving for my freedom. I pray for all prisoners and captives.

Consciousness

Knowing that God loves me unconditionally, I look honestly over the past day, its events, and my feelings. Do I have something to be grateful for? Then I give thanks. Is there something I am sorry for? Then I ask forgiveness.

The Word

Now I turn to the Scripture set out for me this day. I read slowly over the words and see if any sentence or sentiment appeals to me. (Please turn to the Scripture on the following pages. Inspiration points are there, should you need them. When you are ready, return here to continue.)

Conversation

I know with certainty that there were times when you carried me, Lord. There were times when it was through your strength that I got through the dark times in my life.

Conclusion

Glory be to the Father, and to the Son, and to the Holy Spirit,
As it was in the beginning, is now and ever shall be,
World without end. Amen.

Sunday 17th March

Luke 9:28b–36

Now about eight days after these sayings Jesus took with him Peter and John and James, and went up on the mountain to pray. And while he was praying, the appearance of his face changed, and his clothes became dazzling white. Suddenly they saw two men, Moses and Elijah, talking to him. They appeared in glory and were speaking of his departure, which he was about to accomplish at Jerusalem. Now Peter and his companions were weighed down with sleep; but since they had stayed awake, they saw his glory and the two men who stood with him. Just as they were leaving him, Peter said to Jesus, "Master, it is good for us to be here; let us make three dwellings, one for you, one for Moses, and one for Elijah"—not knowing what he said. While he was saying this, a cloud came and overshadowed them; and they were terrified as they entered the cloud. Then from the cloud came a voice that said, "This is my Son, my Chosen; listen to him!" When the voice had spoken, Jesus was found alone. And they kept silent and in those days told no one any of the things they had seen.

- Peter and John and James were privileged to see Jesus in his full dignity. We can see one another in the same way, with the enlightenment of the Holy Spirit. At all sacramental moments, we see those we love in their true dignity as human beings beloved of God. The dreams for this perfect infant at baptism, the blessing with gifts at confirmation, the beauty of forgiveness at reconciliation, the warmth of communion, the hope for healing at the sacrament of the anointing of the sick, the dignity of covenant love at matrimony, the beauty of service at ordination. Fine clothing sometimes makes us even gasp with admiration.

- When have your eyes been opened to the full dignity of another person? Recall that moment and savor it, thanking God for the gift of his vision.

Monday 18th March

Luke 6:36–38

[Jesus said to the disciples,] "Be merciful, just as your Father is merciful. Do not judge, and you will not be judged; do not condemn, and you will not be condemned. Forgive, and you will be forgiven; give, and it will be given to you. A good measure, pressed down, shaken together, running over, will be put into your lap; for the measure you give will be the measure you get back."

- Jesus invites us to be as God is—nothing less! He does not intend to overwhelm us or cause us to feel frustrated by such an enormous invitation; he wants us to wonder at the immensity of God's capacity to love. In our humanity, we are not infinite, but we are called to great love and hope. The invitation reaches to us *as we are*, calling us into the life of God.

- Judgment, condemnation, and lack of forgiveness inhibit good and bind up the spirit. Lord, help me to be generous, not by forcing anything from myself but by sharing fully what you give to me.

Tuesday 19th March
Saint Joseph, Spouse of the Blessed Virgin Mary
Matthew 1:16, 18–21, 24

Jacob was the father of Joseph the husband of Mary, of whom Jesus was born, who is called the Messiah. Now the birth of Jesus the Messiah took place in this way. When his mother Mary had been engaged to Joseph, but before they lived together, she was found to be with child from the Holy Spirit. Her husband Joseph, being a righteous man and unwilling to expose her to public disgrace, planned to dismiss her quietly. But just when he had resolved to do this, an angel of the Lord appeared to him in a dream and said, "Joseph, son of David, do not be afraid to take Mary as your wife, for the child conceived in her is from the Holy Spirit. She will bear a son, and you are to name him Jesus, for he will save his people from their sins." When Joseph awoke from sleep, he did as the angel of the Lord commanded him; he took her as his wife.

- What do we know about St. Joseph? That he loved Mary so much that he suppressed his doubts about her chastity and allowed himself to be regarded as the father of her child, knowing that he wasn't (when Jesus took the floor in the Nazareth synagogue, the begrudgers remarked: "Is not this the son of Joseph?"); that he brought up that child as his own, despite great difficulties and dangers, particularly at the start; that he taught him his trade; that he loved him; and that Jesus' robust health as an adult (physical stamina, courage, strength of purpose, and attractiveness to women, men, and children) is proof of good parenting by his foster father. Joseph is the obvious patron of adoptive fathers.

• I pray for all the men I know who are foster fathers, stepfathers, adoptive fathers, single fathers, and father figures to others.

Wednesday 20th March
Matthew 20:17–28

While Jesus was going up to Jerusalem, he took the twelve disciples aside by themselves, and said to them on the way, "See, we are going up to Jerusalem, and the Son of Man will be handed over to the chief priests and scribes, and they will condemn him to death; then they will hand him over to the Gentiles to be mocked and flogged and crucified; and on the third day he will be raised." Then the mother of the sons of Zebedee came to him with her sons, and kneeling before him, she asked a favor of him. And he said to her, "What do you want?" She said to him, "Declare that these two sons of mine will sit, one at your right hand and one at your left, in your kingdom." But Jesus answered, "You do not know what you are asking. Are you able to drink the cup that I am about to drink?" They said to him, "We are able." He said to them, "You will indeed drink my cup, but to sit at my right hand and at my left, this is not mine to grant, but it is for those for whom it has been prepared by my Father." When the ten heard it, they were angry with the two brothers. But Jesus called them to him and said, "You know that the rulers of the Gentiles lord it over them, and their great ones are tyrants over them. It will not be so among you; but whoever wishes to be great among you must be your servant, and whoever wishes to be first among you must be your slave; just as the Son of Man came not to be served but to serve, and to give his life a ransom for many."

• Our prayer often finds us asking for what we want. As we grow in awareness of the presence of God, we realize how God wants for us something greater. It may appear that we are asked to let go of our requests, but we soon realize that nothing we really want is lost in God.

• Jesus was clear about his relationship with God; he knew who he was and what was his to give. Lord, help me know more clearly what is mine to do and what I might best leave to you.

Thursday 21st March

Luke 16:19–31

[Jesus said to the Pharisees,] "There was a rich man who was dressed in purple and fine linen and who feasted sumptuously every day. And at his gate lay a poor man named Lazarus, covered with sores, who longed to satisfy his hunger with what fell from the rich man's table; even the dogs would come and lick his sores. The poor man died and was carried away by the angels to be with Abraham. The rich man also died and was buried. In Hades, where he was being tormented, he looked up and saw Abraham far away with Lazarus by his side. He called out, 'Father Abraham, have mercy on me, and send Lazarus to dip the tip of his finger in water and cool my tongue; for I am in agony in these flames.' But Abraham said, 'Child, remember that during your lifetime you received your good things, and Lazarus in like manner evil things; but now he is comforted here, and you are in agony. Besides all this, between you and us a great chasm has been fixed, so that those who might want to pass from here to you cannot do so, and no one can cross from there to us.' He said, 'Then, father, I beg you to send him to my father's house—for I have five brothers—that he may warn them, so that they will not also come into this place of torment.' Abraham replied, 'They have Moses and the prophets; they should listen to them.' He said, 'No, father Abraham; but if someone goes to them from the dead, they will repent.' He said to him, 'If they do not listen to Moses and the prophets, neither will they be convinced even if someone rises from the dead.'"

- Take some time to speak to Jesus about this story; consider the situation that was in his mind and recognize how his heart was moved. Look, with Jesus, at your situation, at your world: Who are the self-satisfied rich, who are the overlooked poor?

- Jesus describes Lazarus as being forgotten by people, cared for only by dogs. The wealthy in our world often lavish more care on pets than on their brothers and sisters. I ask God to open my heart and to help me look with compassion on the poor so that I become more like Jesus.

Friday 22nd March

Matthew 21:33–43, 45–46

[Jesus said,] "Listen to another parable. There was a landowner who planted a vineyard, put a fence around it, dug a wine press in it, and built a watchtower. Then he leased it to tenants and went to another country. When the harvest time had come, he sent his slaves to the tenants to collect his produce. But the tenants seized his slaves and beat one, killed another, and stoned another. Again he sent other slaves, more than the first; and they treated them in the same way. Finally he sent his son to them, saying, 'They will respect my son.' But when the tenants saw the son, they said to themselves, 'This is the heir; come, let us kill him and get his inheritance.' So they seized him, threw him out of the vineyard, and killed him. Now when the owner of the vineyard comes, what will he do to those tenants?" They said to him, "He will put those wretches to a miserable death, and lease the vineyard to other tenants who will give him the produce at the harvest time." Jesus said to them, "Have you never read in the scriptures: 'The stone that the builders rejected has become the cornerstone; this was the Lord's doing, and it is amazing in our eyes'? Therefore I tell you, the kingdom of God will be taken away from you and given to a people that produces the fruits of the kingdom." . . . When the chief priests and the Pharisees heard his parables, they realized that he was speaking about them. They wanted to arrest him, but they feared the crowds, because they regarded him as a prophet.

- Jesus speaks about the landlord whose absence causes the tenants to forget themselves. I pray for all those who overlook signs of God's care and imagine God's absence; may my prayer for them and my action this day witness to God's presence and love.

- Jesus—the Son—comes to us so that we might receive our inheritance; we do not need to take anything by force but can trust in Jesus' promise, message, and presence.

Saturday 23rd March

Luke 15:1–3, 11–32

Now all the tax collectors and sinners were coming near to listen to him. And the Pharisees and the scribes were grumbling and saying, "This fellow welcomes sinners and eats with them." So he told them this parable: . . . "There was a man who had two sons. The younger of them said to his father, 'Father, give me the share of the property that will belong to me.' So he divided his property between them. A few days later the younger son gathered all he had and traveled to a distant country, and there he squandered his property in dissolute living. When he had spent everything, a severe famine took place throughout that country, and he began to be in need. So he went and hired himself out to one of the citizens of that country, who sent him to his fields to feed the pigs. He would gladly have filled himself with the pods that the pigs were eating; and no one gave him anything. But when he came to himself he said, 'How many of my father's hired hands have bread enough and to spare, but here I am dying of hunger! I will get up and go to my father, and I will say to him, "Father, I have sinned against heaven and before you; I am no longer worthy to be called your son; treat me like one of your hired hands."' So he set off and went to his father. But while he was still far off, his father saw him and was filled with compassion; he ran and put his arms around him and kissed him. Then the son said to him, 'Father, I have sinned against heaven and before you; I am no longer worthy to be called your son.' But the father said to his slaves, 'Quickly, bring out a robe—the best one—and put it on him; put a ring on his finger and sandals on his feet. And get the fatted calf and kill it, and let us eat and celebrate; for this son of mine was dead and is alive again; he was lost and is found!' And they began to celebrate. Now his elder son was in the field; and when he came and approached the house, he heard music and dancing. He called one of the slaves and asked what was going on. He replied, 'Your brother has come, and your father has killed the fatted calf, because he has got him back safe and sound.' Then he became angry and refused to go in. His father came out and began to plead with him. But he answered his father, 'Listen! For all these years I have been working like a slave for you, and I have never disobeyed your command; yet you have never given me even a young goat so that I might celebrate with my friends. But when this son of yours came back, who has devoured your property with prostitutes, you killed the fatted calf for him!' Then the father said to him, 'Son, you are always with me, and all that is mine is yours. But we had to celebrate and rejoice, because this brother of yours was dead and has come to life; he was lost and has been found.'"

- This story is often told to highlight forgiveness or to focus on our need for repentance. It seems that Jesus told it so that we might relish God's abiding mercy. The loving Father desires only to bless and to restore to love and dignity.

- Lord, help me, this Lent, not to focus entirely on my sin but to keep my heart fixed on your love. Don't let me be distracted by any false image of myself, but allow me to hear your invitation to grow in your image, to reflect your love.

March 24—March 30

Something to think and pray about each day this week:

You may ask yourself, *Why don't I have a relationship with God?* or *Am I too late?* You may think to yourself, *I've been away for a long time* or *I want to go deeper.* Wherever you are on your faith journey, fear not. Rest assured of this: God desires a true and intimate relationship with you. Pope Francis implores us to understand that God is waiting for us: "When you have the strength to say, 'I want to come home,' you will find the door open. God will come to meet you because he is always waiting for you—God is always waiting for you. God embraces you, kisses you, and celebrates." I invite you now to reflect on your life. Do you notice a sense of restlessness? Do you feel a hunger for something more? Do you desire a relationship with God but don't know where to start? Do you wonder how God can show up in the everyday details of the normal life you live? God wants to spend time with us, and we can start sharing that time with God today.

—Becky Eldredge, *Busy Lives & Restless Souls*

The Presence of God

I pause for a moment and think of the love and the grace that God showers on me. I am created in the image and likeness of God; I am God's dwelling place.

Freedom

Lord, you granted me the great gift of freedom. In these times, O Lord, grant that I may be free from any form of racism or intolerance. Remind me that we are all equal in your loving eyes.

Consciousness

Knowing that God loves me unconditionally, I can afford to be honest about how I am.

How has the day been, and how do I feel now? I share my feelings openly with the Lord.

The Word

I take my time to read the word of God slowly, a few times, allowing myself to dwell on anything that strikes me. (Please turn to the Scripture on the following pages. Inspiration points are there, should you need them. When you are ready, return here to continue.)

Conversation

Sometimes I wonder what I might say if I were to meet you in person, Lord. I think I might say "Thank you" because you are always there for me.

Conclusion

I thank God for these moments we have spent together and for any insights I have been given concerning the text.

Sunday 24th March

John 4:5–15, 19b–26, 39a, 40–42

So he came to a Samaritan city called Sychar, near the plot of ground that Jacob had given to his son Joseph. Jacob's well was there, and Jesus, tired out by his journey, was sitting by the well. It was about noon. A Samaritan woman came to draw water, and Jesus said to her, "Give me a drink." (His disciples had gone to the city to buy food.) The Samaritan woman said to him, "How is it that you, a Jew, ask a drink of me, a woman of Samaria?" (Jews do not share things in common with Samaritans.) Jesus answered her, "If you knew the gift of God, and who it is that is saying to you, 'Give me a drink,' you would have asked him, and he would have given you living water." The woman said to him, "Sir, you have no bucket, and the well is deep. Where do you get that living water? Are you greater than our ancestor Jacob, who gave us the well, and with his sons and his flocks drank from it?" Jesus said to her, "Everyone who drinks of this water will be thirsty again, but those who drink of the water that I will give them will never be thirsty. The water that I will give will become in them a spring of water gushing up to eternal life." The woman said to him, "Sir, give me this water, so that I may never be thirsty or have to keep coming here to draw water. . . . I see that you are a prophet. Our ancestors worshiped on this mountain, but you say that the place where people must worship is in Jerusalem." Jesus said to her, "Woman, believe me, the hour is coming when you will worship the Father neither on this mountain nor in Jerusalem. You worship what you do not know; we worship what we know, for salvation is from the Jews. But the hour is coming, and is now here, when the true worshipers will worship the Father in spirit and truth, for the Father seeks such as these to worship him. God is spirit, and those who worship him must worship in spirit and truth." The woman said to him, "I know that Messiah is coming" (who is called Christ). "When he comes, he will proclaim all things to us." Jesus said to her, "I am he, the one who is speaking to you." . . . Many Samaritans from that city believed in him because of the woman's testimony. . . . So when the Samaritans came to him, they asked him to stay with them; and he stayed there for two days. And many more believed because of his word. They said to the woman, "It is no longer because of what you said that we believe, for we have heard for ourselves, and we know that this is truly the Savior of the world."

- The thought of Jesus sitting alone by the well is an invitation to be with him. As he looked at the woman, he looks at me: he longs to offer me life; he invites me to see the deeper meaning in what I do; he respects my dignity, asking me to do what I can for him.

- When Jesus says, "If you knew . . . ," he reveals his desire to draw us into knowing God as he does. His open and generous heart is the heart of God, inviting us all to rest where we are known and loved, to find enduring life and lasting refreshment.

Monday 25th March
The Annunciation of the Lord
Luke 1:26–38

In the sixth month the angel Gabriel was sent by God to a town in Galilee called Nazareth, to a virgin engaged to a man whose name was Joseph, of the house of David. The virgin's name was Mary. And he came to her and said, "Greetings, favored one! The Lord is with you." But she was much perplexed by his words and pondered what sort of greeting this might be. The angel said to her, "Do not be afraid, Mary, for you have found favor with God. And now, you will conceive in your womb and bear a son, and you will name him Jesus. He will be great, and will be called the Son of the Most High, and the Lord God will give to him the throne of his ancestor David. He will reign over the house of Jacob for ever, and of his kingdom there will be no end." Mary said to the angel, "How can this be, since I am a virgin?" The angel said to her, "The Holy Spirit will come upon you, and the power of the Most High will overshadow you; therefore the child to be born will be holy; he will be called Son of God. And now, your relative Elizabeth in her old age has also conceived a son; and this is the sixth month for her who was said to be barren. For nothing will be impossible with God." Then Mary said, "Here am I, the servant of the Lord; let it be with me according to your word." Then the angel departed from her.

- As Christians we hope for great things, humanly impossible things, for ourselves individually, for the church and society. As we ask insistently, we remember that "Nothing will be impossible with God."

- If things are difficult for me now, I try to say with Mary, "Let it be with me according to your word."

Tuesday 26th March

Matthew 18:21–35

Then Peter came and said to him, "Lord, if another member of the church sins against me, how often should I forgive? As many as seven times?" Jesus said to him, "Not seven times, but, I tell you, seventy-seven times. For this reason the kingdom of heaven may be compared to a king who wished to settle accounts with his slaves. When he began the reckoning, one who owed him ten thousand talents was brought to him; and, as he could not pay, his lord ordered him to be sold, together with his wife and children and all his possessions, and payment to be made. So the slave fell on his knees before him, saying, 'Have patience with me, and I will pay you everything.' And out of pity for him, the lord of that slave released him and forgave him the debt. But that same slave, as he went out, came upon one of his fellow slaves who owed him a hundred denarii; and seizing him by the throat, he said, 'Pay what you owe.' Then his fellow slave fell down and pleaded with him, 'Have patience with me, and I will pay you.' But he refused; then he went and threw him into prison until he would pay the debt. When his fellow slaves saw what had happened, they were greatly distressed, and they went and reported to their lord all that had taken place. Then his lord summoned him and said to him, 'You wicked slave! I forgave you all that debt because you pleaded with me. Should you not have had mercy on your fellow slave, as I had mercy on you?' And in anger his lord handed him over to be tortured until he would pay his entire debt. So my heavenly Father will also do to every one of you, if you do not forgive your brother or sister from your heart."

- Forgiveness can be very hard. C. S. Lewis wrote: "Everyone says forgiveness is a lovely idea, until they have something to forgive." But when I fail to forgive, I am shackled to the evil that has been done to me. I cannot move forward. How free am I this moment? What resentments tie me up?

- If we must be prepared to forgive seventy-seven times, then we must also be ready to ask for forgiveness—and believe we are forgiven—seventy-seven times. When was the last time I asked for forgiveness? I ask the Lord to help me search my heart for any unfinished business.

tthew 5:17–19*

[Jesus said to the crowds,] "Do not think that I have come to abolish the law or the prophets; I have come not to abolish but to fulfill. For truly I tell you, until heaven and earth pass away, not one letter, not one stroke of a letter, will pass from the law until all is accomplished. Therefore, whoever breaks one of the least of these commandments, and teaches others to do the same, will be called least in the kingdom of heaven; but whoever does them and teaches them will be called great in the kingdom of heaven."

- Lord, you criticized the petty regulations that had been added to the law of God. You summed up the law and the prophets in the love of God and our neighbor. You were not turning your back on the past but deepening our sense of where we stand before God: not as scrupulous rule keepers, but as loving children.

- End your prayer with the writer of the Psalms: "Make me to know your ways, O LORD; teach me your paths. Lead me in your truth, and teach me, for you are the God of my salvation" (Psalm 25:4–5).

Thursday 28th March

Luke 11:14–23

[Jesus] was casting out a demon that was mute; when the demon had gone out, the one who had been mute spoke, and the crowds were amazed. But some of them said, "He casts out demons by Beelzebul, the ruler of the demons." Others, to test him, kept demanding from him a sign from heaven. But he knew what they were thinking and said to them, "Every kingdom divided against itself becomes a desert, and house falls on house. If Satan also is divided against himself, how will his kingdom stand?—for you say that I cast out the demons by Beelzebul. Now if I cast out the demons by Beelzebul, by whom do your exorcists cast them out? Therefore they will be your judges. But if it is by the finger of God that I cast out the demons, then the kingdom of God has come to you. When a strong man, fully armed, guards his castle, his property is safe. But when one stronger than he attacks him and overpowers him, he takes away his armor in which he trusted and divides his plunder. Whoever is not with me is against me, and whoever does not gather with me scatters."

- You know how painful it is if your motives are misunderstood, if a twisted interpretation is put on your good intentions. Such experiences help you identify with Jesus and feel with him. Be there with him; share your experiences with him.

- Some listeners, who have just witnessed Jesus curing a mute man, refuse to think well of him, and invent a slanderous story. It prods me: Do I think ill of others more readily than I credit them with good? Lord, give me the grace to see the best in others, as I'd wish them to see the best in me.

Friday 29th March

Mark 12:28–34

One of the scribes came near and heard them disputing with one another, and seeing that he answered them well, he asked him, "Which commandment is the first of all?" Jesus answered, "The first is, 'Hear, O Israel: the Lord our God, the Lord is one; you shall love the Lord your God with all your heart, and with all your soul, and with all your mind, and with all your strength.' The second is this, 'You shall love your neighbor as yourself.' There is no other commandment greater than these." Then the scribe said to him, "You are right, Teacher; you have truly said that 'he is one, and besides him there is no other'; and 'to love him with all the heart, and with all the understanding, and with all the strength,' and 'to love one's neighbor as oneself,'—this is much more important than all whole burnt offerings and sacrifices." When Jesus saw that he answered wisely, he said to him, "You are not far from the kingdom of God." After that no one dared to ask him any question.

- Why with all our hearts? Because that is the way the Lord loves us. Parents and grandparents have their children constantly on their minds. They are concerned for them even when they are separated geographically. You are ever in God's mind.

- The second commandment, "You shall love your neighbor as yourself," makes your love of God real. "Those who do not love a brother or sister whom they have seen, cannot love God whom they have not seen" (1 John 4:20). Lord Jesus, keep teaching me to love.

Saturday 30th March
Luke 18:9–14

[Jesus] also told this parable to some who trusted in themselves that they were righteous and regarded others with contempt: "Two men went up to the temple to pray, one a Pharisee and the other a tax collector. The Pharisee, standing by himself, was praying thus, 'God, I thank you that I am not like other people: thieves, rogues, adulterers, or even like this tax collector. I fast twice a week; I give a tenth of all my income.' But the tax collector, standing far off, would not even look up to heaven, but was beating his breast and saying, 'God, be merciful to me, a sinner!' I tell you, this man went down to his home justified rather than the other; for all who exalt themselves will be humbled, but all who humble themselves will be exalted."

- Can I ever get rid completely of the Pharisee in me? I find it so easy to feel superior to others in one way or another while being blind to my own shortcomings. Only by making my own the humble prayer of the publican can I be protected from this danger: "God, be merciful to me, a sinner!"

- How does the story hit me? I would hate to be the object of people's contempt. But Lord, if they knew me as you do, they might be right to feel contempt. And I have no right to look down on those whose sins are paraded in the media. Be merciful to me.

Fourth Week of Lent
March 31—April 6

Something to think and pray about each day this week:

We need to know that we can access God at any time and in any place. We carry a chapel within us—a sacred space—and we can call on God at any moment. God is a friend we can talk to throughout the day: as we wake, as we cook, as we eat, as we drive/commute to work, as we play and hang out with our friends. God is available to talk to us as we do laundry, change diapers, run carpool, shuffle kids to activities, oversee homework, and co-ordinate our families' calendars. *Everything* is holy because our days hold a multitude of ways God can break in and point us back to God as we ponder, pray, and consider.

—Becky Eldredge, *Busy Lives & Restless Souls*

The Presence of God

I pause for a moment and think of the love and the grace that God showers on me. I am created in the image and likeness of God; I am God's dwelling place.

Freedom

Lord, you granted me the great gift of freedom. In these times, O Lord, grant that I may be free from any form of racism or intolerance. Remind me that we are all equal in your loving eyes.

Consciousness

Knowing that God loves me unconditionally, I can afford to be honest about how I am.

How has the day been, and how do I feel now? I share my feelings openly with the Lord.

The Word

I take my time to read the word of God slowly, a few times, allowing myself to dwell on anything that strikes me. (Please turn to the Scripture on the following pages. Inspiration points are there, should you need them. When you are ready, return here to continue.)

Conversation

Sometimes I wonder what I might say if I were to meet you in person, Lord. I think I might say "Thank you" because you are always there for me.

Conclusion

I thank God for these moments we have spent together and for any insights I have been given concerning the text.

Sunday 31st March

John 9:1, 6–9, 13–17, 34–38

As he walked along, he saw a man blind from birth. . . . [Jesus] spat on the ground and made mud with the saliva and spread the mud on the man's eyes, saying to him, "Go, wash in the pool of Siloam" (which means Sent). Then he went and washed and came back able to see. The neighbors and those who had seen him before as a beggar began to ask, "Is this not the man who used to sit and beg?" Some were saying, "It is he." Others were saying, "No, but it is someone like him." He kept saying, "I am the man." . . . They brought to the Pharisees the man who had formerly been blind. Now it was a sabbath day when Jesus made the mud and opened his eyes. Then the Pharisees also began to ask him how he had received his sight. He said to them, "He put mud on my eyes. Then I washed, and now I see." Some of the Pharisees said, "This man is not from God, for he does not observe the sabbath." But others said, "How can a man who is a sinner perform such signs?" And they were divided. So they said again to the blind man, "What do you say about him? It was your eyes he opened." He said, "He is a prophet." . . . They answered him, "You were born entirely in sins, and are you trying to teach us?" And they drove him out. Jesus heard that they had driven him out, and when he found him, he said, "Do you believe in the Son of Man?" He answered, "And who is he, sir? Tell me, so that I may believe in him." Jesus said to him, "You have seen him, and the one speaking with you is he." He said, "Lord, I believe." And he worshiped him.

• The blind man not only receives his sight but the courage to acknowledge what Jesus has done for him: "I am the man." In the full story in (John 9:1–38), when the Pharisees argue with him about how Jesus is a sinner breaking the law by healing on the Sabbath, he fearlessly replies, "He is a prophet." Finally, when he is driven out of the temple and Jesus goes looking for him, we hear him say, "Lord, I believe." He now sees with the eyes of faith as well.

• Ask the Lord to give you courage to witness to your faith: sometimes seriously, other times humorously! "Always be ready to make your defense to anyone who demands from you an accounting for the hope that is in you, yet do it with gentleness and reverence" (1 Peter 3:15–16).

Monday 1st April

John 4:43–54

When the two days were over, he went from that place to Galilee (for Jesus himself had testified that a prophet has no honor in the prophet's own country). When he came to Galilee, the Galileans welcomed him, since they had seen all that he had done in Jerusalem at the festival; for they too had gone to the festival. Then he came again to Cana in Galilee where he had changed the water into wine. Now there was a royal official whose son lay ill in Capernaum. When he heard that Jesus had come from Judea to Galilee, he went and begged him to come down and heal his son, for he was at the point of death. Then Jesus said to him, "Unless you see signs and wonders you will not believe." The official said to him, "Sir, come down before my little boy dies." Jesus said to him, "Go; your son will live." The man believed the word that Jesus spoke to him and started on his way. As he was going down, his slaves met him and told him that his child was alive. So he asked them the hour when he began to recover, and they said to him, "Yesterday at one in the afternoon the fever left him." The father realized that this was the hour when Jesus had said to him, "Your son will live." So he himself believed, along with his whole household. Now this was the second sign that Jesus did after coming from Judea to Galilee.

- Think of the sick people for whom you have prayed. Perhaps your prayer and that of others played its part in their recovery—or had no visible result. Yet no prayer is made in vain. Prayer for another strengthens bonds, softens hearts, and is heard by God.

- For whom do I want to pray now? I trust that the Lord will answer my prayer in the way that is best.

Tuesday 2nd April

John 5:1–16

After this there was a festival of the Jews, and Jesus went up to Jerusalem. Now in Jerusalem by the Sheep Gate there is a pool, called in Hebrew Beth-zatha, which has five porticoes. In these lay many invalids—blind, lame, and paralyzed. One man was there who had been ill for thirty-eight years. When Jesus saw him lying there and knew that he had been there a long time, he said to him, "Do you want to be made well?" The sick man answered him, "Sir, I have no one to put me into the pool when the water is stirred up; and while I am making my way, someone else steps down ahead of me." Jesus said to him, "Stand up, take your mat and walk." At once the man was made well, and he took up his mat and began to walk. Now that day was a sabbath. So the Jews said to the man who had been cured, "It is the sabbath; it is not lawful for you to carry your mat." But he answered them, "The man who made me well said to me, 'Take up your mat and walk.'" They asked him, "Who is the man who said to you, 'Take it up and walk'?" Now the man who had been healed did not know who it was, for Jesus had disappeared in the crowd that was there. Later Jesus found him in the temple and said to him, "See, you have been made well! Do not sin any more, so that nothing worse happens to you." The man went away and told the Jews that it was Jesus who had made him well. Therefore the Jews started persecuting Jesus, because he was doing such things on the sabbath.

- Thirty-eight years of waiting! Did Jesus single out this man, knowing that he had endured his illness longer than anyone else? Jesus speaks with him patiently and allows the man to reveal the pain of his isolation, but he also ignites his desire to be healed. Jesus tells us of his desire for the man: "Do not sin any more . . ."

- Are there sick people in your family, among your friends? Bring them one by one before the Lord, asking him to do what is best for them. Maybe you are worried about your own health? Tell the Lord of your anxieties and leave them with him. "Cast all your anxiety on him, because he cares for you" (1 Peter 5:7).

Wednesday 3rd April

John 5:17–30

[Jesus said,] "My Father is still working, and I also am working." For this reason the Jews were seeking all the more to kill him, because he was not only breaking the sabbath, but was also calling God his own Father, thereby making himself equal to God. Jesus said to them, "Very truly, I tell you, the Son can do nothing on his own, but only what he sees the Father doing; for whatever the Father does, the Son does likewise. The Father loves the Son and shows him all that he himself is doing; and he will show him greater works than these, so that you will be astonished. Indeed, just as the Father raises the dead and gives them life, so also the Son gives life to whomever he wishes. The Father judges no one but has given all judgment to the Son, so that all may honor the Son just as they honor the Father. Anyone who does not honor the Son does not honor the Father who sent him. Very truly, I tell you, anyone who hears my word and believes him who sent me has eternal life, and does not come under judgment, but has passed from death to life. Very truly, I tell you, the hour is coming, and is now here, when the dead will hear the voice of the Son of God, and those who hear will live. For just as the Father has life in himself, so he has granted the Son also to have life in himself; and he has given him authority to execute judgment, because he is the Son of Man. Do not be astonished at this; for the hour is coming when all who are in their graves will hear his voice and will come out—those who have done good, to the resurrection of life, and those who have done evil, to the resurrection of condemnation. I can do nothing on my own. As I hear, I judge; and my judgment is just, because I seek to do not my own will but the will of him who sent me."

• When John's Gospel speaks of "the Jews," it means those Jews who reject-ed Jesus; after all, Jesus and his disciples were Jews. When Jesus said that the Sabbath was made for man, and when he called God his Father, he was challenging his own people's vision of God, proclaiming that God is not so much a lawmaker as a loving father to all his children.

• "My Father is still working, and I also am working." St. Ignatius Loyola used say that the Lord is ever laboring on our behalf: we receive an unex-pected outcome, or we are in the right place at the right time. These are signs of God's providence at work. Thank the Lord for these moments.

Thursday 4th April
John 5:31–47

[Jesus said,] "If I testify about myself, my testimony is not true. There is another who testifies on my behalf, and I know that his testimony to me is true. You sent messengers to John, and he testified to the truth. Not that I accept such human testimony, but I say these things so that you may be saved. He was a burning and shining lamp, and you were willing to rejoice for a while in his light. But I have a testimony greater than John's. The works that the Father has given me to complete, the very works that I am doing, testify on my behalf that the Father has sent me. And the Father who sent me has himself testified on my behalf. You have never heard his voice or seen his form, and you do not have his word abiding in you, because you do not believe him whom he has sent. You search the scriptures because you think that in them you have eternal life; and it is they that testify on my behalf. Yet you refuse to come to me to have life. I do not accept glory from human beings. But I know that you do not have the love of God in you. I have come in my Father's name, and you do not accept me; if another comes in his own name, you will accept him. How can you believe when you accept glory from one another and do not seek the glory that comes from the one who alone is God? Do not think that I will accuse you before the Father; your accuser is Moses, on whom you have set your hope. If you believed Moses, you would believe me, for he wrote about me. But if you do not believe what he wrote, how will you believe what I say?"

- This is a difficult text. However, praying is not study. Focus on what you understand! Jesus is ever aware of having been sent by his Father. The only approval that matters is his Father's, which he received at his baptism and transfiguration. "This is my Son, the Beloved, with whom I am well pleased" (Matthew 3:17; 17:5). While Jesus has the freedom to speak of the Father and his kingdom despite opposition, he is, like us, sensitive to ridicule and hostility.

- Thank the Lord for the encouragement that came from home, school, and friends. Seek to forgive those who were a source of discouragement.

Friday 5th April
John 7:1–2, 10, 25–30

Jesus went about in Galilee. He did not wish to go about in Judea because the Jews were looking for an opportunity to kill him. Now the Jewish festival of Booths was near. . . . But after his brothers had gone to the festival, then he also went, not publicly but as it were in secret. . . . Now some of the people of Jerusalem were saying, "Is not this the man whom they are trying to kill? And here he is, speaking openly, but they say nothing to him! Can it be that the authorities really know that this is the Messiah? Yet we know where this man is from; but when the Messiah comes, no one will know where he is from." Then Jesus cried out as he was teaching in the temple, "You know me, and you know where I am from. I have not come on my own. But the one who sent me is true, and you do not know him. I know him, because I am from him, and he sent me." Then they tried to arrest him, but no one laid hands on him, because his hour had not yet come.

- Notice "as it were in secret." Jesus never made himself the center. He was ever pointing to his Father and, toward the end of his life, speaking of the Spirit who was to come. "They tried to arrest him . . ." On the horizon was the day when "his hour" would come, the hour of his death, the hour of his glory. "Having loved his own who were in the world, he loved them to the end." (John 13:1)

- Bow in silence before the mystery that is God: Father, Son, and Holy Spirit, and pray slowly, "Glory be to the Father and to the Son and to the Holy Spirit."

Saturday 6th April
John 7:40–53

When they heard these words, some in the crowd said, "This is really the prophet." Others said, "This is the Messiah." But some asked, "Surely the Messiah does not come from Galilee, does he? Has not the scripture said that the Messiah is descended from David and comes from Bethlehem, the village where David lived?" So there was a division in the crowd because of him. Some of them wanted to arrest him, but no one laid hands on him. Then the temple police went back to the chief priests and Pharisees, who asked them, "Why did you not arrest him?" The police answered, "Never has anyone spoken like this!" Then the Pharisees replied, "Surely you have not been deceived too, have you? Has any one of the authorities or of the Pharisees believed in him? But this crowd, which does not know the law— they are accursed." Nicodemus, who had gone to Jesus before, and who was one of them, asked, "Our law does not judge people without first giving them a hearing to find out what they are doing, does it?" They replied, "Surely you are not also from Galilee, are you? Search and you will see that no prophet is to arise from Galilee." Then each of them went home.

- Here are two ways of approaching Jesus: some hear him, see how he lives, and love and enjoy him. Others go back to their books and argue about his pedigree. Lord, save me from losing you in the babble of books and arguments. May I meet and know and enjoy you.

- "Never has anyone spoken like this!" I can hear Jesus speak to me from the Scriptures anytime I want—but perhaps the words have been dulled through familiarity? I ask the Holy Spirit to help me regain my sense of wonder at the newness of God.

April 7—April 13

Something to think and pray about each day this week:

People ask me all the time, "How do I know if I'm hearing God's voice or not?" While I don't have the million-dollar answer to this question, I *can* tell you this: A way to recognize God's voice is to spend time praying with Scripture. Scripture is truly the word of God and voice of God. If we want to tune our ear to God's voice, why not start with what we know is God's word? Think about it this way. In a room of young children, I distinctly know when one of my own children is calling out, "Mom!" or when it's another child. Why? Because I've spent hours and hours and hours listening to my children's voices. My ear is finely attuned to what their voices sound like. I can also typically discern which of my children is calling me. I do not think about this anymore; it's just something that naturally happens in motherhood—training our ear to our children's voices. In the same way, as we continue to meditate on God's word, we become more and more attuned to what God's voice sounds like to us.

—Becky Eldredge, *Busy Lives & Restless Souls*

The Presence of God
Dear Jesus, today I call on you, but not to ask for anything. I'd like only to dwell in your presence. May my heart respond to your love.

Freedom
God my creator, you gave me life and the gift of freedom. Through your love I exist in this world. May I never take the gift of life for granted. May I always respect others' right to life.

Consciousness
I ask how I am today. Am I particularly tired, stressed, or anxious? If any of these characteristics apply, can I try to let go of the concerns that disturb me?

The Word
The word of God comes down to us through the Scriptures. May the Holy Spirit enlighten my mind and my heart to respond to the gospel teachings. (Please turn to the Scripture on the following pages. Inspiration points are there, should you need them. When you are ready, return here to continue.)

Conversation
I begin to talk with Jesus about the Scripture I have just read. What part of it strikes a chord in me? Perhaps the words of a friend—or some story I have heard recently—will rise to the surface in my consciousness. If so, does the story throw light on what the Scripture passage may be saying to me?

Conclusion
Glory be to the Father, and to the Son, and to the Holy Spirit,
As it was in the beginning, is now and ever shall be,
World without end. Amen.

Sunday 7th April

John 11:3–7, 17, 20–27, 33–45

So the sisters sent a message to Jesus, "Lord, he whom you love is ill." But when Jesus heard it, he said, "This illness does not lead to death; rather it is for God's glory, so that the Son of God may be glorified through it." Accordingly, though Jesus loved Martha and her sister and Lazarus, after having heard that Lazarus was ill, he stayed two days longer in the place where he was. Then after this he said to the disciples, "Let us go to Judea again." . . . When Jesus arrived, he found that Lazarus had already been in the tomb four days. . . . When Martha heard that Jesus was coming, she went and met him, while Mary stayed at home. Martha said to Jesus, "Lord, if you had been here, my brother would not have died. But even now I know that God will give you whatever you ask of him." Jesus said to her, "Your brother will rise again." Martha said to him, "I know that he will rise again in the resurrection on the last day." Jesus said to her, "I am the resurrection and the life. Those who believe in me, even though they die, will live, and everyone who lives and believes in me will never die. Do you believe this?" She said to him, "Yes, Lord, I believe that you are the Messiah, the Son of God, the one coming into the world." . . . When Jesus saw [Mary] weeping, and the Jews who came with her also weeping, he was greatly disturbed in spirit and deeply moved. He said, "Where have you laid him?" They said to him, "Lord, come and see." Jesus began to weep. So the Jews said, "See how he loved him!" But some of them said, "Could not he who opened the eyes of the blind man have kept this man from dying?" Then Jesus, again greatly disturbed, came to the tomb. It was a cave, and a stone was lying against it. Jesus said, "Take away the stone." Martha, the sister of the dead man, said to him, "Lord, already there is a stench because he has been dead four days." Jesus said to her, "Did I not tell you that if you believed, you would see the glory of God?" So they took away the stone. And Jesus looked upward and said, "Father, I thank you for having heard me. I knew that you always hear me, but I have said this for the sake of the crowd standing here, so that they may believe that you sent me." When he had said this, he cried with a loud voice, "Lazarus, come out!" The dead man came out, his hands and feet bound with strips of cloth, and his face wrapped in a cloth. Jesus said to them, "Unbind him, and let him go." Many of the Jews therefore, who had come with Mary and had seen what Jesus did, believed in him.

- Jesus reminds us many times that, if we have faith, nothing is impossible. Martha's faith is indomitable. Knowing that the tomb contains the decomposing body of her beloved brother, she can still summon up the words, "even now I know that God will give you whatever you ask of him." Do I truly believe that anything is possible for one who believes?

- When I am entombed in hopelessness, grant that I may hear the voice of Jesus, as Lazarus did. Let me hear those blessed words he uttered at Lazarus' grave: "Unbind him, and let him go."

Monday 8th April
John 8:12–20

Again Jesus spoke to them, saying, "I am the light of the world. Whoever follows me will never walk in darkness but will have the light of life." Then the Pharisees said to him, "You are testifying on your own behalf; your testimony is not valid." Jesus answered, "Even if I testify on my own behalf, my testimony is valid because I know where I have come from and where I am going, but you do not know where I come from or where I am going. You judge by human standards; I judge no one. Yet even if I do judge, my judgment is valid; for it is not I alone who judge, but I and the Father who sent me. In your law it is written that the testimony of two witnesses is valid. I testify on my own behalf, and the Father who sent me testifies on my behalf." Then they said to him, "Where is your Father?" Jesus answered, "You know neither me nor my Father. If you knew me, you would know my Father also." He spoke these words while he was teaching in the treasury of the temple, but no one arrested him, because his hour had not yet come.

- We revisit the question of Jesus' identity. The passage begins with one of the "I am" sayings that John attributes to Jesus. These are meant to recall the answer God gave to Moses when he asked God's name: "I AM WHO I AM." Then Moses is told to say to the Israelites: "I AM has sent me to you" (Exodus 3:13–14). Jesus, by using this "I am" language, is claiming to share in God's own identity.

- Christian faith is not primarily in a doctrine but in a person. Through this person, Jesus Christ, we enter the mystery of God. Thank you, Lord, for welcoming me.

Tuesday 9th April

John 8:21–30

Again he said to them, "I am going away, and you will search for me, but you will die in your sin. Where I am going, you cannot come." Then the Jews said, "Is he going to kill himself? Is that what he means by saying, 'Where I am going, you cannot come'?" He said to them, "You are from below, I am from above; you are of this world, I am not of this world. I told you that you would die in your sins, for you will die in your sins unless you believe that I am he." They said to him, "Who are you?" Jesus said to them, "Why do I speak to you at all? I have much to say about you and much to condemn; but the one who sent me is true, and I declare to the world what I have heard from him." They did not understand that he was speaking to them about the Father. So Jesus said, "When you have lifted up the Son of Man, then you will realize that I am he, and that I do nothing on my own, but I speak these things as the Father instructed me. And the one who sent me is with me; he has not left me alone, for I always do what is pleasing to him." As he was saying these things, many believed in him.

- It is when we see Jesus lifted up on the cross that we realize who he is and why he lived. The rest of the Gospels are like a preface to the Passion. On the cross we see the triumph of love over evil, and our best help in coping with the reality of evil.

- Jesus spoke to the world what he heard from the Father. Am I aware, day to day, that I can listen for God's voice and then repeat to others what I hear? Am I that confident in my relationship with the Father? Father, help me settle into my role as son or daughter with comfort, hope, and courage.

Wednesday 10th April

John 8:31–42

Then Jesus said to the Jews who had believed in him, "If you continue in my word, you are truly my disciples; and you will know the truth, and the truth will make you free." They answered him, "We are descendants of Abraham and have never been slaves to anyone. What do you mean by saying, 'You will be made free'?" Jesus answered them, "Very truly, I tell you, everyone who commits sin is a slave to sin. The slave does not have a permanent place in the household; the son has a place there forever. So if the Son makes you free, you will be free indeed. I know that you are descendants of Abraham; yet you look for an opportunity to kill me, because there is no place in you for my word. I declare what I have seen in the Father's presence; as for you, you should do what you have heard from the Father." They answered him, "Abraham is our father." Jesus said to them, "If you were Abraham's children, you would be doing what Abraham did, but now you are trying to kill me, a man who has told you the truth that I heard from God. This is not what Abraham did. You are indeed doing what your father does." They said to him, "We are not illegitimate children; we have one father, God himself." Jesus said to them, "If God were your Father, you would love me, for I came from God and now I am here. I did not come on my own, but he sent me."

- Jesus' promise is that the truth will make us free. Lord, I do want to be free, so let me listen to those who tell me the truth about myself. Let me listen also to your word, which reaches into my heart to liberate me. Let me start with the great truth of which you try to convince me: I am endlessly loved by you.

- When in my life have I had an experience that made me truly see Jesus as the one sent by God?

Thursday 11th April
John 8:51–59

[Jesus said,] "Very truly, I tell you, whoever keeps my word will never see death." The Jews said to him, "Now we know that you have a demon. Abraham died, and so did the prophets; yet you say, 'Whoever keeps my word will never taste death.' Are you greater than our father Abraham, who died? The prophets also died. Who do you claim to be?" Jesus answered, "If I glorify myself, my glory is nothing. It is my Father who glorifies me, he of whom you say, 'He is our God,' though you do not know him. But I know him; if I were to say that I do not know him, I would be a liar like you. But I do know him and I keep his word. Your ancestor Abraham rejoiced that he would see my day; he saw it and was glad." Then the Jews said to him, "You are not yet fifty years old, and have you seen Abraham?" Jesus said to them, "Very truly, I tell you, before Abraham was, I am." So they picked up stones to throw at him, but Jesus hid himself and went out of the temple.

- Lord I am praying here on the edge of what I can grasp, reaching for the eternal Now. What matters to me is that you are as much my contemporary as you were of Pilate and the stone-throwing Jews.

- Abraham's life marks the beginning of salvation history. His immense journey through the wilderness was made in response to God's call. The biblical desert was a place of passage and purification. In our own passage to the Promised Land, we must learn that God is with us at every stage of the journey, as he was with Abraham.

Friday 12th April
John 10:31–42

The Jews took up stones again to stone him. Jesus replied, "I have shown you many good works from the Father. For which of these are you going to stone me?" The Jews answered, "It is not for a good work that we are going to stone you, but for blasphemy, because you, though only a human being, are making yourself God." Jesus answered, "Is it not written in your law, 'I said, you are gods'? If those to whom the word of God came were called 'gods'— and the scripture cannot be annulled—can you say that the one whom the Father has sanctified and sent into the world is blaspheming because I said, 'I am God's Son'? If I am not doing the works of my Father, then do not believe me. But if I do them, even though you do not believe me, believe the works, so that you may know and understand that the Father is in me and I am in the Father." Then they tried to arrest him again, but he escaped from their hands. He went away again across the Jordan to the place where John had been baptizing earlier, and he remained there. Many came to him, and they were saying, "John performed no sign, but everything that John said about this man was true." And many believed in him there.

- Lord, you told the Jews to look at your works, if they did not believe your words. Compassion, kindness, and courage in my life are what make my words credible. May my life reflect what I profess.

- The people in today's reading condemn Jesus because of their particular image of God. What is my image of God? The best image is to see God as Pure Love. Have I ever condemned someone because I nursed a warped image of God?

Saturday 13th April

John 11:45–56

Many of the Jews therefore, who had come with Mary and had seen what Jesus did, believed in him. But some of them went to the Pharisees and told them what he had done. So the chief priests and the Pharisees called a meeting of the council, and said, "What are we to do? This man is performing many signs. If we let him go on like this, everyone will believe in him, and the Romans will come and destroy both our holy place and our nation." But one of them, Caiaphas, who was high priest that year, said to them, "You know nothing at all! You do not understand that it is better for you to have one man die for the people than to have the whole nation destroyed." He did not say this on his own, but being high priest that year he prophesied that Jesus was about to die for the nation, and not for the nation only, but to gather into one the dispersed children of God. So from that day on they planned to put him to death. Jesus therefore no longer walked about openly among the Jews, but went from there to a town called Ephraim in the region near the wilderness; and he remained there with the disciples. Now the Passover of the Jews was near, and many went up from the country to Jerusalem before the Passover to purify themselves. They were looking for Jesus and were asking one another as they stood in the temple, "What do you think? Surely he will not come to the festival, will he?"

- Pope Francis, reflecting on this text, noted that Jesus died for his people and for everyone. But this, the Pope stressed, must not be applied generically; it means that Jesus died specifically for each and every one of us individually. And this is the ultimate expression of Jesus' love for all people.

- The religious leaders were caught up in the politics of the day, which included dealing with the Roman occupiers. From a political standpoint, Caiaphas's conclusion made sense. How do politics or other details in my life press upon the way I make decisions or discern my next steps?

April 14—April 20

Something to think and pray about each day this week:

We kneel before a crucifix and recall that death, a consequence of sin, has no power over Jesus of Nazareth. He hangs on a cross embracing death. At the end, *crying out in a loud voice*, Jesus deliberately *yielded up his spirit* (Matt. 27:50, NJB). What can we believe about this faith handed on to us, so utterly contradictory to the human instincts and our sophisticated culture? We can believe that we contemplate a love so entire that the Son would want to embrace everything human—even suffering and death. We know what the faith teaches us: Jesus "sacrificed his life" for love of us. We struggle, though, to believe in a love so entire that it remains faithful when not returned. Unreturned love is a profound form of suffering. And Jesus' unreturned love was not just not returned; it was violently, disdainfully rejected. No one will understand so great a love who has not experienced it. God knows that is true. He knew it about his own people. So God sent the Son to show us that love, and Jesus did so, publicly suffering rejection and execution. Then he invited us to *love one another as I have loved you* (John 15:12).

—Joseph A. Tetlow, SJ, *Always Discerning*

The Presence of God
God is with me, but even more astounding, God is within me.
Let me dwell for a moment on God's life-giving presence
in my body, in my mind, in my heart,
as I sit here, right now.

Freedom
Lord, may I never take the gift of freedom for granted. You gave me the great blessing of freedom of spirit. Fill my spirit with your peace and joy.

Consciousness
I remind myself that I am in the presence of God, who is my strength in times of weakness and my comforter in times of sorrow.

The Word
I take my time to read the word of God slowly, a few times, allowing myself to dwell on anything that strikes me. (Please turn to the Scripture on the following pages. Inspiration points are there, should you need them. When you are ready, return here to continue.)

Conversation
Jesus, you always welcomed little children when you walked on this earth. Teach me to have a childlike trust in you. Teach me to live in the knowledge that you will never abandon me.

Conclusion
Glory be to the Father, and to the Son, and to the Holy Spirit,
As it was in the beginning, is now and ever shall be,
World without end. Amen.

Sunday 14th April
Palm Sunday of the Passion of the Lord
Luke 23:1–49

Then the assembly rose as a body and brought Jesus before Pilate. They began to accuse him, saying, "We found this man perverting our nation, forbidding us to pay taxes to the emperor, and saying that he himself is the Messiah, a king." Then Pilate asked him, "Are you the king of the Jews?" He answered, "You say so." Then Pilate said to the chief priests and the crowds, "I find no basis for an accusation against this man." But they were insistent and said, "He stirs up the people by teaching throughout all Judea, from Galilee where he began even to this place."

When Pilate heard this, he asked whether the man was a Galilean. And when he learned that he was under Herod's jurisdiction, he sent him off to Herod, who was himself in Jerusalem at that time. When Herod saw Jesus, he was very glad, for he had been wanting to see him for a long time, because he had heard about him and was hoping to see him perform some sign. He questioned him at some length, but Jesus gave him no answer. The chief priests and the scribes stood by, vehemently accusing him. Even Herod with his soldiers treated him with contempt and mocked him; then he put an elegant robe on him, and sent him back to Pilate. That same day Herod and Pilate became friends with each other; before this they had been enemies.

Pilate then called together the chief priests, the leaders, and the people, and said to them, "You brought me this man as one who was perverting the people; and here I have examined him in your presence and have not found this man guilty of any of your charges against him. Neither has Herod, for he sent him back to us. Indeed, he has done nothing to deserve death. I will therefore have him flogged and release him."

Then they all shouted out together, "Away with this fellow! Release Barabbas for us!" (This was a man who had been put in prison for an insurrection that had taken place in the city, and for murder.) Pilate, wanting to release Jesus, addressed them again; but they kept shouting, "Crucify, crucify him!" A third time he said to them, "Why, what evil has he done? I have found in him no ground for the sentence of death; I will therefore have him flogged and then release him." But they kept urgently demanding with loud shouts that he should be crucified; and their voices prevailed. So Pilate gave his verdict that their demand should be granted. He released the man they asked for, the one who had been put in prison for insurrection and murder, and he handed Jesus over as they wished.

As they led him away, they seized a man, Simon of Cyrene, who was coming from the country, and they laid the cross on him, and made him carry it behind Jesus. A great number of the people followed him, and among them were women who were beating their breasts and wailing for him. But Jesus turned to them and said, "Daughters of Jerusalem, do not weep for me, but weep for yourselves and for your children. For the days are surely coming when they will say, 'Blessed are the barren, and the wombs that never bore, and the breasts that never nursed.' Then they will begin to say to the mountains, 'Fall on us'; and to the hills, 'Cover us.' For if they do this when the wood is green, what will happen when it is dry?"

Two others also, who were criminals, were led away to be put to death with him. When they came to the place that is called The Skull, they crucified Jesus there with the criminals, one on his right and one on his left. Then Jesus said, "Father, forgive them; for they do not know what they are doing." And they cast lots to divide his clothing. And the people stood by, watching; but the leaders scoffed at him, saying, "He saved others; let him save himself if he is the Messiah of God, his chosen one!" The soldiers also mocked him, coming up and offering him sour wine, and saying, "If you are the King of the Jews, save yourself!" There was also an inscription over him, "This is the King of the Jews."

One of the criminals who were hanged there kept deriding him and saying, "Are you not the Messiah? Save yourself and us!" But the other rebuked him, saying, "Do you not fear God, since you are under the same sentence of condemnation? And we indeed have been condemned justly, for we are getting what we deserve for our deeds, but this man has done nothing wrong." Then he said, "Jesus, remember me when you come into your kingdom." He replied, "Truly I tell you, today you will be with me in Paradise."

It was now about noon, and darkness came over the whole land until three in the afternoon, while the sun's light failed; and the curtain of the temple was torn in two. Then Jesus, crying with a loud voice, said, "Father, into your hands I commend my spirit." Having said this, he breathed his last. When the centurion saw what had taken place, he praised God and said, "Certainly this man was innocent." And when all the crowds who had gathered there for this spectacle saw what had taken place, they returned home, beating their breasts. But all his acquaintances, including the women who had followed him from Galilee, stood at a distance, watching these things.

- I choose a moment or a scene from this long story of Jesus' Passion, and I stay with Jesus. I tell him how I feel about what is happening. I try to comfort him.

- Lord Jesus, show me how to be present to people who are suffering— people I know who are being persecuted or mistreated or misunderstood and ostracized.

Monday 15th April
John 12:1–11

Six days before the Passover Jesus came to Bethany, the home of Lazarus, whom he had raised from the dead. There they gave a dinner for him. Martha served, and Lazarus was one of those at the table with him. Mary took a pound of costly perfume made of pure nard, anointed Jesus' feet, and wiped them with her hair. The house was filled with the fragrance of the perfume. But Judas Iscariot, one of his disciples (the one who was about to betray him), said, "Why was this perfume not sold for three hundred denarii and the money given to the poor?" (He said this not because he cared about the poor, but because he was a thief; he kept the common purse and used to steal what was put into it.) Jesus said, "Leave her alone. She bought it so that she might keep it for the day of my burial. You always have the poor with you, but you do not always have me." When the great crowd of the Jews learned that he was there, they came not only because of Jesus but also to see Lazarus, whom he had raised from the dead. So the chief priests planned to put Lazarus to death as well, since it was on account of him that many of the Jews were deserting and were believing in Jesus.

- Where Judas sees waste, Jesus sees love. Mary's love anticipates the love of Jesus. She pours her tears on the feet of the one who will pour himself out on the world. Lord, may I honor the vision and wisdom you have given me to understand events with my deepest self.

- Mary is praying with her body and with her heart. It is a way we seldom pray. Her prayer is part of a tradition as old as the passionate, lyrical, and sensuous Song of Solomon. Yet there is nothing to stop us praying this way. A gentle touch of understanding, a hug of reassurance, a smile of love—these, too, are prayers.

Tuesday 16th April
John 13:21–33, 36–38

After saying this Jesus was troubled in spirit, and declared, "Very truly, I tell you, one of you will betray me." The disciples looked at one another, uncertain of whom he was speaking. One of his disciples—the one whom Jesus loved—was reclining next to him; Simon Peter therefore motioned to him to ask Jesus of whom he was speaking. So while reclining next to Jesus, he asked him, "Lord, who is it?" Jesus answered, "It is the one to whom I give this piece of bread when I have dipped it in the dish." So when he had dipped the piece of bread, he gave it to Judas son of Simon Iscariot. After he received the piece of bread, Satan entered into him. Jesus said to him, "Do quickly what you are going to do." Now no one at the table knew why he said this to him. Some thought that, because Judas had the common purse, Jesus was telling him, "Buy what we need for the festival"; or, that he should give something to the poor. So, after receiving the piece of bread, he immediately went out. And it was night. When he had gone out, Jesus said, "Now the Son of Man has been glorified, and God has been glorified in him. If God has been glorified in him, God will also glorify him in himself and will glorify him at once. Little children, I am with you only a little longer. You will look for me; and as I said to the Jews so now I say to you, 'Where I am going, you cannot come.'" . . . Simon Peter said to him, "Lord, where are you going?" Jesus answered, "Where I am going, you cannot follow me now; but you will follow afterward." Peter said to him, "Lord, why can I not follow you now? I will lay down my life for you." Jesus answered, "Will you lay down your life for me? Very truly, I tell you, before the cock crows, you will have denied me three times."

- "And it was night" is not simply a description of the time of day; it is a stark image of the gloom of sin and rejection. Judas walks into the darkness—away from Jesus, the true light that the darkness cannot overcome. He will die in despair, in a pride so stiff-necked that it selects the misery of damnation rather than the happiness offered by a kindly God.

- Peter hit deep points of his life here. His sureness of following Jesus was challenged by Jesus himself. He would later find himself weak and failing. But even when Peter said later that he didn't know Jesus, there would be time for taking it back and speaking it with his life. We oscillate in our following of the Lord; these days let us know in the certainty of Jesus' love that there is always another day, another chance, another joy in our following of Jesus.

Wednesday 17th April
Matthew 26:14–25

Then one of the twelve, who was called Judas Iscariot, went to the chief priests and said, "What will you give me if I betray him to you?" They paid him thirty pieces of silver. And from that moment he began to look for an opportunity to betray him. On the first day of Unleavened Bread the disciples came to Jesus, saying, "Where do you want us to make the preparations for you to eat the Passover?" He said, "Go into the city to a certain man, and say to him, 'The Teacher says, My time is near; I will keep the Passover at your house with my disciples.'" So the disciples did as Jesus had directed them, and they prepared the Passover meal. When it was evening, he took his place with the twelve; and while they were eating, he said, "Truly I tell you, one of you will betray me." And they became greatly distressed and began to say to him one after another, "Surely not I, Lord?" He answered, "The one who has dipped his hand into the bowl with me will betray me. The Son of Man goes as it is written of him, but woe to that one by whom the Son of Man is betrayed! It would have been better for that one not to have been born." Judas, who betrayed him, said, "Surely not I, Rabbi?" He replied, "You have said so."

- Holy Week is an invitation to walk closely with Jesus: we fix our gaze on him and accompany him in his suffering; we let him look closely at us and see us as we really are. We do not have to present a brave face to him but can tell him about where we have been disappointed, let down, perhaps even betrayed. We avoid getting stuck in our own misfortune by seeing as he sees, by learning from his heart.

- Help me to see, Jesus, how you do not condemn. You invite each of us to embrace the truth of our own discipleship. You invite us to follow you willingly, freely, forgiven.

Thursday 18th April
Holy Thursday

John 13:1–15

Now before the festival of the Passover, Jesus knew that his hour had come to depart from this world and go to the Father. Having loved his own who were in the world, he loved them to the end. The devil had already put it into the heart of Judas son of Simon Iscariot to betray him. And during supper Jesus, knowing that the Father had given all things into his hands, and that he had come from God and was going to God, got up from the table, took off his outer robe, and tied a towel around himself. Then he poured water into a basin and began to wash the disciples' feet and to wipe them with the towel that was tied around him. He came to Simon Peter, who said to him, "Lord, are you going to wash my feet?" Jesus answered, "You do not know now what I am doing, but later you will understand." Peter said to him, "You will never wash my feet." Jesus answered, "Unless I wash you, you have no share with me." Simon Peter said to him, "Lord, not my feet only but also my hands and my head!" Jesus said to him, "One who has bathed does not need to wash, except for the feet, but is entirely clean. And you are clean, though not all of you." For he knew who was to betray him; for this reason he said, "Not all of you are clean." After he had washed their feet, had put on his robe, and had returned to the table, he said to them, "Do you know what I have done to you? You call me Teacher and Lord—and you are right, for that is what I am. So if I, your Lord and Teacher, have washed your feet, you also ought to wash one another's feet. For I have set you an example, that you also should do as I have done to you.

- It may be important for us to think of what we want to do for Jesus, to let him know and to seek his approval. Jesus smiles and invites us to listen first—to notice. He asks if we can allow him to serve us. "See what I do," he seems to say. "Accept who I am. Then be who you are!"

- Jesus says, "Later you will understand." Sometimes that's not enough for me! I want to understand now. Help me, Jesus, to live as you did even when I don't fully comprehend what you are asking of me.

Friday 19th April
Friday of the Passion of the Lord (Good Friday)
John 18:1—19:42

After Jesus had spoken these words, he went out with his disciples across the Kidron valley to a place where there was a garden, which he and his disciples entered. Now Judas, who betrayed him, also knew the place, because Jesus often met there with his disciples. So Judas brought a detachment of soldiers together with police from the chief priests and the Pharisees, and they came there with lanterns and torches and weapons. Then Jesus, knowing all that was to happen to him, came forward and asked them, "Whom are you looking for?" They answered, "Jesus of Nazareth." Jesus replied, "I am he." Judas, who betrayed him, was standing with them. When Jesus said to them, "I am he," they stepped back and fell to the ground. Again he asked them, "Whom are you looking for?" And they said, "Jesus of Nazareth." Jesus answered, "I told you that I am he. So if you are looking for me, let these men go." This was to fulfill the word that he had spoken, "I did not lose a single one of those whom you gave me." Then Simon Peter, who had a sword, drew it, struck the high priest's slave, and cut off his right ear. The slave's name was Malchus. Jesus said to Peter, "Put your sword back into its sheath. Am I not to drink the cup that the Father has given me?"

So the soldiers, their officer, and the Jewish police arrested Jesus and bound him. First they took him to Annas, who was the father-in-law of Caiaphas, the high priest that year. Caiaphas was the one who had advised the Jews that it was better to have one person die for the people.

Simon Peter and another disciple followed Jesus. Since that disciple was known to the high priest, he went with Jesus into the courtyard of the high priest, but Peter was standing outside at the gate. So the other disciple, who was known to the high priest, went out, spoke to the woman who guarded the gate, and brought Peter in. The woman said to Peter, "You are not also one of this man's disciples, are you?" He said, "I am not." Now the slaves and the police had made a charcoal fire because it was cold, and they were standing around it and warming themselves. Peter also was standing with them and warming himself.

Then the high priest questioned Jesus about his disciples and about his teaching. Jesus answered, "I have spoken openly to the world; I have always taught in synagogues and in the temple, where all the Jews come together. I have said nothing in secret. Why do you ask me? Ask those who heard what I said to them; they know what I said." When he had said this, one of the police standing nearby struck Jesus on the face, saying, "Is that how you answer the high priest?" Jesus answered, "If I have spoken wrongly, testify to the wrong. But if I have spoken rightly, why do you strike me?" Then Annas sent him bound to Caiaphas the high priest.

Now Simon Peter was standing and warming himself. They asked him, "You are not also one of his disciples, are you?" He denied it and said, "I am not." One of the slaves of the high priest, a relative of the man whose ear Peter had cut off, asked, "Did I not see you in the garden with him?" Again Peter denied it, and at that moment the cock crowed.

Then they took Jesus from Caiaphas to Pilate's headquarters. It was early in the morning. They themselves did not enter the headquarters, so as to avoid ritual defilement and to be able to eat the Passover. So Pilate went out to them and said, "What accusation do you bring against this man?" They answered, "If this man were not a criminal, we would not have handed him over to you." Pilate said to them, "Take him yourselves and judge him according to your law." The Jews replied, "We are not permitted to put anyone to death." (This was to fulfill what Jesus had said when he indicated the kind of death he was to die.)

Then Pilate entered the headquarters again, summoned Jesus, and asked him, "Are you the King of the Jews?" Jesus answered, "Do you ask this on your own, or did others tell you about me?" Pilate replied, "I am not a Jew, am I? Your own nation and the chief priests have handed you over to me. What have you done?" Jesus answered, "My kingdom is not from this world. If my kingdom were from this world, my followers would be fighting to keep me from being handed over to the Jews. But as it is, my kingdom is not from here." Pilate asked him, "So you are a king?" Jesus answered, "You say that I am a king. For this I was born, and for this I came into the world, to testify to the truth. Everyone who belongs to the truth listens to my voice." Pilate asked him, "What is truth?"

After he had said this, he went out to the Jews again and told them, "I find no case against him. But you have a custom that I release someone for you at the Passover. Do you want me to release for you the King of the Jews?" They shouted in reply, "Not this man, but Barabbas!" Now Barabbas was a bandit.

Then Pilate took Jesus and had him flogged. And the soldiers wove a crown of thorns and put it on his head, and they dressed him in a purple robe. They kept coming up to him, saying, "Hail, King of the Jews!" and striking him on the face. Pilate went out again and said to them, "Look, I am bringing him out to you to let you know that I find no case against him." So Jesus came out, wearing the crown of thorns and the purple robe. Pilate said to them, "Here is the man!" When the chief priests and the police saw him, they shouted, "Crucify him! Crucify him!" Pilate said to them, "Take him yourselves and crucify him; I find no case against him." The Jews answered him, "We have a law, and according to that law he ought to die because he has claimed to be the Son of God."

Now when Pilate heard this, he was more afraid than ever. He entered his headquarters again and asked Jesus, "Where are you from?" But Jesus gave him no answer. Pilate therefore said to him, "Do you refuse to speak to me? Do you not know that I have power to release you, and power to crucify you?" Jesus answered him, "You would have no power over me unless it had been given you from above; therefore the one who handed me over to you is guilty of a greater sin." From then on Pilate tried to release him, but the Jews cried out, "If you release this man, you are no friend of the emperor. Everyone who claims to be a king sets himself against the emperor."

When Pilate heard these words, he brought Jesus outside and sat on the judge's bench at a place called The Stone Pavement, or in Hebrew Gabbatha. Now it was the day of Preparation for the Passover; and it was about noon. He said to the Jews, "Here is your King!" They cried out, "Away with him! Away with him! Crucify him!" Pilate asked them, "Shall I crucify your King?" The chief priests answered, "We have no king but the emperor." Then he handed him over to them to be crucified.

So they took Jesus; and carrying the cross by himself, he went out to what is called The Place of the Skull, which in Hebrew is called Golgotha. There they crucified him, and with him two others, one on either side, with Jesus between them. Pilate also had an inscription written and put on the cross. It read, "Jesus of Nazareth, the King of the Jews." Many of the Jews read this inscription, because the place where Jesus was crucified was near the city; and it was written in Hebrew, in Latin, and in Greek. Then the chief priests of the Jews said to Pilate, "Do not write, 'The King of the Jews,' but, 'This man said, I am King of the Jews.'" Pilate answered, "What I have written I have written." When the soldiers had crucified Jesus, they took his clothes and divided them into four parts, one for each soldier. They also took his tunic; now the tunic was seamless, woven in one piece from the top. So they said to one another, "Let us not tear it, but cast lots for it to see who will get it." This was to fulfill what the scripture says, "They divided my clothes among themselves, and for my clothing they cast lots." And that is what the soldiers did.

Meanwhile, standing near the cross of Jesus were his mother, and his mother's sister, Mary the wife of Clopas, and Mary Magdalene. When Jesus saw his mother and the disciple whom he loved standing beside her, he said to his mother, "Woman, here is your son." Then he said to the disciple, "Here is your mother." And from that hour the disciple took her into his own home.

After this, when Jesus knew that all was now finished, he said (in order to fulfill the scripture), "I am thirsty." A jar full of sour wine was standing there. So they put a sponge full of the wine on a branch of hyssop and held it to his mouth. When Jesus had received the wine, he said, "It is finished." Then he bowed his head and gave up his spirit.

Since it was the day of Preparation, the Jews did not want the bodies left on the cross during the sabbath, especially because that sabbath was a day of great solemnity. So they asked Pilate to have the legs of the crucified men broken and the bodies removed. Then the soldiers came and broke the legs of the first and of the other who had been crucified with him. But when they came to Jesus and saw that he was already dead, they did not break his legs. Instead, one of the soldiers pierced his side with a spear, and at once blood and water came out. (He who saw this has testified so that you also may believe. His testimony is true, and he knows that he tells the truth.) These things occurred so that the scripture might be fulfilled, "None of his bones shall be broken." And again another passage of scripture says, "They will look on the one whom they have pierced."

After these things, Joseph of Arimathea, who was a disciple of Jesus, though a secret one because of his fear of the Jews, asked Pilate to let him take away the body of Jesus. Pilate gave him permission; so he came and removed his body. Nicodemus, who had at first come to Jesus by night, also came, bringing a mixture of myrrh and aloes, weighing about a hundred pounds. They took the body of Jesus and wrapped it with the spices in linen cloths, according to the burial custom of the Jews. Now there was a garden in the place where he was crucified, and in the garden there was a new tomb in which no one had ever been laid. And so, because it was the Jewish day of Preparation, and the tomb was nearby, they laid Jesus there.

• Jesus allows himself to be caught up in a sequence of events fueled by hatred, racism (Romans against Jews), pride, fear, and political expediency. He does not use his power to change anyone's mind or will. Lord, help me give myself to this day of my own life, willing to be who I am in you and yet not striving to force change in others.

• Linger with Jesus at any point in this sequence of events. Watch his face and body, say what you long to say to him.

Saturday 20th April
Holy Saturday
Luke 24:1–12

But on the first day of the week, at early dawn, they came to the tomb, taking the spices that they had prepared. They found the stone rolled away from the tomb, but when they went in, they did not find the body. While they were perplexed about this, suddenly two men in dazzling clothes stood beside them. The women were terrified and bowed their faces to the ground, but the men said to them, "Why do you look for the living among the dead? He is not here, but has risen. Remember how he told you, while he was still in Galilee, that the Son of Man must be handed over to sinners, and be crucified, and on the third day rise again." Then they remembered his words, and returning from the tomb, they told all this to the eleven and to all the rest. Now it was Mary Magdalene, Joanna, Mary the mother of James, and the other women with them who told this to the apostles. But these words seemed to them an idle tale, and they did not believe them. But Peter got up and ran to the tomb; stooping and looking in, he saw the linen cloths by themselves; then he went home, amazed at what had happened.

• Holy Saturday is a day of waiting for what is to come (whatever that may be). The emptiness in our hearts left by the death of a loved one is mirrored by the emptiness of the tomb. Not only do we no longer have a living Jesus, neither do we have his dead body. It is the women disciples who first hear the news that Jesus is risen. But this only throws them into greater confusion as they cannot understand what it might mean, and the apostles think their whole story is "an idle tale." What would my response be to what the women say?

- Yet Peter, impulsive as ever, and still feeling overwhelmed by guilt because of his denial of Jesus, runs to the tomb to check out the story. He too finds it empty. What does that empty tomb say to me?

April 21—April 27

Something to think and pray about each day this week:

The sun is up now, and you look up to feel the warmth of the rays against your face. Looking ahead, you notice some women running down the path. They seem to be in a joyful panic, like something frightening but wonderful has happened. As you get closer to where they came from, there is a man standing there. He is standing so tall, so confident. It's as if he has accomplished something impossible. Getting closer, you realize it's him. It's Jesus. You know you saw him die. How can he be standing there? He looks at you with eyes that are clear and sure. He speaks to you. What does Jesus say to you? How do you respond? Standing closer to Jesus, you feel a strength coming from him. You want to reach over and embrace him, to touch him to be sure it is really Jesus. He seems to know your mind and the questions swimming around in your head. Jesus reaches over and touches your hand. You feel a surge of energy rush through you. "It is you," you say to Jesus. "It is you!" Tears stream down your face. Jesus says something to you. What does Jesus say? What do you want to say to Jesus? . . . Easter Sunday is a day when life conquers death. How does my belief in the Resurrection change how I live my life? Who do I need to share the hope and joy of the Resurrection with today?

—Steve Connor on *dotMagis*, the blog of *IgnatianSpirituality.com*

The Presence of God
Dear Lord, as I come to you today, fill my heart, my whole being, with the wonder of your presence. Help me remain receptive to you as I put aside the cares of this world. Fill my mind with your peace.

Freedom
Lord, grant me the grace to be free from the excesses of this life. Let me not get caught up with the desire for wealth. Keep my heart and mind free to love and serve you.

Consciousness
I exist in a web of relationships: links to nature, people, God.
I trace out these links, giving thanks for the life that flows through them.
Some links are twisted or broken; I may feel regret, anger, disappointment.
I pray for the gift of acceptance and forgiveness.

The Word
God speaks to each of us individually. I listen attentively to hear what he is saying to me. Read the text a few times; then listen. (Please turn to the Scripture on the following pages. Inspiration points are there, should you need them. When you are ready, return here to continue.)

Conversation
Jesus, you speak to me through the words of the Gospels. May I respond to your call today. Teach me to recognize your hand at work in my daily living.

Conclusion
I thank God for these moments we have spent together and for any insights I have been given concerning the text.

Sunday 21st April
Easter Sunday of the Resurrection of the Lord
John 20:1–9

Early on the first day of the week, while it was still dark, Mary Magdalene came to the tomb and saw that the stone had been removed from the tomb. So she ran and went to Simon Peter and the other disciple, the one whom Jesus loved, and said to them, "They have taken the Lord out of the tomb, and we do not know where they have laid him." Then Peter and the other disciple set out and went toward the tomb. The two were running together, but the other disciple outran Peter and reached the tomb first. He bent down to look in and saw the linen wrappings lying there, but he did not go in. Then Simon Peter came, following him, and went into the tomb. He saw the linen wrappings lying there, and the cloth that had been on Jesus' head, not lying with the linen wrappings but rolled up in a place by itself. Then the other disciple, who reached the tomb first, also went in, and he saw and believed; for as yet they did not understand the scripture, that he must rise from the dead.

- Mary went to do her best, to tend to Jesus' mortal remains. She accepted the reality as she saw it but was determined to do what she could to bring dignity and honor to her loved one and her teacher. Help me, O God, to do what I can as I remain alert, noticing the movement of your Spirit. May I receive life as you offer it, even if in unexpected ways.

- As described by Benedict XVI in his Easter Vigil homily, April 15, 2006, "The Resurrection was like an explosion of light," a "cosmic event" linking heaven and earth. But above all, it was "an explosion of love." "It ushered in a new dimension of being . . . through which a new world emerges." It is a "leap in the history of 'evolution' and of life in general towards a new future life, a new world which, starting from Christ, already continuously permeates this world of ours, transforms it, and draws it to itself." The Resurrection unites us with God and others. "If we live in this way, we transform the world." I sit with this paragraph and allow it to become my prayer.

Monday 22nd April

Matthew 28:8–15

So they left the tomb quickly with fear and great joy, and ran to tell his disciples. Suddenly Jesus met them and said, "Greetings!" And they came to him, took hold of his feet, and worshiped him. Then Jesus said to them, "Do not be afraid; go and tell my brothers to go to Galilee; there they will see me." While they were going, some of the guard went into the city and told the chief priests everything that had happened. After the priests had assembled with the elders, they devised a plan to give a large sum of money to the soldiers, telling them, "You must say, 'His disciples came by night and stole him away while we were asleep.' If this comes to the governor's ears, we will satisfy him and keep you out of trouble." So they took the money and did as they were directed. And this story is still told among the Jews to this day.

- The women left the tomb with joy, interpreting the emptiness positively; having gone to care for the dead, they realized their task was to announce the living. So it was that they were able to meet Jesus and to receive from him a new mission. I pray that I may have the same space in my life— that, by laying aside my own preoccupations, I might be free to proclaim good news.

- The invitation of Jesus is to go to Galilee and there "they will see me." It's the same invitation he gives to us. Galilee can be the neighborhood, the family, the prayer space, the poor, and the many moments we find ourselves aware of Jesus' presence. Prayer is one of them; prayer will heighten our awareness of times we meet the Lord.

Tuesday 23rd April

John 20:11–18

But Mary stood weeping outside the tomb. As she wept, she bent over to look into the tomb; and she saw two angels in white, sitting where the body of Jesus had been lying, one at the head and the other at the feet. They said to her, "Woman, why are you weeping?" She said to them, "They have taken away my Lord, and I do not know where they have laid him." When she had said this, she turned around and saw Jesus standing there, but she did not know that it was Jesus. Jesus said to her, "Woman, why are you weeping?

Whom are you looking for?" Supposing him to be the gardener, she said to him, "Sir, if you have carried him away, tell me where you have laid him, and I will take him away." Jesus said to her, "Mary!" She turned and said to him in Hebrew, "Rabbouni!" (which means Teacher). Jesus said to her, "Do not hold on to me, because I have not yet ascended to the Father. But go to my brothers and say to them, 'I am ascending to my Father and your Father, to my God and your God.'" Mary Magdalene went and announced to the disciples, "I have seen the Lord"; and she told them that he had said these things to her.

- There is a journey here from the darkness of unfaith to partial faith and finally to perfect faith. Mary's seeing is clouded by disappointment, grief, and unspeakable loss. But the sound of Jesus' voice and the use of her name gives her new vision. I ask to hear Jesus say my name, today and every day.

- Lord, the Easter event bids me to leave my tomb of self-absorption and hopelessness. I am called to walk with Easter eyes. Let me bear witness to your risen presence in our shadowed and fractured world. May my humble efforts of advocacy and solidarity enable others to rise from their tombs and live.

Wednesday 24th April
Luke 24:13–35

Now on that same day two of them were going to a village called Emmaus, about seven miles from Jerusalem, and talking with each other about all these things that had happened. While they were talking and discussing, Jesus himself came near and went with them, but their eyes were kept from recognizing him. And he said to them, "What are you discussing with each other while you walk along?" They stood still, looking sad. Then one of them, whose name was Cleopas, answered him, "Are you the only stranger in Jerusalem who does not know the things that have taken place there in these days?" He asked them, "What things?" They replied, "The things about Jesus of Nazareth, who was a prophet mighty in deed and word before God and all the people, and how our chief priests and leaders handed him over to be condemned to death and crucified him. But we had hoped that he was the one to redeem Israel. Yes, and besides all this, it is now the third day since these things took place. Moreover, some women of our group astounded us. They were at the tomb early this morning, and when they did not find his body there, they came back and told us that they had indeed seen a vision of angels who said that he was alive. Some of those who were with us went to the tomb and found it just as the women had said; but they did not see him." Then he said to them, "Oh, how foolish you are, and how slow of heart to believe all that the prophets have declared! Was it not necessary that the Messiah should suffer these things and then enter into his glory?" Then beginning with Moses and all the prophets, he interpreted to them the things about himself in all the scriptures. As they came near the village to which they were going, he walked ahead as if he were going on. But they urged him strongly, saying, "Stay with us, because it is almost evening and the day is now nearly over." So he went in to stay with them. When he was at the table with them, he took bread, blessed and broke it, and gave it to them. Then their eyes were opened, and they recognized him; and he vanished from their sight. They said to each other, "Were not our hearts burning within us while he was talking to us on the road, while he was opening the scriptures to us?" That same hour they got up and returned to Jerusalem; and they found the eleven and their companions gathered together. They were saying, "The Lord has risen indeed, and he has appeared to Simon!" Then they told what had happened on the road, and how he had been made known to them in the breaking of the bread.

• The trudging disciples had turned their backs on Jerusalem and were picking over the story as they knew it. So it was that Jesus found them, coming near and walking with them. I let him fall in step with me now.

• Jesus, find me where I am. Draw near and walk with me. Help me see how my story comes to life as I listen to yours. Let me so hear your good news that my heart may glow. Let me forget myself and receive your Spirit. You bring me the message of Life, and you trust me to do for others what you want to do for me.

Thursday 25th April
Luke 24:35–48

Then they told what had happened on the road, and how he had been made known to them in the breaking of the bread. While they were talking about this, Jesus himself stood among them and said to them, "Peace be with you." They were startled and terrified, and thought that they were seeing a ghost.

He said to them, "Why are you frightened, and why do doubts arise in your hearts? Look at my hands and my feet; see that it is I myself. Touch me and see; for a ghost does not have flesh and bones as you see that I have." And when he had said this, he showed them his hands and his feet. While in their joy they were disbelieving and still wondering, he said to them, "Have you anything here to eat?" They gave him a piece of broiled fish, and he took it and ate in their presence. Then he said to them, "These are my words that I spoke to you while I was still with you—that everything written about me in the law of Moses, the prophets, and the psalms must be fulfilled." Then he opened their minds to understand the scriptures, and he said to them, "Thus it is written, that the Messiah is to suffer and to rise from the dead on the third day, and that repentance and forgiveness of sins is to be proclaimed in his name to all nations, beginning from Jerusalem. You are witnesses of these things."

- Pope Francis, in a homily (April 24, 2014) on this passage, said, "We are afraid of joy, and Jesus, by his Resurrection, gives us joy: the joy of being Christians, the joy of following him closely, the joy of taking the road of the beatitudes, the joy of being with him." He described the fear of joy as "a Christian illness."

- Let us pray with Pope Francis "that the Lord may open our minds and make us understand that he is a living reality, that he has a body, that he is with us and that he accompanies us, that he has conquered: let us ask the Lord for the grace not to be afraid of joy."

Friday 26th April

John 21:1–14

After these things Jesus showed himself again to the disciples by the Sea of Tiberias; and he showed himself in this way. Gathered there together were Simon Peter, Thomas called the Twin, Nathanael of Cana in Galilee, the sons of Zebedee, and two others of his disciples. Simon Peter said to them, "I am going fishing." They said to him, "We will go with you." They went out and got into the boat, but that night they caught nothing. Just after daybreak, Jesus stood on the beach; but the disciples did not know that it was Jesus. Jesus said to them, "Children, you have no fish, have you?" They answered him, "No." He said to them, "Cast the net to the right side of the boat, and you will find some." So they cast it, and now they were not able to haul it in because there were so many fish. That disciple whom Jesus loved said to Peter, "It is the Lord!" When Simon Peter heard that it was the Lord, he put on some clothes, for he was naked, and jumped into the sea. But the other disciples came in the boat, dragging the net full of fish, for they were not far from the land, only about a hundred yards off. When they had gone ashore, they saw a charcoal fire there, with fish on it, and bread. Jesus said to them, "Bring some of the fish that you have just caught." So Simon Peter went aboard and hauled the net ashore, full of large fish, a hundred fifty-three of them; and though there were so many, the net was not torn. Jesus said to them, "Come and have breakfast." Now none of the disciples dared to ask him, "Who are you?" because they knew it was the Lord. Jesus came and took the bread and gave it to them, and did the same with the fish. This was now the third time that Jesus appeared to the disciples after he was raised from the dead.

- Peter was not one for sitting around moping; he knew where Jesus had found him before and was confident that his busyness would not hide him from the Lord. We see him now, directing the activity of the others yet remaining open to the direction of the stranger. What does this say to me about my own life? In what ways should I take initiative? In what ways can I be open to a voice that calls me beyond myself?

- Peter was not the first to recognize Jesus, but he was the first to respond. I pray that I might hear good news spoken to me by those around me.

Saturday 27th April
Mark 16:9–15

Now after he rose early on the first day of the week, he appeared first to Mary Magdalene, from whom he had cast out seven demons. She went out and told those who had been with him, while they were mourning and weeping. But when they heard that he was alive and had been seen by her, they would not believe it. After this he appeared in another form to two of them, as they were walking into the country. And they went back and told the rest, but they did not believe them. Later he appeared to the eleven themselves as they were sitting at the table; and he upbraided them for their lack of faith and stubbornness, because they had not believed those who saw him after he had risen. And he said to them, "Go into all the world and proclaim the good news to the whole creation."

- Mary Magdalene might not have seemed the most likely of witnesses to those who would not believe. I draw inspiration from her as a witness to life, an announcer of truth.

- The light dawned gradually for the disciples: the message of Easter was not received immediately or wholeheartedly by all. Sometimes outwardly confident yet harboring doubts, at other times hesitant to proclaim what seems certain to me, I am like the disciples. Jesus invites me to a fullness of faith. He sees and understands my stubbornness and reluctance yet trusts me. Calmly and gently he sends me to "the whole world."

April 28—May 4

Something to think and pray about each day this week:

In the spring, we plant seeds, but we also notice all kinds of plants sprouting without any help from us. Right now, we have lettuce coming up in a patch of the backyard close to where the lettuce container plant sat last year. Some of the lettuce went to seed and fell into the ground, and we have small bright green leaves now, popping up with the regular grass. I don't mind lettuce on the lawn, but I do mind certain weeds in the flowerbed or space where the vegetables need their growing room. Today I ask myself: *What is sprouting in my life, and is it helpful or not?* The best time to weed is when the plants are young and the roots haven't grown too deep. Have I developed a habit lately of talking about a coworker who irritates me? This is especially easy if he irritates other colleagues as well—very easy to begin talking about that irritating person with the small club of people he's angered lately. As I review my day at work, can I look closely at the words that have come out of my mouth? Am I willing to be honest and identify my own gossip and backbiting? All kinds of activities sprout when we're not paying attention. . . . One of the simplest ways to discover the unwanted "sprouts" in your life is to do the daily Examen—a prayer St. Ignatius devised to help us review the day.

—Vinita Hampton Wright on *dotMagis*,
the blog of *IgnatianSpirituality.com*

The Presence of God

Dear Jesus, I come to you today longing for your presence. I desire to love you as you love me. May nothing ever separate me from you.

Freedom

Lord grant me the grace to have freedom of the spirit. Cleanse my heart and soul so that I may live joyously in your love.

Consciousness

Where am I with God? With others?
Do I have something to be grateful for? Then I give thanks.
Is there something I am sorry for? Then I ask forgiveness.

The Word

The word of God comes down to us through the Scriptures. May the Holy Spirit enlighten my mind and my heart to respond to the gospel teachings. (Please turn to the Scripture on the following pages. Inspiration points are there, should you need them. When you are ready, return here to continue.)

Conversation

How has God's word moved me? Has it left me cold?
Has it consoled me or moved me to act in a new way?
I imagine Jesus standing or sitting beside me;
I turn and share my feelings with him

Conclusion

I thank God for these moments we have spent together and for any insights I have been given concerning the text.

Sunday 28th April
Second Sunday of Easter (or Sunday of Divine Mercy)

John 20:19–31

When it was evening on that day, the first day of the week, and the doors of the house where the disciples had met were locked for fear of the Jews, Jesus came and stood among them and said, "Peace be with you." After he said this, he showed them his hands and his side. Then the disciples rejoiced when they saw the Lord. Jesus said to them again, "Peace be with you. As the Father has sent me, so I send you." When he had said this, he breathed on them and said to them, "Receive the Holy Spirit. If you forgive the sins of any, they are forgiven them; if you retain the sins of any, they are retained." But Thomas (who was called the Twin), one of the twelve, was not with them when Jesus came. So the other disciples told him, "We have seen the Lord." But he said to them, "Unless I see the mark of the nails in his hands, and put my finger in the mark of the nails and my hand in his side, I will not believe." A week later his disciples were again in the house, and Thomas was with them. Although the doors were shut, Jesus came and stood among them and said, "Peace be with you." Then he said to Thomas, "Put your finger here and see my hands. Reach out your hand and put it in my side. Do not doubt but believe." Thomas answered him, "My Lord and my God!" Jesus said to him, "Have you believed because you have seen me? Blessed are those who have not seen and yet have come to believe." Now Jesus did many other signs in the presence of his disciples, which are not written in this book. But these are written so that you may come to believe that Jesus is the Messiah, the Son of God, and that through believing you may have life in his name.

- Thomas places his hands in the wounds of Jesus, and the experience draws from him the first, ringing affirmation of Christ's divinity: "My Lord and my God!" Fully human, and fully divine. Eternally human, eternally divine. His human nature is glorified, just as his divinity is humanized. Our human nature will be forever in him; his divinity dwells within us and will remain with us even to the consummation of the world.

- Help me, Lord, to be before you and to hear your word in this time of prayer. You know the needs of my mind. You have heard my words. Now, let me listen for your voice and know your presence. I lay aside my demands so that I can receive what you offer to me.

Monday 29th April
John 3:1–8

Now there was a Pharisee named Nicodemus, a leader of the Jews. He came to Jesus by night and said to him, "Rabbi, we know that you are a teacher who has come from God; for no one can do these signs that you do apart from the presence of God." Jesus answered him, "Very truly, I tell you, no one can see the kingdom of God without being born from above." Nicodemus said to him, "How can anyone be born after having grown old? Can one enter a second time into the mother's womb and be born?" Jesus answered, "Very truly, I tell you, no one can enter the kingdom of God without being born of water and Spirit. What is born of the flesh is flesh, and what is born of the Spirit is spirit. Do not be astonished that I said to you, 'You must be born from above.' The wind blows where it chooses, and you hear the sound of it, but you do not know where it comes from or where it goes. So it is with everyone who is born of the Spirit."

• Nicodemus was a logical and reasonable man; he was prepared to give time to considering what Jesus said. Yet his logical and reasonable habits came against him; the idea of being born again confounded him, and he failed to see how he could achieve what Jesus suggested. But Jesus was not suggesting that he do anything! Just as a baby is not born of its own efforts, Jesus was inviting him—and us—to relax, to realize that we are held by God. Our origin is in God, it is God who brings us to life, and it is in responding to God's call to life that we will come to life.

• I pray always in the Spirit, recalling the words of Pope Francis: "The Holy Spirit alone gives us the strength to change our attitude, to change the history of our life, to change our belonging."

Tuesday 30th April
John 3:7–15

[Jesus said,] "Do not be astonished that I said to you, 'You must be born from above.' The wind blows where it chooses, and you hear the sound of it, but you do not know where it comes from or where it goes. So it is with everyone who is born of the Spirit." Nicodemus said to him, "How can these things be?" Jesus answered him, "Are you a teacher of Israel, and yet you do not understand these things? Very truly, I tell you, we speak of what we know and testify to what we have seen; yet you do not receive our testimony. If I have told you about earthly things and you do not believe, how can you believe if I tell you about heavenly things? No one has ascended into heaven except the one who descended from heaven, the Son of Man. And just as Moses lifted up the serpent in the wilderness, so must the Son of Man be lifted up, that whoever believes in him may have eternal life."

- Nicodemus was a clever teacher but lacked a certain wisdom. Used to citing authorities, he was unable to recognize the authority of Jesus who spoke of what he knew. Before God, I acknowledge my habits, my preferences, and my inclinations; I ask God to give me the freedom I need to be touched by Jesus' word, to awaken to his imagination, to want for myself the freedom that he desires for me.

- Jesus states that what he speaks of is a mystery; being born of the Spirit happens in God's way. I pray for an openness to the Holy Spirit's work in me.

Wednesday 1st May

John 3:16–21

[Jesus said,] "For God so loved the world that he gave his only Son, so that everyone who believes in him may not perish but may have eternal life. Indeed, God did not send the Son into the world to condemn the world, but in order that the world might be saved through him. Those who believe in him are not condemned; but those who do not believe are condemned already, because they have not believed in the name of the only Son of God. And this is the judgment, that the light has come into the world, and people loved darkness rather than light because their deeds were evil. For all who do evil hate the light and do not come to the light, so that their deeds may not be exposed. But those who do what is true come to the light, so that it may be clearly seen that their deeds have been done in God."

- The words *Father* and *Son* are human metaphors for the mysterious dynamic of the Blessed Trinity. We believe that God intervened in human history and gave his only Son to show that his attitude toward us is that of a loving parent.

- Considering how God so loves the world, I pray for God's creation, for all God's people; listening to Jesus, may we experience growing abundance.

Thursday 2nd May

John 3:31–36

[Jesus said,] "The one who comes from above is above all; the one who is of the earth belongs to the earth and speaks about earthly things. The one who comes from heaven is above all. He testifies to what he has seen and heard, yet no one accepts his testimony. Whoever has accepted his testimony has certified this, that God is true. He whom God has sent speaks the words of God, for he gives the Spirit without measure. The Father loves the Son and has placed all things in his hands. Whoever believes in the Son has eternal life; whoever disobeys the Son will not see life, but must endure God's wrath."

- Call some words to mind: think of *flight, light, air*—things that come "from above." Then consider *gravity, weighty, plodding,* and what it is to be earthbound. Jesus models for us a way of being in balance: he knows that his identity is from above even as he moves on the earth.

- Our daily prayer helps us search out where there is inspiration, promise, and hope in daily life. We acknowledge light where we find it, acknowledging that it is from God and is a call to us to receive the good news in our hearts. May I hear God's voice and respond in trust to the movement of the Spirit.

Friday 3rd May

John 14:6–14

Jesus said to him, "I am the way, and the truth, and the life. No one comes to the Father except through me. If you know me, you will know my Father also. From now on you do know him and have seen him." Philip said to him, "Lord, show us the Father, and we will be satisfied." Jesus said to him, "Have I been with you all this time, Philip, and you still do not know me? Whoever has seen me has seen the Father. How can you say, 'Show us the Father'? Do you not believe that I am in the Father and the Father is in me? The words that I say to you I do not speak on my own; but the Father who dwells in me does his works. Believe me that I am in the Father and the Father is in me; but if you do not, then believe me because of the works themselves. Very truly, I tell you, the one who believes in me will also do the works that I do and, in fact, will do greater works than these, because I am going to the Father. I will do whatever you ask in my name, so that the Father may be glorified in the Son. If in my name you ask me for anything, I will do it."

- The way Jesus lived his life was that no one was excluded from the circle of his love. He lived for the good of all. Even if we exclude one person from the circle of our love, our way to the Father is barred. Our love needs to grow from self-interest, to national interest, to international interest, to love of the whole of creation.

- Jesus sees not with human eyes but with the eyes of the Spirit. He looks, not at outward appearances, but at the heart. Lord, grant that I may look at my brothers and sisters with your eyes, as equally valuable and deeply lovable members of your earthly family.

Saturday 4th May

John 6:16–21

When evening came, his disciples went down to the sea, got into a boat, and started across the sea to Capernaum. It was now dark, and Jesus had not yet come to them. The sea became rough because a strong wind was blowing. When they had rowed about three or four miles, they saw Jesus walking on the sea and coming near the boat, and they were terrified. But he said to them, "It is I; do not be afraid." Then they wanted to take him into the boat, and immediately the boat reached the land toward which they were going.

- Pope Saint John Paul II repeated in his first homily as pontiff the words "Do not be afraid!" Today, in a world full of fear, anxiety, and paralysis, we need to take that powerful advice to heart and to "open wide the doors for Christ."

- I pray for all people who are in trouble or in need, that they might recognize Jesus' approach in the form of others' care. May they not be afraid of Jesus' embrace.

Third Week of Easter
May 5—May 11

Something to think and pray about each day this week:

It is tempting to always keep busy; there's so much to do and there are so many in need. But the point of all this running around is to support the real work of life. "You are anxious and worried about many things," Jesus once told Martha, who was "burdened with much serving." And then he said, "There is need of only one thing." Mary, Martha's sister, instead sat at his feet, and today she washes them with oil. It's not easy to know how to direct our energies, but if our busy lives, even lived in service to others, never allow us to stop and be with the ones we love, then our purpose is defeated. It is Holy Week, a time for contemplation. So take a break from much serving and find the one thing that is most needed.

—Amy Andrews, *2017: A Book of Grace-Filled Days*

The Presence of God

As I sit here, the beating of my heart,
the ebb and flow of my breathing, the movements of my mind
are all signs of God's ongoing creation of me.
I pause for a moment and become aware
of this presence of God within me.

Freedom

I will ask God's help
to be free from my own preoccupations,
to be open to God in this time of prayer,
to come to know, love, and serve God more.

Consciousness

At this moment, Lord, I turn my thoughts to you.
I will leave aside my chores and preoccupations.
I will take rest and refreshment in your presence.

The Word

Now I turn to the Scripture set out for me this day. I read slowly over the words and see if any sentence or sentiment appeals to me. (Please turn to the Scripture on the following pages. Inspiration points are there, should you need them. When you are ready, return here to continue.)

Conversation

Begin to talk to Jesus about the Scripture you have just read. What part of it strikes a chord in you? Perhaps the words of a friend—or some story you have heard recently—will slowly rise to the surface of your consciousness. If so, does the story throw light on what the Scripture passage may be saying to you?

Conclusion

Glory be to the Father, and to the Son, and to the Holy Spirit,
As it was in the beginning, is now and ever shall be,
World without end. Amen.

Sunday 5th May
Third Sunday of Easter

John 21:1–14

After these things Jesus showed himself again to the disciples by the Sea of Tiberias; and he showed himself in this way. Gathered there together were Simon Peter, Thomas called the Twin, Nathanael of Cana in Galilee, the sons of Zebedee, and two others of his disciples. Simon Peter said to them, "I am going fishing." They said to him, "We will go with you." They went out and got into the boat, but that night they caught nothing. Just after daybreak, Jesus stood on the beach; but the disciples did not know that it was Jesus. Jesus said to them, "Children, you have no fish, have you?" They answered him, "No." He said to them, "Cast the net to the right side of the boat, and you will find some." So they cast it, and now they were not able to haul it in because there were so many fish. That disciple whom Jesus loved said to Peter, "It is the Lord!" When Simon Peter heard that it was the Lord, he put on some clothes, for he was naked, and jumped into the lake. But the other disciples came in the boat, dragging the net full of fish, for they were not far from the land, only about a hundred yards off. When they had gone ashore, they saw a charcoal fire there, with fish on it, and bread. Jesus said to them, "Bring some of the fish that you have just caught." So Simon Peter went aboard and hauled the net ashore, full of large fish, a hundred and fifty-three of them; and though there were so many, the net was not torn. Jesus said to them, "Come and have breakfast." Now none of the disciples dared to ask him, "Who are you?" because they knew it was the Lord. Jesus came and took the bread and gave it to them, and did the same with the fish. This was now the third time that Jesus appeared to the disciples after he was raised from the dead.

- This intervention of Jesus suits Peter perfectly as a fisherman. Jesus knows what will catch Peter's attention and make him happy. He tries to catch my attention too. Am I open to be happily surprised by God today?

- Here I am at prayer right now: Is it a dull event, or do I catch on to the fact that Jesus is saying to me, "Come and have breakfast"?

Monday 6th May

John 6:22–29

The next day the crowd that had stayed on the other side of the lake saw that there had been only one boat there. They also saw that Jesus had not got into the boat with his disciples, but that his disciples had gone away alone. Then some boats from Tiberias came near the place where they had eaten the bread after the Lord had given thanks. So when the crowd saw that neither Jesus nor his disciples were there, they themselves got into the boats and went to Capernaum looking for Jesus. When they found him on the other side of the lake, they said to him, "Rabbi, when did you come here?" Jesus answered them, "Very truly, I tell you, you are looking for me, not because you saw signs, but because you ate your fill of the loaves. Do not work for the food that perishes, but for the food that endures for eternal life, which the Son of Man will give you. For it is on him that God the Father has set his seal." Then they said to him, "What must we do to perform the works of God?" Jesus answered them, "This is the work of God, that you believe in him whom he has sent."

- There is a lot of activity on the side of the lake: boats come and go, the people watch for Jesus, wonder where he might be, and set off to find him. But somehow, even when found, Jesus eludes them. He doesn't allow them much satisfaction or relief in catching up with him but calls them to question what is in their hearts. Our prayer teaches us something like this: we will never capture Jesus or pin him down; engaging with Jesus helps us see what is really in our hearts; our first call is not to do, but to believe.

- Help me, Lord, to approach you with reverence and to allow you to meet me where I am. Purify my searching for you; let me not seek you for my own sake but so that you may find life in me.

Tuesday 7th May

John 6:30–35

So they said to him, "What sign are you going to give us then, so that we may see it and believe you? What work are you performing? Our ancestors ate the manna in the wilderness; as it is written, 'He gave them bread from heaven to eat.'" Then Jesus said to them, "Very truly, I tell you, it was not

Moses who gave you the bread from heaven, but it is my Father who gives you the true bread from heaven. For the bread of God is that which comes down from heaven and gives life to the world." They said to him, "Sir, give us this bread always." Jesus said to them, "I am the bread of life. Whoever comes to me will never be hungry, and whoever believes in me will never be thirsty."

- The people were sure about what they wanted, clear about how God had worked in the past. They had a template, and they wanted to see if Jesus fitted it. We sometimes approach Jesus in the same way, asking for what we need, expecting a particular answer. Jesus wants to open our hearts to receive what God is offering.

- Help me, Lord, when I am limited by my past. When I know how I have been blessed, help me stay before you in trust, aware of how little I deserve but ready to receive your grace in new ways.

Wednesday 8th May
John 6:35–40

Jesus said to them, "I am the bread of life. Whoever comes to me will never be hungry, and whoever believes in me will never be thirsty. But I said to you that you have seen me and yet do not believe. Everything that the Father gives me will come to me, and anyone who comes to me I will never drive away; for I have come down from heaven, not to do my own will, but the will of him who sent me. And this is the will of him who sent me, that I should lose nothing of all that he has given me, but raise it up on the last day. This is indeed the will of my Father, that all who see the Son and believe in him may have eternal life; and I will raise them up on the last day."

- It is not unusual nowadays for bread to be presented as "artisan," "craft," or "specialty." It ceases to be a humble food. When Jesus speaks about bread, he is asking us to identify our essential nourishment and to recognize that it lies in him.

- I will understand what I really need when I spend time in prayer and reflection. If I look beyond my preferences and temporary wants, the Holy Spirit will point me to the deeper desires—and those lead me to the Source of life.

Thursday 9th May

John 6:44–51

Jesus said to the people, "No one can come to me unless drawn by the Father who sent me; and I will raise that person up on the last day. It is written in the prophets, 'And they shall all be taught by God.' Everyone who has heard and learned from the Father comes to me. Not that anyone has seen the Father except the one who is from God; he has seen the Father. Very truly, I tell you, whoever believes has eternal life. I am the bread of life. Your ancestors ate the manna in the wilderness, and they died. This is the bread that comes down from heaven, so that one may eat of it and not die. I am the living bread that came down from heaven. Whoever eats of this bread will live forever; and the bread that I will give for the life of the world is my flesh."

• Slow down and listen for inner guidance. Being drawn to the Father simultaneously draws us to Jesus and, through him, to the Father. Next time you marvel at how a GPS system guides you to your destination, remember that you have an inner GPS that is guiding you home to God.

• All our practices of prayer—our liturgies, disciplines, and habits—are like school buses; they bring us to where a special kind of learning happens. But we need to be present, ready, and eager to receive truth. Jesus tells us that God wants to be the teacher of each person and desires to speak to us, heart to heart.

Friday 10th May

John 6:52–59

The Jews then disputed among themselves, saying, "How can this man give us his flesh to eat?" So Jesus said to them, "Very truly, I tell you, unless you eat the flesh of the Son of Man and drink his blood, you have no life in you. Those who eat my flesh and drink my blood have eternal life, and I will raise them up on the last day; for my flesh is true food and my blood is true drink. Those who eat my flesh and drink my blood abide in me, and I in them. Just as the living Father sent me, and I live because of the Father, so whoever eats me will live because of me. This is the bread that came down from heaven, not like that which your ancestors ate, and they died. But the one who eats this bread will live forever." He said these things while he was teaching in the synagogue at Capernaum.

• Jesus did not want the people simply to agree with him, to assent to his ideas. He wanted them to be drawn fully into the life of God, just as he was. He invites us to be consumed by God, to let go of our reservations and hesitations and to trust in the one who gives life.

• John tells us that Jesus' words created acrimony, setting the people against one another in argument. But Jesus was resolute: sharing in the life of God is not a part-time or trivial thing; God wants nothing less than to give us eternal life.

Saturday 11th May
John 6:60–69

When many of his disciples heard it, they said, "This teaching is difficult; who can accept it?" But Jesus, being aware that his disciples were complaining about it, said to them, "Does this offend you? Then what if you were to see the Son of Man ascending to where he was before? It is the spirit that gives life; the flesh is useless. The words that I have spoken to you are spirit and life. But among you there are some who do not believe." For Jesus knew from the first who were the ones that did not believe, and who was the one that would betray him. And he said, "For this reason I have told you that no one can come to me unless it is granted by the Father." Because of this many of his disciples turned back and no longer went about with him. So Jesus asked the twelve, "Do you also wish to go away?" Simon Peter answered him, "Lord, to whom can we go? You have the words of eternal life. We have come to believe and know that you are the Holy One of God."

• Just when Jesus had fully revealed himself, when he was at his most vulnerable, people walked away. Can you imagine what that must be like, to reveal yourself truly to others, only to have them reject you and walk away?

• On what grounds do people walk away from Jesus today? How much is he and his message distorted by a flawed Church? To what extent have you walked away from Jesus, and what draws you to him?

May 12—May 18

Something to think and pray about each day this week:

We're culturally conditioned, in other words, to expect the same worldly results from prayer—"balance," calm, self-satisfaction—that we try to get from eating well and exercising. There's nothing wrong with working toward physical health; in fact, we're called in a general way to be good stewards of our body. But Fr. Mandić didn't sit in the confessional for up to sixteen hours a day in the hope that he'd be relieved of his chronic arthritis, or of his stammer. He sat in the confessional because that was his vocation and because his deepest desire was to serve God whether or not he was in pain, whether or not he looked good in the eyes of the world. . . . What the world means by "balance" is straddling two worlds: having our cake and eating it, too. Prayer consists in presenting ourselves, whole and entire, to receive the stupendous gift of God's love. Prayer consists in an utter surrender to God's will and an offering of our entire selves to his service.

—Heather King, *Holy Desperation*

The Presence of God

"Be still and know that I am God!" Lord, your words lead us to the calmness and greatness of your presence.

Freedom

God is not foreign to my freedom. The Spirit breathes life into my most intimate desires, gently nudging me toward all that is good. I ask for the grace to let myself be enfolded by the Spirit.

Consciousness

Where do I sense hope, encouragement, and growth in my life? By looking back over the past few months, I may be able to see which activities and occasions have produced rich fruit. If I do notice such areas, I will determine to give those areas both time and space in the future.

The Word

The word of God comes down to us through the Scriptures. May the Holy Spirit enlighten my mind and my heart to respond to the gospel teachings. (Please turn to the Scripture on the following pages. Inspiration points are there, should you need them. When you are ready, return here to continue.)

Conversation

What is stirring in me as I pray? Am I consoled, troubled, left cold? I imagine Jesus standing or sitting at my side, and I share my feelings with him.

Conclusion

Glory be to the Father, and to the Son, and to the Holy Spirit,
As it was in the beginning, is now and ever shall be,
World without end. Amen.

Sunday 12th May
Fourth Sunday of Easter
John 10:27–30

[Jesus said,] "My sheep hear my voice. I know them, and they follow me. I give them eternal life, and they will never perish. No one will snatch them out of my hand. What my Father has given me is greater than all else, and no one can snatch it out of the Father's hand. The Father and I are one."

- Once again, Lord, your words ease our aching hearts. You know us; you give us your best gift, which is eternal life; you will defend us from anyone who tries to snatch us away from you. What more can we ask?

- On my side is the invitation to follow you. But do I think of myself as your follower? My daily prayer helps me keep you always in view, to listen to your voice, and to deepen the relationship that exists between us. Thank you for this graced time.

Monday 13th May
John 10:1–10

"Very truly, I tell you, anyone who does not enter the sheepfold by the gate but climbs in by another way is a thief and a bandit. The one who enters by the gate is the shepherd of the sheep. The gatekeeper opens the gate for him, and the sheep hear his voice. He calls his own sheep by name and leads them out. When he has brought out all his own, he goes ahead of them, and the sheep follow him because they know his voice. They will not follow a stranger, but they will run from him because they do not know the voice of strangers." Jesus used this figure of speech with them, but they did not understand what he was saying to them. So again Jesus said to them, "Very truly, I tell you, I am the gate for the sheep. All who came before me are thieves and bandits; but the sheep did not listen to them. I am the gate. Whoever enters by me will be saved, and will come in and go out and find pasture. The thief comes only to steal and kill and destroy. I came that they may have life, and have it abundantly."

- What lifts your spirit, satisfies your soul, gives you lasting peace, and fills you with life? What seems to be just the right fit for you? These are moments that come from the presence of Christ in you.

- On the other hand, what drains you, steals your energy, leaves you life-less and empty, kills your spirit, treats you like a statistic rather than a unique person? These are moments indicative of the thief, the enemy of our human nature.

Tuesday 14th May

John 15:9–17

[Jesus said to the disciples,] "As the Father has loved me, so I have loved you; abide in my love. If you keep my commandments, you will abide in my love, just as I have kept my Father's commandments and abide in his love. I have said these things to you so that my joy may be in you, and that your joy may be complete. This is my commandment, that you love one another as I have loved you. No one has greater love than this, to lay down one's life for one's friends. You are my friends if you do what I command you. I do not call you servants any longer, because the servant does not know what the master is doing; but I have called you friends, because I have made known to you everything that I have heard from my Father. You did not choose me but I chose you. And I appointed you to go and bear fruit, fruit that will last, so that the Father will give you whatever you ask him in my name. I am giving you these commands so that you may love one another."

- You pray, Lord, that my joy may be complete. This is not the joy based on the illusion that everything in the garden is lovely. It is wide-eyed joy, knowing that there is hatred, corruption, and murder in this world, but that you, Lord, have faced all that evil, and by dint of your love have enabled us to keep joy in our hearts. On our faces, too. When you have paid such a price for us, there is nothing Christian about long faces.

- Today, sit in a comfortable place with a cup of tea or whatever your favorite beverage is and spend twenty minutes talking with Jesus as friend to friend. He has called us friends—but how often do we treat him like a friend—with trust, happiness in our conversation, an ease of presence?

Wednesday 15th May

John 12:44–50

Then Jesus cried aloud: "Whoever believes in me believes not in me but in him who sent me. And whoever sees me sees him who sent me. I have come as light into the world, so that everyone who believes in me should not remain in the darkness. I do not judge anyone who hears my words and does not keep them, for I came not to judge the world, but to save the world. The one who rejects me and does not receive my word has a judge; on the last day the word that I have spoken will serve as judge, for I have not spoken on my own, but the Father who sent me has himself given me a commandment about what to say and what to speak. And I know that his commandment is eternal life. What I speak, therefore, I speak just as the Father has told me."

- Jesus is always pointing us to his Father. Their relationship is good beyond our imagining. They are ecstatic about one another, they share everything and work perfectly together. They think the world of one another. Imagine the most harmonious relationship you have, expand it a thousand times, and then you have a dim sense of how Father and Son get along!

- The great revelation is that all of us are invited into the family life of God. We will be swept off our feet and made radiantly happy when we meet God directly. If I want this to begin even now, I can open myself more and more to God in my daily prayer.

Thursday 16th May
John 13:16–20

[Jesus said,] "Very truly, I tell you, servants are not greater than their master, nor are messengers greater than the one who sent them. If you know these things, you are blessed if you do them. I am not speaking of all of you; I know whom I have chosen. But it is to fulfill the scripture, 'The one who ate my bread has lifted his heel against me.' I tell you this now, before it occurs, so that when it does occur, you may believe that I am he. Very truly, I tell you, whoever receives one whom I send receives me; and whoever receives me receives him who sent me."

- Saint Ignatius reminds us that love is shown more in deeds than in words. I ask God for the help that I need to allow the words in my mind and heart to become evident in my feet and my hands, that I might recognize where God wants me to be and do what God wants me to do.

- Jesus recognizes that knowing and understanding are important but are only part of God's work in us. God blesses us, too, in what we do. My prayer helps me to be enlightened by God's light and moves me to do what I can to bring light to the world through how I live.

Friday 17th May
John 14:1–6

[Jesus said to his disciples:] "Do not let your hearts be troubled. Believe in God, believe also in me. In my Father's house there are many dwelling places. If it were not so, would I have told you that I go to prepare a place for you? And if I go and prepare a place for you, I will come again and will take you to myself, so that where I am, there you may be also. And you know the way to the place where I am going." Thomas said to him, "Lord, we do not know where you are going. How can we know the way?" Jesus said to him, "I am the way, and the truth, and the life. No one comes to the Father except through me."

• When we hold on to negativity from hurts that were inflicted on us in the past, even if we were wronged and unjustly treated, we are letting ourselves be defined by what happened to us in the past rather than by what we choose to do now and in the future. This is a crucial choice that hugely determines the quality of our lives. Pray for the grace and wisdom to let go of negativity from past events and to choose to be defined by what you will do now and in the future.

• Jesuit mystic Pierre Teilhard de Chardin was fond of reminding us, "We are not human beings having a spiritual experience; we are spiritual beings having a human experience." The spiritual embraces and transcends the human dimension of our lives. "Do you have a sense that your life includes and is more than your span of life on earth?"

Saturday 18th May
John 14:7–14

[Jesus said to the disciples,] "If you know me, you will know my Father also. From now on you do know him and have seen him." Philip said to him, "Lord, show us the Father, and we will be satisfied." Jesus said to him, "Have I been with you all this time, Philip, and you still do not know me? Whoever has seen me has seen the Father. How can you say, 'Show us the Father'? Do you not believe that I am in the Father and the Father is in me? The words that I say to you I do not speak on my own; but the Father who dwells in me does his works. Believe me that I am in the Father and the Father is in me; but if you do not, then believe me because of the works themselves. Very truly, I tell you, the one who believes in me will also do the works that I do and, in fact, will do greater works than these, because I am going to the Father. I will do whatever you ask in my name, so that the Father may be glorified in the Son. If in my name you ask me for anything, I will do it."

- We need to be very humble and patient about embodying the presence of Jesus in the world. Because we have so much false conditioning to shed, we are in constant need of purification, we are always a work in progress. Each day we need to invite the Spirit of Jesus to take us over.

- I could start each day with this prayer and then, at evening, reflect over the day to see how I lived this offering: "Lord Jesus, I give you my hands to do your work. I give you my feet to go your way. I give you my tongue to speak your words. I give you my mind that you may think in me. I give you my spirit that you may pray in me. Above all, I give you my heart that you may love in me your Father and all humankind. I give you my whole self that you may grow in me, so that it is you, Lord Jesus, who live and work and pray in me" (The Grail Prayer).

May 19—May 25

Something to think and pray about each day this week:

We have to develop some practice where we're not flying solo. We're called to participate. If we try to get away to some place where it's just us and Jesus, or us and God, we're headed for trouble. Participation is the essence of true spirituality: in particular, participation that is (1) not to our specifications, and (2) with people we did not handpick. That means we're called to open our hearts to everybody, to welcome everybody, to be available to everybody—if and when they want us. That is part of our vocation of love—and it is not for the faint of heart.

—Heather King, *Holy Desperation*

The Presence of God

"Come to me, all you who are weary and are carrying heavy burdens, and I will give you rest." Here I am, Lord. I come to seek your presence. I long for your healing power.

Freedom

By God's grace I was born to live in freedom. Free to enjoy the pleasures he created for me. Dear Lord, grant that I may live as you intended, with complete confidence in your loving care.

Consciousness

Knowing that God loves me unconditionally, I look honestly over the past day, its events, and my feelings. Do I have something to be grateful for? Then I give thanks. Is there something I am sorry for? Then I ask forgiveness.

The Word

God speaks to each of us individually. I listen attentively to hear what he is saying to me. Read the text a few times; then listen. (Please turn to the Scripture on the following pages. Inspiration points are there, should you need them. When you are ready, return here to continue.)

Conversation

I know with certainty that there were times when you carried me, Lord. There were times when it was through your strength that I got through the dark times in my life.

Conclusion

Glory be to the Father, and to the Son, and to the Holy Spirit,
As it was in the beginning, is now and ever shall be,
World without end. Amen.

Sunday 19th May
Fifth Sunday of Easter
John 13:31–33a, 34–35

When he had gone out, Jesus said, "Now the Son of Man has been glorified, and God has been glorified in him. If God has been glorified in him, God will also glorify him in himself and will glorify him at once. Little children, I am with you only a little longer. . . . I give you a new commandment, that you love one another. Just as I have loved you, you also should love one another. By this everyone will know that you are my disciples, if you have love for one another."

- Judas had "gone out." Lord, may I never go away from you. May no human being be lost to you. Everyone is a brother or sister for whom you died, as St. Paul says. Let me become more like you by loving everyone and commending them to you. Stretch my heart till all my fellow humans are gathered in.

- "O, that my monk's robe were wide enough to gather up the suffering people of this floating world" (Ryokan, a Zen monk who died in 1831).

Monday 20th May
John 14:21–26

[Jesus said,] "They who have my commandments and keep them are those who love me; and those who love me will be loved by my Father, and I will love them and reveal myself to them." Judas (not Iscariot) said to him, "Lord, how is it that you will reveal yourself to us, and not to the world?" Jesus answered him, "Those who love me will keep my word, and my Father will love them, and we will come to them and make our home with them. Whoever does not love me does not keep my words; and the word that you hear is not mine, but is from the Father who sent me. I have said these things to you while I am still with you. But the Advocate, the Holy Spirit, whom the Father will send in my name, will teach you everything, and remind you of all that I have said to you."

- By keeping the commandments, we love—in specific ways—God and neighbor. Can I identify a commandment that has helped me live out God's love for others?

- To be permeated with the awareness of being loved by God is a prerequisite to loving God. We can't love what isn't ultimately lovable. Allowing ourselves to be loved unconditionally means that we let God take up residence in us and allow him to radiate through us. His presence in us will show up as a spirit of nonviolence, justice, mercy, and love of the poor.

Tuesday 21st May

John 14:27–31a

"Peace I leave with you; my peace I give to you. I do not give to you as the world gives. Do not let your hearts be troubled, and do not let them be afraid. You heard me say to you, 'I am going away, and I am coming to you.' If you loved me, you would rejoice that I am going to the Father, because the Father is greater than I. And now I have told you this before it occurs, so that when it does occur, you may believe. I will no longer talk much with you, for the ruler of this world is coming. He has no power over me; but I do as the Father has commanded me, so that the world may know that I love the Father. Rise, let us be on our way."

- The peace that Jesus promises is not an escape from trouble—the peace that the world gives—but rather the courage to face it calmly. As he spoke these words of peace, he was walking out to Gethsemane and his Passion.

- Lord, I need your gift of peace! So often I find myself unsure, anxious, worried, angry. Talk to me about how you coped when things were out of control in your life, especially at the end. What kept you going? You seem to have had such a deep sense that your Father was with you, and that he was asking you to reveal the limitless scope of divine love for the world.

Wednesday 22nd May

John 15:1–8

[Jesus said,] "I am the true vine, and my Father is the vinegrower. He removes every branch in me that bears no fruit. Every branch that bears fruit he prunes to make it bear more fruit. You have already been cleansed by the word that I have spoken to you. Abide in me as I abide in you. Just as the branch cannot bear fruit by itself unless it abides in the vine, neither can you unless you abide in me. I am the vine, you are the branches. Those who abide in me and I in them bear much fruit, because apart from me you can do nothing. Whoever does not abide in me is thrown away like a branch and withers; such branches are gathered, thrown into the fire, and burned. If you abide in me, and my words abide in you, ask for whatever you wish, and it will be done for you. My Father is glorified by this, that you bear much fruit and become my disciples."

• Through the analogy of the vine and the branches, Jesus invites us to be united to him. We are the branches, and if we allow the life of the vine to infuse us fully, it will bear much fruit of patience, kindness, compassion, and forgiveness.

• In a homily during the Easter season, Pope Francis noted, "A beautiful question for us Christians is this: do I abide in Jesus or am I far from Jesus? Am I united to the vine that gives me life, or am I a dead branch that is incapable of bearing fruit, giving witness?"

Thursday 23rd May
John 15:9–11

[Jesus said to his disciples,] "As the Father has loved me, so I have loved you; abide in my love. If you keep my commandments, you will abide in my love, just as I have kept my Father's commandments and abide in his love. I have said these things to you so that my joy may be in you, and that your joy may be complete."

• Jesus didn't issue commandments to control and dominate us but offered them as paths to true happiness. His sole intention is that "my joy may be in you, and that your joy may be complete" (John 15:11). The mark of a true Christian then surely is joy. There is no purpose in setting out to love others without first trusting in how greatly we ourselves are loved. That is how Jesus went about it: "As the Father has loved me, so I have loved you." We need to abide in Jesus' love to learn how we are to love others.

• St. Ignatius would have us begin our prayer by considering how God sees us. There is no better place to begin, and no better place to end! Each of us can say, "You see me as your well-beloved." Much of our prayer time can be taken up in simply savoring this delightful truth about ourselves. If we pray like this, the joy of God will fill our hearts. In the Gospels, joy is always linked with closeness to the Lord.

Friday 24th May

John 15:12–17

[Jesus said,] "This is my commandment, that you love one another as I have loved you. No one has greater love than this, to lay down one's life for one's friends. You are my friends if you do what I command you. I do not call you servants any longer, because the servant does not know what the master is doing; but I have called you friends, because I have made known to you everything that I have heard from my Father. You did not choose me but I chose you. And I appointed you to go and bear fruit, fruit that will last, so that the Father will give you whatever you ask him in my name. I am giving you these commands so that you may love one another."

- A sign of love is that we share everything with the beloved. Jesus holds nothing back from his disciples; he shares with them everything, even the secrets that were revealed to him by his Father, thereby giving the disciples the dignity and privilege of being friends. He would even lay down his life for their well-being.

- Jesus still invites us today into friendship with him. He wants to reveal even more that the Father has revealed to him. Imagine Jesus asking you repeatedly, "Would you be willing to let me be your friend?" and notice your response.

Saturday 25th May

John 15:18–21

[Jesus said to his disciples,] "If the world hates you, be aware that it hated me before it hated you. If you belonged to the world, the world would love you as its own. Because you do not belong to the world, but I have chosen you out of the world—therefore the world hates you. Remember the word that I said to you, 'Servants are not greater than their master.' If they persecuted me, they will persecute you; if they kept my word, they will keep yours also. But they will do all these things to you on account of my name, because they do not know him who sent me."

- "The world" in today's reading doesn't mean the physical world but the world of people who have mistakenly made money, success, reputation, power, and control their gods. They place their worth solely in how much they own, whom they know, and their capacity to exploit others and the earth to their own exclusive benefit. They are ready to use force to gain their ends. Jesus warns us that they hated him and his message: put God and his kingdom first, and everything else will fall into place.

• Forgive me, Lord: at times, I slip into voguish nonsense, trying to keep up with the prejudices and fripperies of fashion, or echoing the cynicism and materialism around me. When "the world" loves me, I need to look hard at myself and remember that you, the most lovable of men, suffered hatred and execution. When people are giving me a hard time, it may well be that I am blessed.

May 26—June 1

Something to think and pray about each day this week:

Talk of "winners" and "warriors" with respect to prayer is, to me, oxymoronic. Christ told us to be willing to take the last place, and for me that's never so much a matter of willingness as acknowledging that I'm there by default pretty much all the time. I'm no prayer warrior, or any other kind of warrior. I'm just a run-of-the-mill, deeply flawed human being who is terrified of not being loved, afraid of dying alone, and surrounded by people *who never act the way I want them to.* And who also really wants to be kind and to contribute—to serve, even. Prayer is like writing. We either do it or we don't. Talking about it, reading books about it, talking to other people who do it isn't writing—and it isn't prayer. Clearly, we're not going to be doing other things while we're praying. Clearly we turn off the TV, step away from the laptop, and put away the phone. I like to light a candle and a stick of incense, a little ritual to mark that I'm about to enter consecrated time and consecrated space. I live in a small one-bedroom apartment in which my consecrated space happens to be The Green Chair. You'll find your own. Then the best way I know is just to sit down and talk to God, or open yourself to him, or do whatever feels comfortable or urgent or natural in the sense that you couldn't hold back even if you wanted to. Love is like that.

—Heather King, *Holy Desperation*

The Presence of God

"Be still and know that I am God!" Lord, your words lead us to the calmness and greatness of your presence.

Freedom

Leave me here / freely all alone / In cell where never sunlight shone / Should no one ever speak to me. / This golden silence makes me free!
  —Part of a poem by Bl. Titus Brandsma, written while he was a prisoner
at Dachau concentration camp

Consciousness

Knowing that God loves me unconditionally, I can afford to be honest about how I am.
How has the day been, and how do I feel now? I share my feelings openly with the Lord.

The Word

I take my time to read the word of God slowly, a few times, allowing myself to dwell on anything that strikes me. (Please turn to the Scripture on the following pages. Inspiration points are there, should you need them. When you are ready, return here to continue.)

Conversation

Sometimes I wonder what I might say if I were to meet you in person, Lord. I think I might say "Thank you" because you are always there for me.

Conclusion

I thank God for these moments we have spent together and for any insights I have been given concerning the text.

Sunday 26th May
Sixth Sunday of Easter

John 14:23–29

Jesus answered him, "Those who love me will keep my word, and my Father will love them, and we will come to them and make our home with them. Whoever does not love me does not keep my words; and the word that you hear is not mine, but is from the Father who sent me. I have said these things to you while I am still with you. But the Advocate, the Holy Spirit, whom the Father will send in my name, will teach you everything, and remind you of all that I have said to you. Peace I leave with you; my peace I give to you. I do not give to you as the world gives. Do not let your hearts be troubled, and do not let them be afraid. You heard me say to you, 'I am going away, and I am coming to you.' If you loved me, you would rejoice that I am going to the Father, because the Father is greater than I. And now I have told you this before it occurs, so that when it does occur, you may believe."

- These words are part of Jesus' great farewell discourse at the Last Supper. The following day will see the immense outpouring of his love on the cross, a love that remains the same yesterday, today, and forever. This unconditional love calls for our unconditional "Yes."

- Lord, help me overcome my guilt, my shame, and my fear. Help me throw open wide the doors to my inmost heart so that my transcendent God can make his home there.

Monday 27th May

John 15:26—16:4

[Jesus said,] "When the Advocate comes, whom I will send to you from the Father, the Spirit of truth who comes from the Father, he will testify on my behalf. You also are to testify because you have been with me from the beginning. I have said these things to you to keep you from stumbling. They will put you out of the synagogues. Indeed, an hour is coming when those who kill you will think that by doing so they are offering worship to God. And they will do this because they have not known the Father or me. But I have said these things to you so that when their hour comes you may remember that I told you about them. I did not say these things to you from the beginning, because I was with you."

- Jesus taught his disciples with his word and prepared them for life when he would no longer be with them. He knew they would face opposition, even danger, because they followed him.

- Jesus reassures us that the Holy Spirit, the Advocate, who comes from the Father, will support us in giving witness to the good news, despite challenges from those who persecute the Christian faith. I ask to know Jesus more closely so that I might testify to his presence in my life through my daily choices, words, and deeds; and I ask the Holy Spirit for the help I need.

Tuesday 28th May

John 16:5–11

[Jesus said,] "Now I am going to him who sent me; yet none of you asks me, 'Where are you going?' But because I have said these things to you, sorrow has filled your hearts. Nevertheless, I tell you the truth: it is to your advantage that I go away, for if I do not go away, the Advocate will not come to you; but if I go, I will send him to you. And when he comes, he will prove the world wrong about sin and righteousness and judgment: about sin, because they do not believe in me; about righteousness, because I am going to the Father and you will see me no longer; about judgment, because the ruler of this world has been condemned."

- A successful master/teacher makes his or her pupils masters in their own right. Jesus tells his disciples, "It is to your advantage that I go away" so that they will discover in themselves the guidance and inspiration of the Holy Spirit who guided him. This Spirit will show up in the shortcomings of the world, lead us into right relationship with God and others, and convince us that love alone is the ultimate value on which we all will be judged.

- How is the Holy Spirit enlightening you and guiding you? Do you find that the Spirit shows you what the world lacks and provides you with a more inclusive integrating vision for humanity?

Wednesday 29th May

John 16:12–15

[Jesus said to his disciples,] "I still have many things to say to you, but you cannot bear them now. When the Spirit of truth comes, he will guide you into all the truth; for he will not speak on his own, but will speak whatever he hears, and he will declare to you the things that are to come. He will glorify me, because he will take what is mine and declare it to you. All that the Father has is mine. For this reason I said that he will take what is mine and declare it to you."

- It is impossible to assimilate in a short period of time all that Jesus has to teach us. As our journey through life continues, the Holy Spirit gradually unfolds God's message so that it speaks to us at appropriate times in our lives. Our capacity to take in what God reveals to us is expandable: when we become more open, the Spirit of truth will reveal more, and guide us into all the truth.

- Jesus wants to draw us into the life of God. He knows how anxious we can be, both to let go of the past and to trust what the future will bring. Can I speak to him about my anxieties?

Thursday 30th May

John 16:16–20

[Jesus said to his disciples,] "A little while, and you will no longer see me, and again a little while, and you will see me." Then some of his disciples said to one another, "What does he mean by saying to us, 'A little while, and you will no longer see me, and again a little while, and you will see me'; and 'Because I am going to the Father'?" They said, "What does he mean by this 'a little while'? We do not know what he is talking about." Jesus knew that they wanted to ask him, so he said to them, "Are you discussing among yourselves what I meant when I said, 'A little while, and you will no longer see me, and again a little while, and you will see me'? Very truly, I tell you, you will weep and mourn, but the world will rejoice; you will have pain, but your pain will turn into joy."

- In today's Gospel, Jesus tells his disciples that he will be gone from them in the form that is familiar to them, but in a little while they will experience him again with them in a mysterious new form. We can sometimes get stuck in trying to fix people in the form that is familiar to us. Life is always changing, and we never meet the same person twice—we need to keep meeting people where they are, always open to the new.

- The phase "a little while" is repeatedly used in this short passage. "A little while" may refer to the three days between the death of Jesus and his Resurrection; but it may also be the time between the first and the second coming of Christ, the time in which we live, and move, and have our being. Jesus does not mince his words; he tells us that our lives will not be free from pain and desolation, but he also promises us that our mourning will turn to hope, and our pain to joy.

Friday 31st May
Luke 1:39–56

In those days Mary set out and went with haste to a Judean town in the hill country, where she entered the house of Zechariah and greeted Elizabeth. When Elizabeth heard Mary's greeting, the child leapt in her womb. And Elizabeth was filled with the Holy Spirit and exclaimed with a loud cry, "Blessed are you among women, and blessed is the fruit of your womb. And why has this happened to me, that the mother of my Lord comes to me? For as soon as I heard the sound of your greeting, the child in my womb leapt for joy. And blessed is she who believed that there would be a fulfillment of what was spoken to her by the Lord." And Mary said, "My soul magnifies the Lord, and my spirit rejoices in God my Savior, for he has looked with favor on the lowliness of his servant. Surely, from now on all generations will call me blessed; for the Mighty One has done great things for me, and holy is his name. His mercy is for those who fear him from generation to generation. He has shown strength with his arm; he has scattered the proud in the thoughts of their hearts. He has brought down the powerful from their thrones, and lifted up the lowly; he has filled the hungry with good things, and sent the rich away empty. He has helped his servant Israel, in remembrance of his mercy, according to the promise he made to our ancestors, to Abraham and to his descendants for ever." And Mary remained with her for about three months and then returned to her home.

- Mary is an archetype for all Christians in how to say yes to God. God desires to have a personal relationship with each of us. Mary models for us how to respond to this great invitation. She trusts that God wants to do this great work in her, and she recognizes what a glorious privilege this is. She sees that it is entirely God's doing; she is merely saying yes, and her response has ramifications for the whole world.

- When two people meet who have said yes to God in their lives, like Mary and her cousin Elizabeth in today's Scripture, the new life of God that is growing in one woman leaps for joy in recognition of the life of God growing in another. It is God in one greeting God in the other. When have I felt this happy movement of recognition in my life?

Saturday 1st June
John 16:23–28

[Jesus said to his disciples,] "Very truly, I tell you, if you ask anything of the Father in my name, he will give it to you. Until now you have not asked for anything in my name. Ask and you will receive, so that your joy may be complete. I have said these things to you in figures of speech. The hour is coming when I will no longer speak to you in figures, but will tell you plainly of the Father. On that day you will ask in my name. I do not say to you that I will ask the Father on your behalf; for the Father himself loves you, because you have loved me and have believed that I came from God. I came from the Father and have come into the world; again, I am leaving the world and am going to the Father."

- The Father himself loves us. This is where we fit into the inner dynamic of the Blessed Trinity. As Jesus is joined to the Father through the Holy Spirit, so too are we because Jesus is our brother.

- We ask often in prayer, and sometimes prayer is answered very directly. Even when this appears not to happen, no prayer, like no act in love, is wasted. The true gift of prayer is always the Father's love, given to us no matter what we ask for. We are always gifted with the Spirit of Jesus, alive in our lives and in our love. We ask always in his name, knowing that in his name God will always hear us, inspire us, direct us, and love us.

June 2—June 8

Something to think and pray about each day this week:

You'll find that Christ spent most of his life healing, teaching, and hanging out with those who wanted to be called to a higher way of life. He got a kick out of all the things we do—eating, drinking, swapping stories, telling jokes—and he got the right kind of kick because he was utterly united to the Father in prayer. He made himself available to all kinds of very unpromising people—just as we're called to do. He had a special heart for those so desperate that they were willing to make holy fools of themselves in their hunger and need. Christ reveals himself in the deeply messy, profoundly awkward world of face-to-face human interaction with people in trouble, conflict, doubt, hunger, thirst, and pain. The real encounter with Christ takes place not when we are all dressed up and polished and nicely groomed and brandishing our résumés but in our broken humanity. Encounter with Christ happens in our longing for a kingdom that is not of this world and that we must search for and work for with all our might in this world.

—Heather King, *Holy Desperation*

The Presence of God

"I am standing at the door, knocking" says the Lord. What a wonderful privilege that the Lord of all creation desires to come to me. I welcome his presence.

Freedom

Everything has the potential to draw forth from me a fuller love and life. Yet my desires are often fixed, caught, on illusions of fulfillment. I ask that God, through my freedom, may orchestrate my desires in a vibrant, loving melody rich in harmony.

Consciousness

To be conscious about something is to be aware of it.
Dear Lord, help me to remember that you gave me life.
Thank you for the gift of life.
Teach me to slow down, to be still and enjoy the pleasures created for me.
To be aware of the beauty that surrounds me: the marvel of mountains, the calmness of lakes, the fragility of a flower petal. I need to remember that all these things come from you.

The Word

I read the word of God slowly, a few times over, and I listen to what God is saying to me. (Please turn to the Scripture on the following pages. Inspiration points are there, should you need them. When you are ready, return here to continue.)

Conversation

What feelings are rising in me as I pray and reflect on God's word? I imagine Jesus himself sitting or standing near me, and I open my heart to him.

Conclusion

I thank God for these moments we have spent together and for any insights I have been given concerning the text.

Sunday 2nd June
The Ascension of the Lord

Luke 24:46–53

[Jesus] said to them, "Thus it is written, that the Messiah is to suffer and to rise from the dead on the third day, and that repentance and forgiveness of sins is to be proclaimed in his name to all nations, beginning from Jerusalem. You are witnesses of these things. And see, I am sending upon you what my Father promised; so stay here in the city until you have been clothed with power from on high." Then he led them out as far as Bethany, and, lifting up his hands, he blessed them. While he was blessing them, he withdrew from them and was carried up into heaven. And they worshiped him, and returned to Jerusalem with great joy; and they were continually in the temple blessing God.

• Lord, strengthen my faith—faith that will give me eyes that see and ears that hear; faith that will reveal your luminous presence at the very heart of myself. Then, I may begin my own long ascent. Grant that one day I may be where you are and behold the glory the Father gave you before the foundation of the world.

• I pray to experience joy in worship and in the work of God's kingdom.

Monday 3rd June

John 16:29–33

His disciples said, "Yes, now you are speaking plainly, not in any figure of speech! Now we know that you know all things, and do not need to have anyone question you; by this we believe that you came from God." Jesus answered them, "Do you now believe? The hour is coming, indeed it has come, when you will be scattered, each one to his home, and you will leave me alone. Yet I am not alone because the Father is with me. I have said this to you, so that in me you may have peace. In the world you face persecution. But take courage; I have conquered the world!"

• How easy it is to identify with the apostles! Fired by enthusiasm, they profess unwavering faith. Jesus knows them better than they know themselves. He warns them that the fervor will quickly wear off and that they will disappear quickly when the storm begins to gather around him. I have so often vowed to turn aside from things that separate me from God, only to fall at the first hurdle.

• Lord, let me take comfort from your patience with your disciples. You looked past their present failures to see what they would become: people who would bear steadfast witness to you as they faced torture and death. Grant me the grace to be forever beginning, forever becoming, not discouraged by my past failures, always open to growth and change.

Tuesday 4th June
John 17:1–11

After Jesus had spoken these words, he looked up to heaven and said, "Father, the hour has come; glorify your Son so that the Son may glorify you, since you have given him authority over all people, to give eternal life to all whom you have given him. And this is eternal life, that they may know you, the only true God, and Jesus Christ whom you have sent. I glorified you on earth by finishing the work that you gave me to do. So now, Father, glorify me in your own presence with the glory that I had in your presence before the world existed. I have made your name known to those whom you gave me from the world. They were yours, and you gave them to me, and they have kept your word. Now they know that everything you have given me is from you; for the words that you gave to me I have given to them, and they have received them and know in truth that I came from you; and they have believed that you sent me. I am asking on their behalf; I am not asking on behalf of the world, but on behalf of those whom you gave me, because they are yours. All mine are yours, and yours are mine; and I have been glorified in them. And now I am no longer in the world, but they are in the world, and I am coming to you. Holy Father, protect them in your name that you have given me, so that they may be one, as we are one."

• The mission of Jesus is about to be accomplished. Saint John sees the Passion and Death of Jesus as the moment in which he is most glorious because his mission is to reveal in human form the infinite love and mercy of God, in all circumstances, for the whole of humanity. I pause to meditate on this great mystery and mercy.

• This love and mercy is most evident when Jesus responds with love and mercy to his being betrayed, rejected, mocked, scourged, and crucified. The message is that nothing can separate us from his love and mercy.

He makes clear the inner nature of God. The evil of the whole human race is transformed in the heart of Jesus crucified. May I recognize these glorious truths today in the life I enjoy through Christ.

Wednesday 5th June
John 17:11–19

[Jesus looked up to heaven and said,] "And now I am no longer in the world, but they are in the world, and I am coming to you. Holy Father, protect them in your name that you have given me, so that they may be one, as we are one. While I was with them, I protected them in your name that you have given me. I guarded them, and not one of them was lost except the one destined to be lost, so that the scripture might be fulfilled. But now I am coming to you, and I speak these things in the world so that they may have my joy made complete in themselves. I have given them your word, and the world has hated them because they do not belong to the world, just as I do not belong to the world. I am not asking you to take them out of the world, but I ask you to protect them from the evil one. They do not belong to the world, just as I do not belong to the world. Sanctify them in the truth; your word is truth. As you have sent me into the world, so I have sent them into the world. And for their sakes I sanctify myself, so that they also may be sanctified in truth."

- No, Lord, do not take me out of the world. I belong there, with all its messiness, just as you belonged there and took all the risks it involved. I do not seek a lily-pure existence untouched by the struggle for survival. But I do beg you to protect me from the evil one, from the malice in my own heart.

- Jesus' prayer reveals his passionate love for his disciples. Read through this passage slowly and hear Jesus praying it for you and your loved ones.

Thursday 6th June
John 17:20–26

[Jesus looked up to heaven and said,] "I ask not only on behalf of these, but also on behalf of those who will believe in me through their word, that they may all be one. As you, Father, are in me and I am in you, may they also be in us, so that the world may believe that you have sent me. The glory that you have given me I have given them, so that they may be one, as we are one, I in them and you in me, that they may become completely one, so that the world may know that you have sent me and have loved them even as you have loved me. Father, I desire that those also, whom you have given me, may be with me where I am, to see my glory, which you have given me because you loved me before the foundation of the world. Righteous Father, the world does not know you, but I know you; and these know that you have sent me. I made your name known to them, and I will make it known, so that the love with which you have loved me may be in them, and I in them."

• Lord, I treasure all the chances of fellowship with others who believe in you. When I work or talk with them, or love them, or serve or pray with them, your grace is at work in us. These occasions may not be labeled *ecumenical events*, but they carry your blessing.

• Jesus' second prayer at the Last Supper is for future generations of believers, including ourselves. His prayer is that all of us will be united with God our Father and with him. He is to share with all of us what is deepest in his heart: the glory he had from the beginning of time. Love wants to share with the beloved all that is best.

Friday 7th June
John 21:15–19

When they had finished breakfast, Jesus said to Simon Peter, "Simon son of John, do you love me more than these?" He said to him, "Yes, Lord; you know that I love you." Jesus said to him, "Feed my lambs." A second time he said to him, "Simon son of John, do you love me?" He said to him, "Yes, Lord; you know that I love you." Jesus said to him, "Tend my sheep." He said to him the third time, "Simon son of John, do you love me?" Peter felt hurt because he said to him the third time, "Do you love me?" And he said to him, "Lord, you know everything; you know that I love you." Jesus said to him, "Feed my sheep. Very truly, I tell you, when you were younger, you used to fasten your own belt and to go wherever you wished. But when you grow old, you will stretch out your hands, and someone else will fasten a belt around you and take you where you do not wish to go." (He said this to indicate the kind of death by which he would glorify God.) After this he said to him, "Follow me."

- Do you ever wonder if you really love the Lord? Did Peter? In the end he had no proof; he just knew that the Lord knew. Jesus sees into the heart and knows love, and he also knows our efforts to love.

- We are called to feed his people in many ways, not because we are perfect but because we do our best to share the best of our lives with others. We can offer the love of our hearts, imperfect as it is, and then we can say, "Lord, you know that I love you," trusting that he knows our true desires.

Saturday 8th June

John 21:20–25

Peter turned and saw the disciple whom Jesus loved following them; he was the one who had reclined next to Jesus at the supper and had said, "Lord, who is it that is going to betray you?" When Peter saw him, he said to Jesus, "Lord, what about him?" Jesus said to him, "If it is my will that he remain until I come, what is that to you? Follow me!" So the rumor spread in the community that this disciple would not die. Yet Jesus did not say to him that he would not die, but, "If it is my will that he remain until I come, what is that to you?" This is the disciple who is testifying to these things and has written them, and we know that his testimony is true. But there are also many other things that Jesus did; if every one of them were written down, I suppose that the world itself could not contain the books that would be written.

- The blank page at the end of a Bible invites us to write our own story of the good news. Our gospel story begins at our birth and continues through our life, during which we meet the Lord and follow him. What would you write of your life story today?

- Maybe today you can give thanks to the Lord for the ways you have found him close to you, in good times and bad times. In our life's journal we record the love and actions of God. And in God's journal—the "book of life"—our names are written.

Tenth Week in Ordinary Time
June 9—June 15

Something to think and pray about each day this week:

What if, instead of more action, what we need is more stillness? What if, instead of more speech, we need more silence? What if all of our words—whether spoken, in an article, blog post, or group message—will make more sense if understood by attending to the Word underneath all words, the Word that gives rise to language itself? Could it be that paying more attention to silence might actually make us more attentive to one another, in the way that paying attention to what we eat makes us more attentive to our health?

Can you be alone with only your thoughts?

Can you live free of screens and wireless Internet?

Can you listen to silence?

What memories emerge in your consciousness when you give yourself time to reflect?

—Tim Muldoon, *Living Against the Grain*

The Presence of God

"Be still and know that I am God!" Lord, your words lead us to the calmness and greatness of your presence.

Freedom

God is not foreign to my freedom. The Spirit breathes life into my most intimate desires, gently nudging me toward all that is good. I ask for the grace to let myself be enfolded by the Spirit.

Consciousness

Where do I sense hope, encouragement, and growth in my life? By looking back over the past few months, I may be able to see which activities and occasions have produced rich fruit. If I do notice such areas, I will determine to give those areas both time and space in the future.

The Word

The word of God comes down to us through the Scriptures. May the Holy Spirit enlighten my mind and my heart to respond to the gospel teachings. (Please turn to the Scripture on the following pages. Inspiration points are there, should you need them. When you are ready, return here to continue.)

Conversation

What is stirring in me as I pray? Am I consoled, troubled, left cold? I imagine Jesus standing or sitting at my side, and I share my feelings with him.

Conclusion

Glory be to the Father, and to the Son, and to the Holy Spirit,
As it was in the beginning, is now and ever shall be,
World without end. Amen.

Sunday 9th June
Pentecost Sunday
John 20:19–23

When it was evening on that day, the first day of the week, and the doors of the house where the disciples had met were locked for fear of the Jews, Jesus came and stood among them and said, "Peace be with you." After he said this, he showed them his hands and his side. Then the disciples rejoiced when they saw the Lord. Jesus said to them again, "Peace be with you. As the Father has sent me, so I send you." When he had said this, he breathed on them and said to them, "Receive the Holy Spirit. If you forgive the sins of any, they are forgiven them; if you retain the sins of any, they are retained."

- Take time today and allow the word *Peace* to echo in your mind and heart. Let the word and all it may mean fill your body and remain within you. Peace is the constant promise of Jesus to his followers. It is a gift nobody can take from us. Give time each day to receive this gift of God's Spirit. He gives it without even being asked. As you receive peace from God, send this peace in a prayer to those close to you or those who may sorely need prayer today.

- The risen Jesus penetrates the disciples' defenses, overcomes their fears, and brings them joy. I ask him to pass through all my security systems and liberate me from whatever prevents me from having life and having it in all its fullness.

Monday 10th June
Matthew 5:1–12

When Jesus saw the crowds, he went up the mountain; and after he sat down, his disciples came to him. Then he began to speak, and taught them, saying:
"Blessed are the poor in spirit, for theirs is the kingdom of heaven.
"Blessed are those who mourn, for they will be comforted.
"Blessed are the meek, for they will inherit the earth.
"Blessed are those who hunger and thirst for righteousness, for they will be filled.
"Blessed are the merciful, for they will receive mercy.
"Blessed are the pure in heart, for they will see God.

"Blessed are the peacemakers, for they will be called children of God.

"Blessed are those who are persecuted for righteousness' sake, for theirs is the kingdom of heaven.

"Blessed are you when people revile you and persecute you and utter all kinds of evil against you falsely on my account. Rejoice and be glad, for your reward is great in heaven, for in the same way they persecuted the prophets who were before you."

- The Beatitudes are blessings or gifts offered by God. They are not to be "observed" as commandments are, but desired and nurtured in prayer. It is in prayer that their strangely paradoxical meanings reveal themselves. So ponder them slowly and see if they resonate with your own experiences. Do you have a favorite among the Beatitudes, one that touches you deeply?

- The Beatitudes show me what is in the heart of Jesus, what he considered to be signs of God's kingdom. I pray that my eyes be blessed to see how the kingdom of God is around and about me.

Tuesday 11th June

Matthew 5:13–16

[Jesus said to his disciples,] "You are the salt of the earth; but if salt has lost its taste, how can its saltiness be restored? It is no longer good for anything, but is thrown out and trampled under foot. You are the light of the world. A city built on a hill cannot be hidden. No one after lighting a lamp puts it under the bushel basket, but on the lampstand, and it gives light to all in the house. In the same way, let your light shine before others, so that they may see your good works and give glory to your Father in heaven."

- I am to let the message of Jesus shine out through my words and actions. Goodness lights up both the giver and the recipient. I stand up for the just rights of God's "little ones." I work for a world of kindness, peace, and love.

- Salt and light are essential elements in the life of humans and animals. When Jesus says that we are "the salt of the earth" and "the light of the world," he means that we Christians have something essential to bring to the world around us. We are to be good news to those we encounter and to shed light on the problems of our world. But to be "salty" and to be light-bearers, we need to keep closely in touch with the One who is both the light of the world and its salt. I ask for this grace.

Wednesday 12th June
Matthew 5:17–19

[Jesus said to the crowds,] "Do not think that I have come to abolish the law or the prophets; I have come not to abolish but to fulfill. For truly I tell you, until heaven and earth pass away, not one letter, not one stroke of a letter, will pass from the law until all is accomplished. Therefore, whoever breaks one of the least of these commandments, and teaches others to do the same, will be called least in the kingdom of heaven; but whoever does them and teaches them will be called great in the kingdom of heaven."

- Jesus came "to fulfill" the law and the prophets. Observing external laws is not enough. Jesus wants listening hearts that are courageous, generous, and discerning. Hearts like his. Are you ever called to be prophetic by rising above peer pressure and speaking the truth in your heart?

- Jesus was a Jew: he lived out the Torah (the Law), which expressed the love relationship between God and the Chosen People. He did this by revealing in his life and death the love of God in a dramatic new way. We too are called to fulfill that sacred relationship. By looking at my life and listening to me, would anyone know that God is at the center of my heart, and that I try like Jesus to "always do what is pleasing to him" (John 8:29)?

Thursday 13th June
Matthew 5:20–26

[Jesus said,] "For I tell you, unless your righteousness exceeds that of the scribes and Pharisees, you will never enter the kingdom of heaven. You have heard that it was said to those of ancient times, 'You shall not murder'; and 'whoever murders shall be liable to judgment.' But I say to you that if you are angry with a brother or sister, you will be liable to judgment; and if you insult a brother or sister, you will be liable to the council; and if you say, 'You fool,' you will be liable to the hell of fire. So when you are offering your gift at the altar, if you remember that your brother or sister has something against you, leave your gift there before the altar and go; first be reconciled to your brother or sister, and then come and offer your gift. Come to terms quickly with your accuser while you are on the way to court with him, or your accuser may hand you over to the judge, and the judge to the guard, and you will be thrown into prison. Truly I tell you, you will never get out until you have paid the last penny."

- What do I do when my sisters or brothers have something against me? Perhaps I have hurt them, made them feel small. What do I do? Perhaps I try to justify myself, but my conscience keeps niggling at me. Jesus is clear: he says to me, "Go and be reconciled." Otherwise, he says, I am walking away from "the kingdom of heaven." He means that because God is a totally forgiving God, those who want to be God's friends must radiate a spirit of forgiveness too.

- Jesus is unhappy with taking the prohibition of murder too literally or restrictively. He wants it to include any kind of psychological or verbal abuse of another human being. Life is meant to be about relationships that are peaceful and harmonious. Hence the need for reconciliation when relationships break down. Am I in need of reconciliation with anyone today? Am I willing to leave my "gift" (whatever it may be) before the altar and seek reconciliation first with my offended brother or sister?

Friday 14th June
Matthew 5:27–32

[Jesus said,] "You have heard that it was said, 'You shall not commit adultery.' But I say to you that everyone who looks at a woman with lust has already committed adultery with her in his heart. If your right eye causes you to sin, tear it out and throw it away; it is better for you to lose one of your members than for your whole body to be thrown into hell. And if your right hand causes you to sin, cut it off and throw it away; it is better for you to lose one of your members than for your whole body to go into hell. It was also said, 'Whoever divorces his wife, let him give her a certificate of divorce.' But I say to you that anyone who divorces his wife, except on the ground of unchastity, causes her to commit adultery; and whoever marries a divorced woman commits adultery."

- I am part of a big gathering of families sitting on a sunny hillside, enthused by the encouraging words Jesus has for the poor, the peacemakers, those concerned for justice. Suddenly the tone changes. He has harsh words for those who undermine marriages and destroy families through lustful glances, adultery, divorce. His image of hell is Gehenna, the foul-smelling, smoking dump close to Jerusalem where refuse from the city was burned.

• Lord, may I value families and relationships with the same love you expressed through these words. They sounded harsh but indicated how much God wants our lives to be whole and fulfilled, protected by faithful love and reliable promises.

Saturday 15th June
Matthew 5:33–37

[Jesus said,] "Again, you have heard that it was said to those of ancient times, 'You shall not swear falsely, but carry out the vows you have made to the Lord.' But I say to you, Do not swear at all, either by heaven, for it is the throne of God, or by the earth, for it is his footstool, or by Jerusalem, for it is the city of the great King. And do not swear by your head, for you cannot make one hair white or black. Let your word be 'Yes, Yes' or 'No, No'; anything more than this comes from the evil one."

• Here Jesus is reinforcing the eighth commandment of God: You shall not bear false witness against your neighbor. In other words, you must never lie. Lies violate justice and charity, undermining trust in the community.

• Do I find myself responding to this call, or can I be devious in what I do or say? I pray for enlightenment.

June 16—June 22

Something to think and pray about each day this week:

How can we develop a greater capacity to see the beauty of the world and to draw meaning from our experiences? The answer is simple: by reflecting on our experiences and memories and attending mindfully to how this practice moves us to see the world in a new way. We can learn something about how this happens from Gerard Manley Hopkins, who wrote a letter to a friend about an insight he had. One day toward the end of summer, he was fishing alone in the Elwy River in Wales, enjoying a gorgeous afternoon. As he walked home, he looked up at the clouds and the hills, and his heart was lifted by the beauty around him. In that moment, the world transformed into a glimpse of God. He saw the hills as the figure of Atlas from Greek mythology—the one who carries the earth on his back. The hills had always been there, but not before this moment had he perceived how majestic they were. His key insight, as he looked around, was that it is easy to miss the beauty around us:

> And the azurous hung hills are his world-wielding shoulder
> Majestic—as a stallion stalwart, very-violet-sweet!—
> These things, these things were here and but the beholder
> Wanting.

The spontaneity of Hopkins's wonder is made possible by his willingness to be in the moment, to be present to the experience of the walk home after a calm afternoon fishing. He recognizes that there is beauty all around but that too often it goes unnoticed.

—Tim Muldoon, *Living Against the Grain*

The Presence of God
As I sit here, the beating of my heart,
the ebb and flow of my breathing, the movements of my mind
are all signs of God's ongoing creation of me.
I pause for a moment and become aware
of this presence of God within me.

Freedom
I will ask God's help
to be free from my own preoccupations,
to be open to God in this time of prayer,
to come to know, love, and serve God more.

Consciousness
At this moment, Lord, I turn my thoughts to you.
I will leave aside my chores and preoccupations.
I will take rest and refreshment in your presence.

The Word
Now I turn to the Scripture set out for me this day. I read slowly over the
words and see if any sentence or sentiment appeals to me. (Please turn to the
Scripture on the following pages. Inspiration points are there, should you
need them. When you are ready, return here to continue.)

Conversation
Begin to talk to Jesus about the Scripture you have just read. What part of
it strikes a chord in you? Perhaps the words of a friend—or some story you
have heard recently—will slowly rise to the surface of your consciousness. If
so, does the story throw light on what the Scripture passage may be saying
to you?

Conclusion
Glory be to the Father, and to the Son, and to the Holy Spirit,
As it was in the beginning, is now and ever shall be,
World without end. Amen.

Sunday 16th June
The Most Holy Trinity
John 16:12–15

[Jesus said to his disciples,] "I still have many things to say to you, but you cannot bear them now. When the Spirit of truth comes, he will guide you into all the truth; for he will not speak on his own, but will speak whatever he hears, and he will declare to you the things that are to come. He will glorify me, because he will take what is mine and declare it to you. All that the Father has is mine. For this reason I said that he will take what is mine and declare it to you."

- *You cannot bear them now*, you said. Lord, you time your interventions for my readiness. They that wait upon you shall renew their strength, says Isaiah. May I learn how to wait upon you.

- The Spirit of truth did indeed come, but how often am I aware of this? Do I address the Holy Spirit in my prayers, asking for help, asking to be guided into the truth of everyday situations? I say such a prayer now.

Monday 17th June
Matthew 5:38–42

[Jesus said,] "You have heard that it was said, 'An eye for an eye and a tooth for a tooth.' But I say to you, Do not resist an evildoer. But if anyone strikes you on the right cheek, turn the other also; and if anyone wants to sue you and take your coat, give your cloak as well; and if anyone forces you to go one mile, go also the second mile. Give to everyone who begs from you, and do not refuse anyone who wants to borrow from you."

- The principle of an eye for an eye and a tooth for a tooth served to prevent excessive retaliation for an offense endured. But Jesus wants no retaliation at all. Instead he looks for a generosity of spirit that forgives the offender and returns good for evil.

- Take each of his examples into your prayer in turn and see how it might apply to you. Ask Jesus to enlighten you.

Tuesday 18th June
Matthew 5:43–48

[Jesus said,] "You have heard that it was said, 'You shall love your neighbor and hate your enemy.' But I say to you, Love your enemies and pray for those who persecute you, so that you may be children of your Father in heaven; for he makes his sun rise on the evil and on the good, and sends rain on the righteous and on the unrighteous. For if you love those who love you, what reward do you have? Do not even the tax collectors do the same? And if you greet only your brothers and sisters, what more are you doing than others? Do not even the Gentiles do the same? Be perfect, therefore, as your heavenly Father is perfect."

• Before Jesus came, God was portrayed as *destroying* the wicked. But Jesus portrays God as pouring out good things on wicked as well as good people. This seems like extravagant madness. But when we come to the Passion, we find Jesus doing what he talks about here. He pours out divine love on everyone, bad and good. He prays for his enemies. On the world scene today, we have plenty of people to love and to pray for!

• I ponder on how Jesus himself modeled this love. Do I want to live and love like him?

Wednesday 19th June
Matthew 6:1–6, 16–18

[Jesus said,] "Beware of practicing your piety before others in order to be seen by them; for then you have no reward from your Father in heaven. So whenever you give alms, do not sound a trumpet before you, as the hypocrites do in the synagogues and in the streets, so that they may be praised by others. Truly I tell you, they have received their reward. But when you give alms, do not let your left hand know what your right hand is doing, so that your alms may be done in secret; and your Father who sees in secret will reward you. And whenever you pray, do not be like the hypocrites; for they love to stand and pray in the synagogues and at the street corners, so that they may be seen by others. Truly I tell you, they have received their reward. But whenever you pray, go into your room and shut the door and pray to your Father who is in secret; and your Father who sees in secret will reward you. . . . And whenever you fast, do not look dismal, like the hypocrites, for they disfigure their faces so as to show others that they are fasting. Truly I tell you, they have received their reward. But when you fast, put oil on your head and wash your face, so that your fasting may be seen not by others but by your Father who is in secret; and your Father who sees in secret will reward you."

- In this passage we find six references here to "your Father"! How does Jesus portray our Father?

- Our consumerist culture lays great store on what is seen outwardly, and often we do catch ourselves being influenced by the widely publicized actions of celebrities, even though we know that most of this is artificial hype. Jesus' words remain a real challenge to me, and I let them shine a light on my actions and choices. I ask for the purity of heart of the beatitudes, and I ask pardon for the frivolities in my life choices.

Thursday 20th June
Matthew 6:7–15

[Jesus said,] "When you are praying, do not heap up empty phrases as the Gentiles do; for they think that they will be heard because of their many words. Do not be like them, for your Father knows what you need before you ask him. Pray then in this way: Our Father in heaven, hallowed be your name. Your kingdom come. Your will be done, on earth as it is in heaven. Give us this day our daily bread. And forgive us our debts, as we also have forgiven our debtors. And do not bring us to the time of trial, but rescue us from the evil one. For if you forgive others their trespasses, your heavenly Father will also forgive you; but if you do not forgive others, neither will your Father forgive your trespasses."

- This prayer can be recited by members of any religion. God is the Father of all. Rather than rattle it off, we could profitably dwell on a phrase at a time, or even just the word *Father*.

- As you pray now, does God seem like a distant figure with little interest in your affairs? And what about your day: is God around, or are you alone? The good news is that God is indescribably close to us as we go about our affairs. "Your Father knows what you need before you ask him." We might say that God is infinite awareness and that his focus is on us. "God is closer to me than I am to myself," says Saint Augustine.

Friday 21st June
Matthew 6:19–23

[Jesus said,] "Do not store up for yourselves treasures on earth, where moth and rust consume and where thieves break in and steal; but store up for yourselves treasures in heaven, where neither moth nor rust consumes and where thieves do not break in and steal. For where your treasure is, there your heart will be also. The eye is the lamp of the body. So, if your eye is healthy, your whole body will be full of light; but if your eye is unhealthy, your whole body will be full of darkness. If then the light in you is darkness, how great is the darkness!"

- Jesus once again reminds us that God looks at the heart, and he challenges us to ask ourselves where our real priorities lie. Where is my heart? My treasure? Is it something that is durable, that cannot be corrupted by moth or by rust, or is it something merely material or ethereal, like money or success or popularity?

- The central teaching here is in the sentence "For where your treasure is, there your heart will be also." Putting your heart into something suggests enthusiasm, energy, determination, and a valuing of whatever is occupying you. Your treasures are what you value. Jesus distinguishes between treasures that are vulnerable to robbery or decay and treasures that endure whatever happens. Such are the values of the Spirit, such as the virtues (above all, love) and our appreciation of all that is good, true, beautiful, and noble. Lord, may I value what you value.

Saturday 22nd June
Matthew 6:24–34

[Jesus said,] "No one can serve two masters; for a slave will either hate the one and love the other, or be devoted to the one and despise the other. You cannot serve God and wealth. Therefore I tell you, do not worry about your life, what you will eat or what you will drink, or about your body, what you will wear. Is not life more than food, and the body more than clothing? Look at the birds of the air; they neither sow nor reap nor gather into barns, and yet your heavenly Father feeds them. Are you not of more value than they? And can any of you by worrying add a single hour to your span of life? And why do you worry about clothing? Consider the lilies of the field, how they grow; they neither toil nor spin, yet I tell you, even Solomon in all his glory was not clothed like one of these. But if God so clothes the grass of the field, which is alive today and tomorrow is thrown into the oven, will he not much more clothe you—you of little faith? Therefore do not worry, saying, 'What will we eat?' or 'What will we drink?' or 'What will we wear?' For it is the Gentiles who strive for all these things; and indeed your heavenly Father knows that you need all these things. But strive first for the kingdom of God and his righteousness, and all these things will be given to you as well. So do not worry about tomorrow, for tomorrow will bring worries of its own. Today's trouble is enough for today."

- Clearly Jesus, the Word of God, had a special feel for the wonders of creation: "He was in the world, and the world came into being through him" (John 1:10).

- This is a teaching about providence: the challenge to accept that, at all times and in every circumstance, God will provide. Jesus uses picturesque imagery to get his point across. He invites you to enter the imagery: *Look* at the birds of the air . . . *Consider* the lilies of the field. What feelings do these images stir in you? Are you one of those "of little faith," or do you believe with conviction that, no matter what difficulties you face, you are in God's hands? Maybe you could pray: "Lord, I believe. But help my unbelief."

June 23—June 29

Something to think and pray about each day this week:

If there is one lesson that becomes clear when we look at the story of Jesus and of the countless saints—not to mention men and women today whose desires lead them to lives of great generosity—it is that a life mission begins with a desire to love authentically and truly. And this mission always blossoms in beauty, regardless of how great or small its fruits. At first, it may be about learning small ways to practice generosity and compassion. But as our desire to listen to God grows, so too do our creativity and resolve in taking on new ideas and ways of serving the world God has made. Over time, we find, the practice of the missioned life moves us in the direction of great desires rooted in the love of God, blossoming in beauty, truth, and goodness—especially among those who need it most.

—Tim Muldoon, *Living Against the Grain*

The Presence of God

At any time of the day or night we can call on Jesus.
He is always waiting, listening for our call.
What a wonderful blessing.
No phone needed, no emails, just a whisper.

Freedom

If God were trying to tell me something, would I know?
If God were reassuring me or challenging me, would I notice?
I ask for the grace to be free of my own preoccupations
and open to what God may be saying to me.

Consciousness

Help me, Lord, become more conscious of your presence. Teach me to recognize your presence in others. Fill my heart with gratitude for the times your love has been shown to me through the care of others.

The Word

In this expectant state of mind, please read the text for the day with confidence. Believe that the Holy Spirit is present and may reveal whatever the passage has to say to you. Read reflectively, listening with a third ear to what may be going on in your heart. (Please turn to the Scripture on the following pages. Inspiration points are there, should you need them. When you are ready, return here to continue.)

Conversation

Conversation requires talking and listening.
As I talk to Jesus, may I also learn to pause and listen.
I picture the gentleness in his eyes and the love in his smile.
I can be totally honest with Jesus as I tell him my worries and cares.
I will open my heart to Jesus as I tell him my fears and doubts.
I will ask him to help me place myself fully in his care, knowing that he always desires good for me.

Conclusion

I thank God for these moments we have spent together and for any insights I have been given concerning the text.

Sunday 23rd June
The Most Holy Body and Blood of Christ
(Corpus Christi)
Luke 9:11–17

When the crowds found out about it, they followed him; and he welcomed them, and spoke to them about the kingdom of God, and healed those who needed to be cured. The day was drawing to a close, and the twelve came to him and said, "Send the crowd away, so that they may go into the surrounding villages and countryside, to lodge and get provisions; for we are here in a deserted place." But he said to them, "You give them something to eat." They said, "We have no more than five loaves and two fish—unless we are to go and buy food for all these people." For there were about five thousand men. And he said to his disciples, "Make them sit down in groups of about fifty each." They did so and made them all sit down. And taking the five loaves and the two fish, he looked up to heaven, and blessed and broke them, and gave them to the disciples to set before the crowd. And all ate and were filled. What was left over was gathered up, twelve baskets of broken pieces.

- Mother Teresa said about Jesus, "He uses us to be his love and compassion in the world in spite of our weaknesses and frailties." In this miracle, Jesus does not produce food out of nowhere. He takes the little that the apostles have, and he multiplies it a thousandfold. No matter how little I think I have to give, once I freely place my gifts in Jesus' service, they become limitless.

- In the miracle of the multiplication of the loaves and fishes, I am reminded that Jesus can also provide spiritual sustenance beyond my imagining. There is a mysterious disproportion between what I give and what the Lord makes of it.

Monday 24th June
The Nativity of Saint John the Baptist
Luke 1:57–66, 80

Now the time came for Elizabeth to give birth, and she bore a son. Her neighbors and relatives heard that the Lord had shown his great mercy to her, and they rejoiced with her. On the eighth day they came to circumcise the child, and they were going to name him Zechariah after his father. But his mother said, "No; he is to be called John." They said to her, "None of your relatives has this name." Then they began motioning to his father to find out what name he wanted to give him. He asked for a writing tablet and wrote, "His name is John." And all of them were amazed. Immediately his mouth was opened and his tongue freed, and he began to speak, praising God. Fear came over all their neighbors, and all these things were talked about throughout the entire hill country of Judea. All who heard them pondered them and said, "What then will this child become?" For, indeed, the hand of the Lord was with him. The child grew and became strong in spirit, and he was in the wilderness until the day he appeared publicly to Israel.

- The story of the birth of John parallels in many ways that of the birth of Jesus. They both evoke feelings of wonder and amazement. The stories are told to throw light on the question: Who is this child, and how does he fit into God's plan for his people?

- Place yourself imaginatively into this scene where Elizabeth's relatives and neighbors gather to celebrate the naming of the newborn. Look at the persons and observe their actions, listen to what they say, and ponder the meaning of it all.

Tuesday 25th June
Matthew 7:6, 12–14

[Jesus said,] "Do not give what is holy to dogs; and do not throw your pearls before swine, or they will trample them under foot and turn and maul you. . . . In everything do to others as you would have them do to you; for this is the law and the prophets. Enter through the narrow gate; for the gate is wide and the road is easy that leads to destruction, and there are many who take it. For the gate is narrow and the road is hard that leads to life, and there are few who find it."

- These three sayings of Jesus are not connected to one another and may have been spoken at different times. In the first the phrase "what is holy" refers to the flesh (and blood) offered in Jewish sacrifices. The whole saying seems to be about preserving the integrity of all that is sacred. The middle saying is a reiteration of the Golden Rule, which is found in some form in all the great religions. Here it is put in a positive form: "do to others" rather than "do not do to others." Jesus asks for active and committed love. The third saying points to the difficulty of the Christian journey toward eternal life—a saying that needs to be balanced by other gentler words of Jesus. Can you recall some of these?

- I sit with the Lord and ask him what traces he finds of these Rules in my life.

Wednesday 26th June

Matthew 7:15–20

[Jesus said,] "Beware of false prophets, who come to you in sheep's clothing but inwardly are ravenous wolves. You will know them by their fruits. Are grapes gathered from thorns, or figs from thistles? In the same way, every good tree bears good fruit, but the bad tree bears bad fruit. A good tree cannot bear bad fruit, nor can a bad tree bear good fruit. Every tree that does not bear good fruit is cut down and thrown into the fire. Thus you will know them by their fruits."

- A tree does not go bad overnight. Rather, decay begins from within, and it takes time to show on the outside. On the other hand, growth in goodness is evident. By my fruits others will know my inner worth.

- St. Irenaeus says: "The glory of God is the human person fully alive!" I am meant to become fully alive myself, and to help others to become fully alive also. There is the agenda for a lifetime!

Thursday 27th June

Matthew 7:21–29

[Jesus said,] "Not everyone who says to me, 'Lord, Lord,' will enter the kingdom of heaven, but only the one who does the will of my Father in heaven. On that day many will say to me, 'Lord, Lord, did we not prophesy in your name, and cast out demons in your name, and do many deeds of power in your name?' Then I will declare to them, 'I never knew you; go away from me, you evildoers.' Everyone then who hears these words of mine and acts on them will be like a wise man who built his house on rock. The rain fell, the floods came, and the winds blew and beat on that house, but it did not fall, because it had been founded on rock. And everyone who hears these words of mine and does not act on them will be like a foolish man who built his house on sand. The rain fell, and the floods came, and the winds blew and beat against that house, and it fell—and great was its fall!" Now when Jesus had finished saying these things, the crowds were astounded at his teaching, for he taught them as one having authority, and not as their scribes.

- St. Ignatius wrote: "Love ought to manifest itself more by deeds than by words." This teaching comes close to that offered by Jesus in today's reading.

- Ponder the two powerful metaphors used by Jesus: the house built on rock and the house built on sand. Where have I built my "house" (my life), and what kind of foundations does it have? Am I a wise person or a foolish one?

Friday 28th June
The Most Sacred Heart of Jesus
Luke 15:3–7

So he told them this parable: "Which one of you, having a hundred sheep and losing one of them, does not leave the ninety-nine in the wilderness and go after the one that is lost until he finds it? When he has found it, he lays it on his shoulders and rejoices. And when he comes home, he calls together his friends and neighbors, saying to them, 'Rejoice with me, for I have found my sheep that was lost.' Just so, I tell you, there will be more joy in heaven over one sinner who repents than over ninety-nine righteous people who need no repentance."

- The message of today's feast and of today's reading is the most basic truth of all: God loves us, and he sent his Son who loved us to the very end, shedding his blood for us. Like love in all its forms, it is something we can never contemplate enough, it is beyond our grasp. Yet I know it is there and makes a huge difference in my life.

- Heaven rejoices and celebrates when one sinner repents. Do I join in the celebration, or am I one of the ninety-nine righteous ones who do not know how to be joyful, too concerned with the evil around them?

Saturday 29th June
Saints Peter and Paul, Apostles
John 21:15–19

When they had finished breakfast, Jesus said to Simon Peter, "Simon son of John, do you love me more than these?" He said to him, "Yes, Lord; you know that I love you." Jesus said to him, "Feed my lambs." A second time he said to him, "Simon son of John, do you love me?" He said to him, "Yes, Lord; you know that I love you." Jesus said to him, "Tend my sheep." He said to him the third time, "Simon son of John, do you love me?" Peter felt hurt because he said to him the third time, "Do you love me?" And he said to him, "Lord, you know everything; you know that I love you." Jesus said to him, "Feed my sheep. Very truly, I tell you, when you were younger, you used to fasten your own belt and to go wherever you wished. But when you grow old, you will stretch out your hands, and someone else will fasten a belt around you and take you where you do not wish to go." (He said this to indicate the kind of death by which he would glorify God.) After this he said to him, "Follow me."

- Imagine Jesus asking you, "Do you love me?" What is your response? What does this question stir up within you?

- "Feed my lambs." Love leads to action, and the actions fueled by our love for God will carry out God's desires. Identify some of the fruits of your love for God.

Thirteenth Week in Ordinary Time
June 30—July 6

Something to think and pray about each day this week:

Once I awakened to God's love for me, something shifted. My life's foundation went from what felt like shifting sand to solid rock that has only continued to strengthen over time. Knowing that I am deeply loved by God is something I cannot un-know, even when I try to forget it. I came to understand God's love for me slowly, just as I came to fully grasp the love my husband had for me and I had for my husband. Both grew over time, nurtured through the gift of spending time together. Coming to know God's love for me happened through the time we spent together and by immersing myself in God's words. Over time, I trained my ear to God's voice, and the words I read from the Bible were not just words on the page. They became words that God was speaking to me and about me.

—Becky Eldredge on *dotMagis*, the blog of *IgnatianSpirituality.com*

The Presence of God

Dear Jesus, as I call on you today, I realize that often I come asking for favors. Today I'd like just to be in your presence. Draw my heart in response to your love.

Freedom

It is so easy to get caught up
with the trappings of wealth in this life.
Grant, O Lord, that I may be free
from greed and selfishness.
Remind me that the best things in life are free:
Love, laughter, caring, and sharing.

Consciousness

How am I really feeling? Lighthearted? Heavyhearted? I may be very much at peace, happy to be here.
Equally, I may be frustrated, worried, or angry.
I acknowledge how I really am. It is the real me whom the Lord loves.

The Word

Lord Jesus, you became human to communicate with me.
You walked and worked on this earth.
You endured the heat and struggled with the cold.
All your time on this earth was spent in caring for humanity.
You healed the sick, you raised the dead.
Most important of all, you saved me from death.
(Please turn to the Scripture on the following pages. Inspiration points are there, should you need them. When you are ready, return here to continue.)

Conversation

Do I notice myself reacting as I pray with the word of God? Do I feel challenged, comforted, angry? Imagining Jesus sitting or standing by me, I speak out my feelings, as one trusted friend to another.

Conclusion

Glory be to the Father, and to the Son, and to the Holy Spirit,
As it was in the beginning, is now and ever shall be,
World without end. Amen.

Sunday 30th June
Luke 9:51–62

When the days drew near for Jesus to be taken up, he set his face to go to Jerusalem. And he sent messengers ahead of him. On their way they entered a village of the Samaritans to make ready for him; but they did not receive him, because his face was set toward Jerusalem. When his disciples James and John saw it, they said, "Lord, do you want us to command fire to come down from heaven and consume them?" But he turned and rebuked them. Then they went on to another village. As they were going along the road, someone said to him, "I will follow you wherever you go." And Jesus said to him, "Foxes have holes, and birds of the air have nests; but the Son of Man has nowhere to lay his head." To another he said, "Follow me." But he said, "Lord, first let me go and bury my father." But Jesus said to him, "Let the dead bury their own dead; but as for you, go and proclaim the kingdom of God." Another said, "I will follow you, Lord; but let me first say farewell to those at my home." Jesus said to him, "No one who puts a hand to the plough and looks back is fit for the kingdom of God."

- The temptation to use violence motivated by religion was present even within the small circle of the apostles. Jesus rebukes them and insists that the struggle must take place within our hearts. Am I really ready to follow him whatever the cost? The enthusiasm of the convert is not enough, for the stakes are high, and I really need to deny myself, and carry my cross every day. It is only by looking at my deeds that I discover how near or far I am from being Jesus' disciple.

- I look at the quality of my commitments and ask for the grace not to look back as I place my hand on the plough.

Monday 1st July
Matthew 8:18–22

Now when Jesus saw great crowds around him, he gave orders to go over to the other side. A scribe then approached and said, "Teacher, I will follow you wherever you go." And Jesus said to him, "Foxes have holes, and birds of the air have nests; but the Son of Man has nowhere to lay his head." Another of his disciples said to him, "Lord, first let me go and bury my father." But Jesus said to him, "Follow me, and let the dead bury their own dead."

- Jesus knew that we humans are poor judges of our own nature. So he periodically made statements that would bring people back to reality. When am I tempted to make grand statements about my commitment to Christ—or to make big plans for my life of faith?

- "[T]he Son of Man has nowhere to lay his head." What do you think Jesus meant by this?

Tuesday 2nd July
Matthew 8:23–27

And when he got into the boat, his disciples followed him. A windstorm arose on the sea, so great that the boat was being swamped by the waves; but he was asleep. And they went and woke him up, saying, "Lord, save us! We are perishing!" And he said to them, "Why are you afraid, you of little faith?" Then he got up and rebuked the winds and the sea; and there was a dead calm. They were amazed, saying, "What sort of man is this, that even the winds and the sea obey him?"

- "Lord, save us! We are perishing!" Like so many other prayers we find in the Gospel, I may find that today this simple prayer resonates in my heart as I look at my family, my community, my country, our world. I stay with these words, pleading for Jesus' help.

- "And he said to them, 'Why are you afraid, you of little faith?'" I acknowledge my weak faith, my fear that Jesus is asleep while the windstorm threatens to overwhelm me. I ask for simple trust, and I share in the apostles' wonder at the power present in the person of Jesus.

Wednesday 3rd July
John 20:24–29

But Thomas (who was called the Twin), one of the twelve, was not with them when Jesus came. So the other disciples told him, "We have seen the Lord." But he said to them, "Unless I see the mark of the nails in his hands, and put my finger in the mark of the nails and my hand in his side, I will not believe." A week later his disciples were again in the house, and Thomas was with them. Although the doors were shut, Jesus came and stood among them and said, "Peace be with you." Then he said to Thomas, "Put your finger here and see my hands. Reach out your hand and put it in my side.

Do not doubt but believe." Thomas answered him, "My Lord and my God!" Jesus said to him, "Have you believed because you have seen me? Blessed are those who have not seen and yet have come to believe."

• We can only imagine how ashamed and angry at themselves the apostles must have been after their desertion of Jesus. To miss Jesus' apparition must have been the last straw for Thomas. Yet Jesus has no words of reproach but of peace. He accepts Thomas's emotional reaction and gently leads him to one of the finest expressions of faith in the whole of the Gospel: "My Lord and my God!" The risen Jesus brings peace to troubled hearts; he heals us and leads us to faith. I imagine him taking me gently by the hand and letting me physically feel his presence at my side. What words well from my grateful heart?

• Thomas's anger led him to discover the deep faith he had in Jesus. Sometimes I might be unaware of how my strong emotions can help me grow as a person and as a believer. I ask to hear the Risen Jesus' favorite greeting: "Peace be with you," words that enable me to look deep into my heart.

Thursday 4th July
Matthew 9:1–8

And after getting into a boat Jesus crossed the sea and came to his own town. And just then some people were carrying a paralyzed man lying on a bed. When Jesus saw their faith, he said to the paralytic, "Take heart, son; your sins are forgiven." Then some of the scribes said to themselves, "This man is blaspheming." But Jesus, perceiving their thoughts, said, "Why do you think evil in your hearts? For which is easier, to say, 'Your sins are forgiven,' or to say, 'Stand up and walk'? But so that you may know that the Son of Man has authority on earth to forgive sins"—he then said to the paralytic—"Stand up, take your bed and go to your home." And he stood up and went to his home. When the crowds saw it, they were filled with awe, and they glorified God, who had given such authority to human beings.

• When Jesus saw their faith, he said to the paralytic, "Take heart, son; your sins are forgiven." This is indeed the good news brought to us by Jesus, the news that he asked the apostles to take to the whole world. I ask myself whether God's mercy is at the center of my understanding of the gospel, of God himself. Does my faith enable me to take heart, or do I feel discouraged at the sin present around me and within me?

- "When the crowds saw it, they were filled with awe, and they glorified God, who had given such authority to human beings." By the time the Gospel of Matthew was written, the early church was certain of its God-given power to forgive sins. It is certainly an awesome power, perhaps too big not to scandalize us. Especially because the human beings to whom this power is given are themselves in need of forgiveness. I too give glory to God for his mercy.

Friday 5th July
Matthew 9:9–13

As Jesus was walking along, he saw a man called Matthew sitting at the tax booth; and he said to him, "Follow me." And he got up and followed him. And as he sat at dinner in the house, many tax collectors and sinners came and were sitting with him and his disciples. When the Pharisees saw this, they said to his disciples, "Why does your teacher eat with tax collectors and sinners?" But when he heard this, he said, "Those who are well have no need of a physician, but those who are sick. Go and learn what this means, 'I desire mercy, not sacrifice.' For I have come to call not the righteous but sinners."

- Despite being concerned with his balances and rates, Matthew was ready to hear a deeper message. How might I preserve a readiness to hear the promptings of Jesus when I am in the midst of my daily occupation?

- "I desire mercy, not sacrifice." Here are two visions of religion put into stark contrast: is religion primarily observation of rules and laws, or a loving and merciful relationship to God and to others? This discussion was as lively in Jesus' time as it is nowadays, as Pope Francis challenges us to put mercy at the center of our Christian life and draw the practical consequences. I ask for the grace to grasp the meaning of all this, to make the right choices.

Saturday 6th July

Matthew 9:14–17

Then the disciples of John came to him, saying, "Why do we and the Pharisees fast often, but your disciples do not fast?" And Jesus said to them, "The wedding guests cannot mourn as long as the bridegroom is with them, can they? The days will come when the bridegroom is taken away from them, and then they will fast. No one sews a piece of unshrunk cloth on an old cloak, for the patch pulls away from the cloak, and a worse tear is made. Neither is new wine put into old wineskins; otherwise, the skins burst, and the wine is spilled, and the skins are destroyed; but new wine is put into fresh wineskins, and so both are preserved."

• John's disciples were more concerned with adhering to the custom of fasting and seemed to neglect the possibility of opening themselves more fully to the teaching of Jesus. Using the example of the wineskins, Jesus indicates how the existing Jewish traditions could be enhanced in the light of his preaching about the kingdom of God.

• Jesus, I pray that I may more readily see the ways through which your teaching offers me new life. Help me to be attentive to receive the newness of your message and the blessings you wish to give me.

July 7—July 13

Something to think and pray about each day this week:

One of my bags was lost in transit, and I couldn't wait for it so continued the trip without it. I had to buy shampoo and some socks. Other than that, I didn't miss the bag. By the time I headed home, the bag was back in my possession. I set it down in the hallway at home and didn't open it for a week because I couldn't remember what was in it. And if I couldn't remember, then could anything in that bag be so important? This makes me wonder how much energy I use up, day in and day out, hauling stuff around that isn't even important. What burdens have I taken upon myself that just take up space and make me tired and anxious? I don't think we were meant to live this way—too many bags, and too much weight. I think God wants us to travel light and to enjoy the trip a lot more.

—Vinita Hampton Wright on *LoyolaPress.com*

The Presence of God

Dear Jesus, I come to you today longing for your presence. I desire to love you as you love me. May nothing ever separate me from you.

Freedom

Lord, grant me the grace to have freedom of the spirit. Cleanse my heart and soul so that I may live joyously in your love.

Consciousness

Where am I with God? With others?
Do I have something to be grateful for? Then I give thanks.
Is there something I am sorry for? Then I ask forgiveness.

The Word

The word of God comes down to us through the Scriptures. May the Holy Spirit enlighten my mind and my heart to respond to the gospel teachings. (Please turn to the Scripture on the following pages. Inspiration points are there, should you need them. When you are ready, return here to continue.)

Conversation

How has God's word moved me? Has it left me cold?
Has it consoled me or moved me to act in a new way?
I imagine Jesus standing or sitting beside me;
I turn and share my feelings with him.

Conclusion

I thank God for these moments we have spent together and for any insights I have been given concerning the text.

Sunday 7th July

Luke 10:1–9

After this the Lord appointed seventy others and sent them on ahead of him in pairs to every town and place where he himself intended to go. He said to them, "The harvest is plentiful, but the laborers are few; therefore ask the Lord of the harvest to send out laborers into his harvest. Go on your way. See, I am sending you out like lambs into the midst of wolves. Carry no purse, no bag, no sandals; and greet no one on the road. Whatever house you enter, first say, 'Peace to this house!' And if anyone is there who shares in peace, your peace will rest on that person; but if not, it will return to you. Remain in the same house, eating and drinking whatever they provide, for the laborer deserves to be paid. Do not move about from house to house. Whenever you enter a town and its people welcome you, eat what is set before you; cure the sick who are there, and say to them, 'The kingdom of God has come near to you.'"

- In many parts of the world I may be "like a lamb in the midst of wolves." The expression of my faith is simply to say, "Peace to this house." My desire is to heal the wounds of division among peoples. I cannot give up this vision of "the kingdom" if I wish to remain in this Gospel scene among those seventy others.

- Jesus' advice to travel light applies to all of us. How many unneeded and unused purses, bags, and other items clutter my closets? Could I carry everything I truly need for a trip?

Monday 8th July

Matthew 9:18–26

While [Jesus was speaking], suddenly a leader of the synagogue came in and knelt before him, saying, "My daughter has just died; but come and lay your hand on her, and she will live." And Jesus got up and followed him, with his disciples. Then suddenly a woman who had been suffering from hemorrhages for twelve years came up behind him and touched the fringe of his cloak, for she said to herself, "If I only touch his cloak, I will be made well." Jesus turned, and seeing her he said, "Take heart, daughter; your faith has made you well." And instantly the woman was made well. When Jesus came to the leader's house and saw the flute players and the crowd making a commotion, he said, "Go away; for the girl is not dead but sleeping." And they laughed at him. But when the crowd had been put outside, he went in and took her by the hand, and the girl got up. And the report of this spread throughout that district.

- Like the woman in today's text, I may be suffering from some malady, physical or spiritual, that has become a permanent feature of my life, holding me back from being my true self. Like her I might feel the urge to seek healing, to touch Jesus discreetly while believing in his power to heal me. I listen to Jesus' reply, affirming my move.

- Jesus came for us to have life, and life in abundance. He raises this girl back to life, and his own story ends in his triumph over death and sin. I pray that I too can believe firmly in life and in all that enhances it, on all levels.

Tuesday 9th July
Matthew 9:32–38

After they had gone away, a demoniac who was mute was brought to him. And when the demon had been cast out, the one who had been mute spoke; and the crowds were amazed and said, "Never has anything like this been seen in Israel." But the Pharisees said, "By the ruler of the demons he casts out the demons." Then Jesus went about all the cities and villages, teaching in their synagogues, and proclaiming the good news of the kingdom, and curing every disease and every sickness. When he saw the crowds, he had compassion for them, because they were harassed and helpless, like sheep without a shepherd. Then he said to his disciples, "The harvest is plentiful, but the laborers are few; therefore ask the Lord of the harvest to send out laborers into his harvest."

- I ask myself what I feel when I look around me and see so much confusion and loneliness: Is it anger or moral superiority, fear perhaps, or is it compassion and a desire to bring the good news of salvation? I ask the Lord to send laborers to his abundant harvest, and I ask to be one of them.

- When we pray to the Lord to send laborers into his harvest, we often think of the religious life and sometimes forget that Jesus calls each person to be a disciple of his love. Help me, Lord, to be caring and compassionate to those around me, remembering that it is often through the small and invisible things I do for others that I can contribute to the building of your kingdom.

Wednesday 10th July
Matthew 10:1–7

Then Jesus summoned his twelve disciples and gave them authority over unclean spirits, to cast them out, and to cure every disease and every sickness. These are the names of the twelve apostles: first, Simon, also known as Peter, and his brother Andrew; James son of Zebedee, and his brother John; Philip and Bartholomew; Thomas and Matthew the tax collector; James son of Alphaeus, and Thaddaeus; Simon the Cananaean, and Judas Iscariot, the one who betrayed him. These twelve Jesus sent out with the following instructions: "Go nowhere among the Gentiles, and enter no town of the Samaritans, but go rather to the lost sheep of the house of Israel. As you go, proclaim the good news, 'The kingdom of heaven has come near.'"

- He called the twelve disciples to him and sent them to others. We cannot be real disciples of Jesus without being also apostles to others. The mission is the same that Jesus received from the Father: Go and tell everyone the good news that the kingdom of heaven is near; bring healing to all who need it, and get involved in the struggle against evil. I ask for the grace not to be deaf to the call to be a disciple and apostle.

- Help me, Lord, to understand how my faith can have a missionary dimension. Show me how I can be an instrument of your love in my encounters with others, so that your kingdom of justice, truth, and love may reign.

Thursday 11th July
Matthew 10:7–15

[Jesus said to his disciples,] "As you go, proclaim the good news, 'The kingdom of heaven has come near.' Cure the sick, raise the dead, cleanse the lepers, cast out demons. You received without payment; give without payment. Take no gold, or silver, or copper in your belts, no bag for your journey, or two tunics, or sandals, or a staff; for laborers deserve their food. Whatever town or village you enter, find out who in it is worthy, and stay there until you leave. As you enter the house, greet it. If the house is worthy, let your peace come upon it; but if it is not worthy, let your peace return to you. If anyone will not welcome you or listen to your words, shake off the dust from your feet as you leave that house or town. Truly I tell you, it will be more tolerable for the land of Sodom and Gomorrah on the day of judgment than for that town."

- I find Jesus' very concrete instructions reassuring: God gets involved in the nitty-gritty of life's challenges as well as dealing with the big issues. For God no problem is too small for me to ask for help and advice. Knock, and the door will be opened.

- "You received without payment; give without payment." What can I give that requires no payment on either side? My time? My expertise? My gifts? My forgiveness? I can give others the benefit of the doubt. I can pray that the person who receives from me will pass on the grace of giving, and that whomever I forgive will likewise forgive someone else.

Friday 12th July
Matthew 10:16–23

[Jesus said to his disciples,] "See, I am sending you out like sheep into the midst of wolves; so be wise as serpents and innocent as doves. Beware of them, for they will hand you over to councils and flog you in their synagogues; and you will be dragged before governors and kings because of me, as a testimony to them and the Gentiles. When they hand you over, do not worry about how you are to speak or what you are to say; for what you are to say will be given to you at that time; for it is not you who speak, but the Spirit of your Father speaking through you. Brother will betray brother to death, and a father his child, and children will rise against parents and have them put to death; and you will be hated by all because of my name. But the one who endures to the end will be saved. When they persecute you in one town, flee to the next; for truly I tell you, you will not have gone through all the towns of Israel before the Son of Man comes."

- Often we struggle with the opposition we face when we try to live an honest Christian life, and with the increasing duplicity that seems to surround us. We do well to listen to Jesus' words about sheep among wolves and the need to know how to be both wise and transparent. Jesus knows all this, yet he still sends us to take the gospel to this difficult world. But he also promises us his assistance: he asks us not to worry!

- Lord, send forth your Holy Spirit when I feel weighed down by struggles and persecutions. Help me trust in the power of your Spirit, the very life of God within me, which guides me into the ways of truth and love.

Saturday 13th July

Matthew 10:24–33

[Jesus said to his disciples,] "A disciple is not above the teacher, nor a slave above the master; it is enough for the disciple to be like the teacher, and the slave like the master. If they have called the master of the house Beelzebul, how much more will they malign those of his household! So have no fear of them; for nothing is covered up that will not be uncovered, and nothing secret that will not become known. What I say to you in the dark, tell in the light; and what you hear whispered, proclaim from the housetops. Do not fear those who kill the body but cannot kill the soul; rather fear him who can destroy both soul and body in hell. Are not two sparrows sold for a penny? Yet not one of them will fall to the ground apart from your Father. And even the hairs of your head are all counted. So do not be afraid; you are of more value than many sparrows. Everyone therefore who acknowledges me before others, I also will acknowledge before my Father in heaven; but whoever denies me before others, I also will deny before my Father in heaven."

- The words of Jesus are an encouragement not to be deterred in the face of challenge or opposition. The loving, attentive care of God the Father extends even to the sparrows, and we are of more value than many sparrows.

- Father God, you have created me in your image and likeness; you have counted every hair on my head. You know all my concerns and accompany me on all life's journeys. Help me to perceive your supporting presence and not to be afraid, for you are with me always.

July 14—July 20

Something to think and pray about each day this week:

When a zebra foal is born, so the ranger informs me, it first staggers to its feet and runs in circles round its mother's legs. Nature's way, no doubt, of getting those spindly newborn limbs strong enough, quickly enough, to flee from predators. But then, exhausted, the newborn foal collapses in a weary heap and lies back, simply gazing, for hours it seems, at its mother. *How very cute*, I think. But this isn't cuteness; it's something else altogether. This is the foal memorizing its mother's stripe pattern. Imagine! Every single zebra on this planet has a unique stripe pattern. Memorizing its mother's pattern is the foal's first act of bonding, its first defense against getting lost in the herd. I believe that God paints a unique pattern of presence in each human life. We discover this pattern as we reflect on what is actually happening in our everyday experience. It is there we will notice God's personal relationship with us, unfolding minute by minute. This reflection becomes an attitude of mindfulness, an ongoing act of bonding, and it holds us in an unbreakable connection with the source of our being through every moment of our living.

—Margaret Silf, *Compass Points*

The Presence of God

Dear Jesus, today I call on you, but not to ask for anything. I'd like only to dwell in your presence. May my heart respond to your love.

Freedom

God my creator, you gave me life and the gift of freedom. Through your love I exist in this world. May I never take the gift of life for granted. May I always respect others' right to life.

Consciousness

I ask how I am today. Am I particularly tired, stressed, or anxious? If any of these characteristics apply, can I try to let go of the concerns that disturb me?

The Word

The word of God comes down to us through the Scriptures. May the Holy Spirit enlighten my mind and my heart to respond to the gospel teachings. (Please turn to the Scripture on the following pages. Inspiration points are there, should you need them. When you are ready, return here to continue.)

Conversation

I begin to talk with Jesus about the Scripture I have just read. What part of it strikes a chord in me? Perhaps the words of a friend—or some story I have heard recently—will rise to the surface in my consciousness. If so, does the story throw light on what the Scripture passage may be saying to me?

Conclusion

Glory be to the Father, and to the Son, and to the Holy Spirit,
As it was in the beginning, is now and ever shall be,
World without end. Amen.

Sunday 14th July

Luke 10:25–37

Just then a lawyer stood up to test Jesus. "Teacher," he said, "what must I do to inherit eternal life?" He said to him, "What is written in the law? What do you read there?" He answered, "You shall love the Lord your God with all your heart, and with all your soul, and with all your strength, and with all your mind; and your neighbor as yourself." And he said to him, "You have given the right answer; do this, and you will live." But wanting to justify himself, he asked Jesus, "And who is my neighbor?" Jesus replied, "A man was going down from Jerusalem to Jericho, and fell into the hands of robbers, who stripped him, beat him, and went away, leaving him half dead. Now by chance a priest was going down that road; and when he saw him, he passed by on the other side. So likewise a Levite, when he came to the place and saw him, passed by on the other side. But a Samaritan while traveling came near him; and when he saw him, he was moved with pity. He went to him and bandaged his wounds, having poured oil and wine on them. Then he put him on his own animal, brought him to an inn, and took care of him. The next day he took out two denarii, gave them to the innkeeper, and said, Take care of him; and when I come back, I will repay you whatever more you spend. Which of these three, do you think, was a neighbor to the man who fell into the hands of the robbers?" He said, "The one who showed him mercy." Jesus said to him, "Go and do likewise."

- Dear Lord, you remind me here that I often seek to justify my own self-ishness. But the knowledge of the lawyer is not what you seek. It is my heart that you seek, and the acts of love and mercy that should flow freely out of my heart. Forgive me and let your flame of love and mercy flare up afresh in my heart and consume my selfish tendencies. I pray this as your disciple. Amen.

- "Grant me, O Lord, to see everything now with new eyes, to discern and test the spirits that help me read the signs of the times, to relish the things that are yours and to communicate them to others. Give me the clarity of understanding that you gave Ignatius" (Pedro Arrupe, SJ).

Monday 15th July

Matthew 10:34—11:1

[Jesus said to his disciples,] "Do not think that I have come to bring peace to the earth; I have not come to bring peace, but a sword. For I have come to set a man against his father, and a daughter against her mother, and a daughter-in-law against her mother-in-law; and one's foes will be members of one's own household. Whoever loves father or mother more than me is not worthy of me; and whoever loves son or daughter more than me is not worthy of me; and whoever does not take up the cross and follow me is not worthy of me. Those who find their life will lose it, and those who lose their life for my sake will find it. Whoever welcomes you welcomes me, and whoever welcomes me welcomes the one who sent me. Whoever welcomes a prophet in the name of a prophet will receive a prophet's reward; and whoever welcomes a righteous person in the name of a righteous person will receive the reward of the righteous; and whoever gives even a cup of cold water to one of these little ones in the name of a disciple—truly I tell you, none of these will lose their reward." Now when Jesus had finished instructing his twelve disciples, he went on from there to teach and proclaim his message in their cities.

- These hard words of Jesus can be understood only in the light of our life experience, the times we had to face the dramatic choices Jesus speaks of. We know there are moments when stark choices need to be made to ensure that we can still call ourselves disciples of Jesus, moments when we wield the sword of division or separation.

- Do I want to save my life or to lose it? Am I ready to lose it, or do I cling on for fear of losing it? This is perhaps the basic condition for discipleship, and no moralistic or perfect obedience to any law or system of rules can replace it. I ask insistently for the grace of real interior freedom and for courage to be true to myself—the person God created—and to my calling.

Tuesday 16th July

Matthew 11:20–24

Then Jesus began to reproach the cities in which most of his deeds of power had been done, because they did not repent. "Woe to you, Chorazin! Woe to you, Bethsaida! For if the deeds of power done in you had been done in Tyre and Sidon, they would have repented long ago in sackcloth and ashes. But I tell you, on the day of judgment it will be more tolerable for Tyre and Sidon than for you. And you, Capernaum, will you be exalted to heaven? No, you will be brought down to Hades. For if the deeds of power done in you had been done in Sodom, it would have remained until this day. But I tell you that on the day of judgment it will be more tolerable for the land of Sodom than for you."

- We might not feel very comfortable with the idea of Jesus as our judge, who thunders terrible threats on big and powerful cities. I try to listen to these words as directed to me and my society's way of life. I also ask for the adequate response to this call for conversion.

- Not only individuals but our whole societies are urgently called to conversion. There are too many innocent victims of systematic evil not to make us ask some very painful questions about the way we are organized. I pray for my society and for its conversion from what I consider the most obnoxious elements in God's eyes. I ask for light to see what part I can play as a responsible citizen.

Wednesday 17th July
Matthew 11:25–27

At that time Jesus said, "I thank you, Father, Lord of heaven and earth, because you have hidden these things from the wise and the intelligent and have revealed them to infants; yes, Father, for such was your gracious will. All things have been handed over to me by my Father; and no one knows the Son except the Father, and no one knows the Father except the Son and anyone to whom the Son chooses to reveal him."

- No matter what happens, Jesus is always present with us. He wants to bless us and reveal the Father's love as we draw closer to him. Can I open my heart more fully to receive the gift of God's love just like the simplicity of a little child longing for the loving embrace of a parent?

- I share Jesus' joy and gratitude for the great gift of the Father's showing himself to us, especially to those who are small. I ask for the grace not to consider myself wise and intelligent before God's greatness, but become like a little child, willing to listen and learn, to be surprised by how and what God tells me about himself.

Thursday 18th July
Matthew 11:28–30

[Jesus said,] "Come to me, all you that are weary and are carrying heavy burdens, and I will give you rest. Take my yoke upon you, and learn from me; for I am gentle and humble in heart, and you will find rest for your souls. For my yoke is easy, and my burden is light."

• Jesus you are sensitive to the crushing demands on ordinary people. You are so very aware of the poor, and the daily burdens they carry. You offer them the solace of taking on your yoke as they try to eke out a daily living.

• I seek quiet in my heart so that I can listen to Jesus' invitation to lay all my heavy burdens at his feet, and so find rest. Then I bring myself to respond by accepting this invitation, going to him and taking my burdens one by one, becoming aware of my need to find rest.

Friday 19th July
Matthew 12:1–8

At that time Jesus went through the cornfields on the sabbath; his disciples were hungry, and they began to pluck heads of grain and to eat. When the Pharisees saw it, they said to him, "Look, your disciples are doing what is not lawful to do on the sabbath." He said to them, "Have you not read what David did when he and his companions were hungry? He entered the house of God and ate the bread of the Presence, which it was not lawful for him or his companions to eat, but only for the priests. Or have you not read in the law that on the sabbath the priests in the temple break the sabbath and yet are guiltless? I tell you, something greater than the temple is here. But if you had known what this means, 'I desire mercy and not sacrifice,' you would not have condemned the guiltless. For the Son of Man is lord of the sabbath."

• Jesus' internal freedom, built on his self-awareness as someone wholly unique, must have confused and irritated his critics. He always refers to a rule of behavior that is higher and purer than the observances his hearers are used to. Sometimes this seems too much for them. Are we still capable of being shocked by Jesus' words and actions, or have we rendered them innocuous?

- Jesus proclaims himself as greater than the temple, even Lord of the Sabbath itself, two of the most sacred Jewish institutions. I ask Jesus to challenge me by his presence and his demands, especially as regards my understanding of Christianity and the church.

Saturday 20th July

Matthew 12:14–21

But the Pharisees went out and conspired against him, how to destroy him. When Jesus became aware of this, he departed. Many crowds followed him, and he cured all of them, and he ordered them not to make him known. This was to fulfill what had been spoken through the prophet Isaiah: "Here is my servant, whom I have chosen, my beloved, with whom my soul is well pleased. I will put my Spirit upon him, and he will proclaim justice to the Gentiles. He will not wrangle or cry aloud, nor will anyone hear his voice in the streets. He will not break a bruised reed or quench a smoldering wick until he brings justice to victory. And in his name the Gentiles will hope."

- Jesus was an advocate of justice who quietly proclaimed a message of love that set his people free. When he encountered hostility as the Pharisees conspired against him, he did not want his followers to make him known. This was to fulfill the prophecy of Isaiah about the suffering servant who was full of gentleness and compassion, which Jesus applies to himself.

- I can pray the words of Isaiah and give thanks. God has chosen me, I am his beloved son or daughter, and he is pleased with me. He has given me his Spirit, and he wants to bless me as I draw closer to him.

Something to think and pray about each day this week:

In the Gospels, Jesus uses the image of scattered seeds to tell a story about the lure of false desires. In the story, the sower spreads seeds along four kinds of ground, where some take root and some do not. On a path, birds eat up the seeds. On rocky ground, the sun's heat scorches the seed and it dies. On ground covered with thorns, the seed grows but then is choked. Finally, on good soil, the seed takes root and grows beautifully, producing enough grain to feed many people. The parable is meant to challenge Jesus' followers about the ways that daily concerns choke out the seeds that bring forth fruit in their lives. We all might start with an intention to become strong, authentic people, building our lives around relationships, good practices of self-care, awareness of others and a desire to serve, and maybe even prayer. But this "seed" of authentic desire can fall on a path of success, in which all choices are secondary to the desire to rise to the top. And so these good intentions wither and die. Similarly, we can allow the seeds of new commitments—say, the resolve to give money to the poor—to be choked by fear of financial stress or job loss. Or we may find that others' demands on us, whether at work, at home, or among friends, slowly draw us away from exploring the inner life that might otherwise grow into a new form of self-giving to the world. Jesus' parable invites us to consider the sources of desire in our lives. Too often, he says, "the cares of the world, and the lure of wealth, and the desire for other things come in and choke the word, and it yields nothing." Developing an authentic self, he suggests, requires cultivating the ground of our inner lives, so that the seed may take root and bring forth all the virtues that lead to a great soul. That cultivation is a daily practice that, little by little, forms us into people capable of great love.

—Tim Muldoon, *Living Against the Grain*

The Presence of God

Dear Lord, as I come to you today, fill my heart, my whole being, with the wonder of your presence. Help me remain receptive to you as I put aside the cares of this world. Fill my mind with your peace.

Freedom

Lord, grant me the grace to be free from the excesses of this life. Let me not get caught up with the desire for wealth. Keep my heart and mind free to love and serve you.

Consciousness

I exist in a web of relationships: links to nature, people, God.
I trace out these links, giving thanks for the life that flows through them.
Some links are twisted or broken; I may feel regret, anger, disappointment.
I pray for the gift of acceptance and forgiveness.

The Word

God speaks to each of us individually. I listen attentively to hear what he is saying to me. Read the text a few times; then listen. (Please turn to the Scripture on the following pages. Inspiration points are there, should you need them. When you are ready, return here to continue.)

Conversation

Jesus, you speak to me through the words of the Gospels. May I respond to your call today. Teach me to recognize your hand at work in my daily living.

Conclusion

I thank God for these moments we have spent together and for any insights I have been given concerning the text.

Sunday 21st July

Luke 10:38–42

Now as they went on their way, [Jesus] entered a certain village, where a woman named Martha welcomed him into her home. She had a sister named Mary, who sat at the Lord's feet and listened to what he was saying. But Martha was distracted by her many tasks; so she came to him and asked, "Lord, do you not care that my sister has left me to do all the work by myself? Tell her then to help me." But the Lord answered her, "Martha, Martha, you are worried and distracted by many things; there is need of only one thing. Mary has chosen the better part, which will not be taken away from her."

- Some Scripture scholars remark that this gospel passage is less about work versus prayer and more about breaking boundaries. They understand that sitting at Jesus' feet or listening to any rabbi was reserved for men only. They in turn would become teachers of faith. But here, Mary has stepped out of the traditional role where she should be in the women's quarters, and Jesus fully approves, inviting Martha to do the same.
- I thank the Lord that I have responded to his invitation today and enjoy listening to him.

Monday 22nd July

John 20:1–2, 11–18

Early on the first day of the week, while it was still dark, Mary Magdalene came to the tomb and saw that the stone had been removed from the tomb. So she ran and went to Simon Peter and the other disciple, the one whom Jesus loved, and said to them, "They have taken the Lord out of the tomb, and we do not know where they have laid him." . . . But Mary stood weeping outside the tomb. As she wept, she bent over to look into the tomb; and she saw two angels in white, sitting where the body of Jesus had been lying, one at the head and the other at the feet. They said to her, "Woman, why are you weeping?" She said to them, "They have taken away my Lord, and I do not know where they have laid him." When she had said this, she turned around and saw Jesus standing there, but she did not know that it was Jesus. Jesus said to her, "Woman, why are you weeping? Whom are you looking for?" Supposing him to be the gardener, she said to him, "Sir, if you have carried him away, tell me where you have laid him, and I will take him away." Jesus said to her, "Mary!" She turned and said to him in Hebrew, "Rabbouni!" (which means Teacher). Jesus said to her, "Do not hold on to me, because I have not yet ascended to the Father. But go to my brothers and say to them, 'I am ascending to my Father and your Father, to my God and your God.'" Mary Magdalene went and announced to the disciples, "I have seen the Lord"; and she told them that he had said these things to her.

- Mary is one of the first witnesses of the Resurrection; she was the one who brought the news of the empty tomb to Peter and John, and later she announced to the disciples, "I have seen the Lord!" I thank God for these witnesses and ask for the grace to be myself a joyful and enthusiastic witness to the presence of the risen Jesus in the world and to the joy and freedom that it radiates.

- The risen Jesus does not let Mary cling to him but sends her on a mission, telling others he is risen. What do I feel Jesus sending me to do, after my personal encounter with him after his Resurrection? I pray for the grace not to be deaf to this call, but ready to respond to it with generosity.

Tuesday 23rd July
Matthew 12:46–50

While [Jesus] was still speaking to the crowds, his mother and his brothers were standing outside, wanting to speak to him. Someone told him, "Look, your mother and your brothers are standing outside, wanting to speak to you." But to the one who had told him this, Jesus replied, "Who is my mother, and who are my brothers?" And pointing to his disciples, he said, "Here are my mother and my brothers! For whoever does the will of my Father in heaven is my brother and sister and mother."

- This text can give rise to criticism of Jesus for being disrespectful to his mother and brothers. However, we should read it in the light of how he wishes to extend his family, so that we are all members of the one family in which God is our father. Families who have adopted sons and daughters can understand this when all are treated equally as belonging to the one family. We are reminded that we are to love God and love our neighbor with one and the self-same love.

- Being brothers and sisters in the Lord implies a call to witness to our faith. Can I bring God's love and compassion to others, especially the poor, marginalized, and vulnerable?

Wednesday 24th July
Matthew 13:1–9

That same day Jesus went out of the house and sat beside the sea. Such great crowds gathered around him that he got into a boat and sat there, while the whole crowd stood on the beach. And he told them many things in parables, saying: "Listen! A sower went out to sow. And as he sowed, some seeds fell on the path, and the birds came and ate them up. Other seeds fell on rocky ground, where they did not have much soil, and they sprang up quickly, since they had no depth of soil. But when the sun rose, they were scorched; and since they had no root, they withered away. Other seeds fell among thorns, and the thorns grew up and choked them. Other seeds fell on good soil and brought forth grain, some a hundredfold, some sixty, some thirty. Let anyone with ears listen!"

- "Let anyone with ears listen." This means me! When I come to pray, do I have the soil of an open heart toward Jesus and his teachings? Am I willing to allow his word to break in and find a good place to grow?

- If I am a normal person, my heart contains all four sorts of ground, being more or less open to the gospel message. I ask for light to see where the hardness and the insecurity lie, and I ask the Sower that my life may bear abundant fruit.

Thursday 25th July
Feast of Saint James, Apostle
Matthew 20:20–28

Then the mother of the sons of Zebedee came to him with her sons, and kneeling before him, she asked a favor of him. And he said to her, "What do you want?" She said to him, "Declare that these two sons of mine will sit, one at your right hand and one at your left, in your kingdom." But Jesus answered, "You do not know what you are asking. Are you able to drink the cup that I am about to drink?" They said to him, "We are able." He said to them, "You will indeed drink my cup, but to sit at my right hand and at my left, this is not mine to grant, but it is for those for whom it has been prepared by my Father." When the ten heard it, they were angry with the two brothers. But Jesus called them to him and said, "You know that the rulers of the Gentiles lord it over them, and their great ones are tyrants over them. It will not be so among you; but whoever wishes to be great among you must be your servant, and whoever wishes to be first among you must be your slave; just as the Son of Man came not to be served but to serve, and to give his life a ransom for many."

- On the feast of Saint James, one of Jesus' inner circle, I rejoice in the faithfulness of these men. They were ready to let the Spirit enable them to overcome their many shortcomings, transforming them into the first apostles of the good news of the kingdom. Thanks to them and their love of Jesus, their readiness to drink the cup he was about to drink, the faith has come to us and to billions of others throughout the world. I ask for gratitude, and for their sense of urgency in spreading the gospel to the whole world.

- We are impressed by how often the gospel portrays even those closest to Jesus struggling with questions of power and service. I look into my own heart and dwell on Jesus' words on the Christian's attitude to such an important aspect of our life together. I ask for the grace to grow in my imitation of him who came to serve and not to be served.

Friday 26th July
Matthew 13:18–23

[Jesus said to his disciples,] "Hear then the parable of the sower. When anyone hears the word of the kingdom and does not understand it, the evil one comes and snatches away what is sown in the heart; this is what was sown on the path. As for what was sown on rocky ground, this is the one who hears the word and immediately receives it with joy; yet such a person has no root, but endures only for a while, and when trouble or persecution arises on account of the word, that person immediately falls away. As for what was sown among thorns, this is the one who hears the word, but the cares of the world and the lure of wealth choke the word, and it yields nothing. But as for what was sown on good soil, this is the one who hears the word and understands it, who indeed bears fruit and yields, in one case a hundredfold, in another sixty, and in another thirty."

- I look at my life in gratitude for the abundant fruit that the word sown in my heart has produced in my relationships, in my freedom and openness to God and others, and in my sensibility to suffering around me. Especially to the place Jesus has in my life.

- I also look at the margins of my heart, those areas where the word finds it difficult to bear lasting fruit, and I ask for light and freedom to remove these obstacles and distractions.

Saturday 27th July
Matthew 13:24–30

He put before them another parable: "The kingdom of heaven may be compared to someone who sowed good seed in his field; but while everybody was asleep, an enemy came and sowed weeds among the wheat, and then went away. So when the plants came up and bore grain, then the weeds appeared as well. And the slaves of the householder came and said to him, 'Master, did you not sow good seed in your field? Where, then, did these weeds come from?' He answered, 'An enemy has done this.' The slaves said to him, 'Then do you want us to go and gather them?' But he replied, 'No; for in gathering the weeds you would uproot the wheat along with them. Let both of them grow together until the harvest; and at harvest time I will tell the reapers, Collect the weeds first and bind them in bundles to be burned, but gather the wheat into my barn.'"

- We are frustrated and baffled by the presence of evil in our midst. In this parable, Jesus tells us that this is the work of the enemy: the struggle between good and evil is to the death, but we can rest assured that God will have the last word. It is never easy to believe this, for often the evidence points in the other direction, so I ask for the grace to believe that God is the just and powerful judge.

- What is my position in this grand struggle between good and evil? Am I a passive spectator, an armchair critic, a mere consumer who cares only about my own well-being? Or am I a coworker with God, as he labors to proclaim and spread his kingdom of truth, justice, and peace?

July 28—August 3

Something to think and pray about each day this week:

It's a very dark night in a very remote village in the hills of northern England. There are no street lights and no stars. Just the very occasional glimmer of light from behind the curtains of scattered cottages. The road is uneven and fraught with bends and potholes—really, a bit like the road of life. I try to discern the way ahead by training the meager beam of my flashlight into the middle distance. Its light is swallowed up immediately by the darkness and disappears into the night without adding in the slightest to my pathfinding. I try a different tack. I shine the little light I have on the few feet of ground immediately ahead of me. The way opens up, step by step. No way of deciphering the mysteries that may lie ahead. Enough simply to trust the light, one step at a time.

—Margaret Silf, *Compass Points*

The Presence of God
God is with me, but even more astounding, God is within me.
Let me dwell for a moment on God's life-giving presence
in my body, in my mind, in my heart,
as I sit here, right now.

Freedom
Lord, may I never take the gift of freedom for granted. You gave me the great blessing of freedom of spirit. Fill my spirit with your peace and joy.

Consciousness
I remind myself that I am in the presence of God, who is my strength in times of weakness and my comforter in times of sorrow.

The Word
I take my time to read the word of God slowly, a few times, allowing myself to dwell on anything that strikes me. (Please turn to the Scripture on the following pages. Inspiration points are there, should you need them. When you are ready, return here to continue.)

Conversation
Jesus, you always welcomed little children when you walked on this earth. Teach me to have a childlike trust in you. Teach me to live in the knowledge that you will never abandon me.

Conclusion
Glory be to the Father, and to the Son, and to the Holy Spirit,
As it was in the beginning, is now and ever shall be,
World without end. Amen.

Sunday 28th July

Luke 11:1–13

[Jesus] was praying in a certain place, and after he had finished, one of his disciples said to him, "Lord, teach us to pray, as John taught his disciples." He said to them, "When you pray, say: Father, hallowed be your name. Your kingdom come. Give us each day our daily bread. And forgive us our sins, for we ourselves forgive everyone indebted to us. And do not bring us to the time of trial." And he said to them, "Suppose one of you has a friend, and you go to him at midnight and say to him, 'Friend, lend me three loaves of bread; for a friend of mine has arrived, and I have nothing to set before him.' And he answers from within, 'Do not bother me; the door has already been locked, and my children are with me in bed; I cannot get up and give you anything.' I tell you, even though he will not get up and give him anything because he is his friend, at least because of his persistence he will get up and give him whatever he needs." So I say to you, Ask, and it will be given to you; search, and you will find; knock, and the door will be opened for you. For everyone who asks receives, and everyone who searches finds, and for everyone who knocks, the door will be opened." Is there anyone among you who, if your child asks for a fish, will give a snake instead of a fish? Or if the child asks for an egg, will give a scorpion? If you then, who are evil, know how to give good gifts to your children, how much more will the heavenly Father give the Holy Spirit to those who ask him!"

- "Do not bother me." The friend had a Do Not Disturb sign on his door handle! That friend loved himself and his warm bed too much. Jesus is different: he promises that "for everyone who knocks, the door will be opened."

- When my prayer is not being answered, the silence of God challenges my faith. I am told here that I must persist in asking, searching, knocking. God will answer in God's own time.

Monday 29th July

John 11:19–27

Many of the Jews had come to Martha and Mary to console them about their brother. When Martha heard that Jesus was coming, she went and met him, while Mary stayed at home. Martha said to Jesus, "Lord, if you had been here, my brother would not have died. But even now I know that God will give you whatever you ask of him." Jesus said to her, "Your brother will rise again." Martha said to him, "I know that he will rise again in the resurrection on the last day." Jesus said to her, "I am the resurrection and the life. Those who believe in me, even though they die, will live, and everyone who lives and believes in me will never die. Do you believe this?" She said to him, "Yes, Lord, I believe that you are the Messiah, the Son of God, the one coming into the world."

- "I am the resurrection and the life." Jesus is Lord of both our physical and spiritual lives. But the greatest miracle of Jesus was not restoring Lazarus to physical life. No, the greatest miracle lies in Jesus' power to give endless spiritual life to us who believe in him.

- Faith in the Resurrection helps me live with an attitude of hope, sharing in the joy of the victory of the risen Christ over sin and death. It is because of the Resurrection that Christ is with me on all my journeys. Can I acknowledge his presence and open my heart to encounter him more fully?

Tuesday 30th July
Matthew 13:36–43

Then he left the crowds and went into the house. And his disciples approached him, saying, "Explain to us the parable of the weeds of the field." He answered, "The one who sows the good seed is the Son of Man; the field is the world, and the good seed are the children of the kingdom; the weeds are the children of the evil one, and the enemy who sowed them is the devil; the harvest is the end of the age, and the reapers are angels. Just as the weeds are collected and burned up with fire, so will it be at the end of the age. The Son of Man will send his angels, and they will collect out of his kingdom all causes of sin and all evildoers, and they will throw them into the furnace of fire, where there will be weeping and gnashing of teeth. Then the righteous will shine like the sun in the kingdom of their Father. Let anyone with ears listen!"

- Jesus uses the image of the field to explain the presence of both good and evil in the world and to illustrate how these forces are manifested at the end of time. The good seed is sown by Jesus, who by his light and love helps me grow and blossom so that I can yield a good harvest and shine like the sun in the heavenly kingdom.

• The world and the individuals in it are a mixture of good and evil. We have within ourselves warring spirits. Am I aware of these spirits within myself?

Wednesday 31st July
Saint Ignatius of Loyola
Matthew 13:44–46

[Jesus said,] "The kingdom of heaven is like treasure hidden in a field, which someone found and hid; then in his joy he goes and sells all that he has and buys that field. Again, the kingdom of heaven is like a merchant in search of fine pearls; on finding one pearl of great value, he went and sold all that he had and bought it."

• Seekers, who may be unclear about what exactly they are seeking but who pursue their search with sincerity, show by this very fact that God is with them. Their peace will be in the seeking, as it will eventually be in the finding.

• "Let me seek you in desiring you; let me desire you in seeking you; let me find you in loving you; let me love you in finding you" (Saint Anselm).

Thursday 1st August
Matthew 13:47–53

[Jesus said,] "Again, the kingdom of heaven is like a net that was thrown into the sea and caught fish of every kind; when it was full, they drew it ashore, sat down, and put the good into baskets but threw out the bad. So it will be at the end of the age. The angels will come out and separate the evil from the righteous and throw them into the furnace of fire, where there will be weeping and gnashing of teeth. Have you understood all this?" They answered, "Yes." And he said to them, "Therefore every scribe who has been trained for the kingdom of heaven is like the master of a household who brings out of his treasure what is new and what is old." When Jesus had finished these parables, he left that place.

• Father, as we weave our way through life, help us discern what is pleasing to you and how we can reach for the heavens in our daily communion with our brothers and sisters. Help us learn from our experience what helps us live lovingly.

• The image that Jesus uses of drawing the fishing net and separating the catch was one that many of his disciples would have been familiar with in their role as fishermen. Putting the good fish into baskets and dispensing with the bad was part of their everyday duty. Jesus was speaking to them in language that they could relate to when describing the kingdom of heaven. What language does Jesus use when speaking to me?

Friday 2nd August
Matthew 13:54–58

He came to his hometown and began to teach the people in their synagogue, so that they were astounded and said, "Where did this man get this wisdom and these deeds of power? Is not this the carpenter's son? Is not his mother called Mary? And are not his brothers James and Joseph and Simon and Judas? And are not all his sisters with us? Where then did this man get all this?" And they took offense at him. But Jesus said to them, "Prophets are not without honor except in their own country and in their own house." And he did not do many deeds of power there, because of their unbelief.

• Are we not inclined to reduce others to the first impressions they made on us, like for instance old school pals we meet at a reunion? Do we allow for how they bloomed and grew in the intervening years? Lord, do I feel threatened by others' growth and success, and, if so, what is the root of those feelings?

• It is strange that nothing in the life of Jesus prepared his friends and relatives for his ministry and teaching. Perhaps this is because Jesus' words required a response. When am I most likely to resist Jesus?

Saturday 3rd August
Matthew 14:1–12

At that time Herod the ruler heard reports about Jesus; and he said to his servants, "This is John the Baptist; he has been raised from the dead, and for this reason these powers are at work in him." For Herod had arrested John, bound him, and put him in prison on account of Herodias, his brother Philip's wife, because John had been telling him, "It is not lawful for you to have her." Though Herod wanted to put him to death, he feared the crowd, because they regarded him as a prophet. But when Herod's birthday came, the daughter of Herodias danced before the company, and she pleased Herod so much that he promised on oath to grant her whatever she might ask. Prompted by her mother, she said, "Give me the head of John the Baptist here on a platter." The king was grieved, yet out of regard for his oaths and for the guests, he commanded it to be given; he sent and had John beheaded in the prison. The head was brought on a platter and given to the girl, who brought it to her mother. His disciples came and took the body and buried it; then they went and told Jesus.

- Do I know what it is like to "cut someone's head off" to avoid hearing the truth from him or her?

- The disciples of John the Baptist did what they could do, and then they went to tell Jesus. I ask God for the strength I need to do what I can, and then turn to Jesus in my prayer.

August 4—August 10

Something to think and pray about each day this week:

The word *saunter* evokes for me the sense of holy ground, where a pilgrim might linger and reflect on the wonder of life. I needed a small child to teach me how to saunter. The day had passed by without my realizing it. Soon it would be dinnertime, and the shops would be closing. Hastily I dressed my little girl in her outdoor clothes and rushed off with her to buy some food for a meal. Rushed? Well no, my child had other ideas. All at once I felt a tug on my hand. Her silent request for a pause in the onward rush was insistent. The journey was well and truly stalled, as she guided me with implacable determination to the edge of the sidewalk, to gaze in rapture as a beetle crossed the road. She was watching this wonder for the first time in her life. She was teaching me to do the same. I needed a little child to read the map of this world's holy ground and to make me take off my shoes as I tread its sacred pathways through the ordinariness of every day. All ground reveals its holiness, if I walk upon it with gentleness and mindfulness. God is in every particle.

—Margaret Silf, *Compass Points*

The Presence of God
God is with me, but more,
God is within me, giving me existence.
Let me dwell for a moment on God's life-giving presence
in my body, my mind, my heart,
and in the whole of my life.

Freedom
Lord, you created me to live in freedom. May your Holy Spirit guide me
to follow you freely. Instill in my heart a desire to know and love you more
each day.

Consciousness
In God's loving presence I unwind the past day,
starting from now and looking back, moment by moment.
I gather in all the goodness and light, in gratitude.
I attend to the shadows and what they say to me,
seeking healing, courage, forgiveness.

The Word
God speaks to each of us individually. I listen attentively to hear what he
is saying to me. Read the text a few times; then listen. (Please turn to the
Scripture on the following pages. Inspiration points are there, should you
need them. When you are ready, return here to continue.)

Conversation
Jesus, you always welcomed little children when you walked on this earth.
Teach me to have a childlike trust in you. Teach me to live in the knowledge
that you will never abandon me.

Conclusion
I thank God for these moments we have spent together and for any insights
I have been given concerning the text.

Sunday 4th August
Luke 12:13–21

Someone in the crowd said to him, "Teacher, tell my brother to divide the family inheritance with me." But he said to him, "Friend, who set me to be a judge or arbitrator over you?" And he said to them, "Take care! Be on your guard against all kinds of greed; for one's life does not consist in the abundance of possessions." Then he told them a parable: "The land of a rich man produced abundantly. And he thought to himself, 'What should I do, for I have no place to store my crops?' Then he said, 'I will do this: I will pull down my barns and build larger ones, and there I will store all my grain and my goods. And I will say to my soul, Soul, you have ample goods laid up for many years; relax, eat, drink, be merry.' But God said to him, 'You fool! This very night your life is being demanded of you. And the things you have prepared, whose will they be?' So it is with those who store up treasures for themselves but are not rich toward God."

- One could argue that the rich man is not foolish because he makes provision for the future. But his own future is his only concern, not that of others. He does not think to use his abundance to help others. Lord, make me a grateful person, aware that all that is good in my life comes from you, and is held in trust for others.

- Saint Ignatius was a mystic who had very enriching ideas about God and about ourselves. He saw God as the great lover and ourselves as God's beloveds. He saw too that God gives us everything and even wants to give his very self to us, so far as he can. Lord, make me grounded enough to want only to love and humbly serve others as best I can. Help me to do everything for the greater glory of God.

Monday 5th August
Matthew 14:13–21

Now when Jesus heard this, he withdrew from there in a boat to a deserted place by himself. But when the crowds heard it, they followed him on foot from the towns. When he went ashore, he saw a great crowd; and he had compassion for them and cured their sick. When it was evening, the disciples came to him and said, "This is a deserted place, and the hour is now late; send the crowds away so that they may go into the villages and buy food for themselves." Jesus said to them, "They need not go away; you give them something to eat." They replied, "We have nothing here but five loaves and two fish." And he said, "Bring them here to me." Then he ordered the crowds to sit down on the grass. Taking the five loaves and the two fish, he looked up to heaven, and blessed and broke the loaves, and gave them to the disciples, and the disciples gave them to the crowds. And all ate and were filled; and they took up what was left over of the broken pieces, twelve baskets full. And those who ate were about five thousand men, besides women and children.

- This is a marvelous scene; pay close attention to the persons, what they say and what they do. How do you imagine the crowd reacted? What impact did this incident make on their lives? Do you think their participation in this event changed them?

- Reflect and pray about the fact that this wonder is a sign of the greater wonder of the Eucharistic meal in which he gives us himself.

Tuesday 6th August
The Transfiguration of the Lord
Luke 9:28–36

Now about eight days after these sayings Jesus took with him Peter and John and James, and went up on the mountain to pray. And while he was praying, the appearance of his face changed, and his clothes became dazzling white. Suddenly they saw two men, Moses and Elijah, talking to him. They appeared in glory and were speaking of his departure, which he was about to accomplish at Jerusalem. Now Peter and his companions were weighed down with sleep; but since they had stayed awake, they saw his glory and the two men who stood with him. Just as they were leaving him, Peter said to Jesus, "Master, it is good for us to be here; let us make three dwellings, one for you, one for Moses, and one for Elijah"—not knowing what he said. While he was saying this, a cloud came and overshadowed them; and they were terrified as they entered the cloud. Then from the cloud came a voice that said, "This is my Son, my Chosen; listen to him!" When the voice had spoken, Jesus was found alone. And they kept silent and in those days told no one any of the things they had seen.

- Peter and John and James were privileged to see Jesus in his full dignity. But we are able to see others' dignity, especially during sacramental moments, when we see those we love in their true dignity as human beings beloved of God. The dreams for this perfect infant at baptism, the blessing with gifts at confirmation, the beauty of forgiveness at reconciliation, the warmth of communion, the hope for healing at the sacrament of the sick, the dignity of covenant love at matrimony, the beauty of service at ordination.

- All we do our whole lives long is go from one little piece of holy ground to the next. Lord, give me the strength to keep going in between.

Wednesday 7th August
Matthew 15:21–28

Jesus left that place and went away to the district of Tyre and Sidon. Just then a Canaanite woman from that region came out and started shouting, "Have mercy on me, Lord, Son of David; my daughter is tormented by a demon." But he did not answer her at all. And his disciples came and urged him, saying, "Send her away, for she keeps shouting after us." He answered, "I was sent only to the lost sheep of the house of Israel." But she came and knelt before him, saying, "Lord, help me." He answered, "It is not fair to take the children's food and throw it to the dogs." She said, "Yes, Lord, yet even the dogs eat the crumbs that fall from their masters' table." Then Jesus answered her, "Woman, great is your faith! Let it be done for you as you wish." And her daughter was healed instantly.

- In the tradition preserved for us in the Scriptures, Jesus is presented to us as a formidable debater, but in this instance the Canaanite woman comfortably wins the debating point. Jesus praises the woman for her faith—but what was her faith? What did she believe about Jesus? One would love to know her subsequent history. Did this act of Jesus mark a turning point in her life? We do not know.

- This woman shows great persistence; she did not allow the disciples' irritation or Jesus' offhand remark to put her off. She knew what she wanted, and she trusted that Jesus could help. I pray that my faith may have something of her clarity and persistence.

Thursday 8th August
Matthew 16:13–23

Now when Jesus came into the district of Caesarea Philippi, he asked his disciples, "Who do people say that the Son of Man is?" And they said, "Some say John the Baptist, but others Elijah, and still others Jeremiah or one of the prophets." He said to them, "But who do you say that I am?" Simon Peter answered, "You are the Messiah, the Son of the living God." And Jesus answered him, "Blessed are you, Simon son of Jonah! For flesh and blood has not revealed this to you, but my Father in heaven. And I tell you, you are Peter, and on this rock I will build my church, and the gates of Hades will not prevail against it. I will give you the keys of the kingdom of heaven, and whatever you bind on earth will be bound in heaven, and whatever you loose on earth will be loosed in heaven." Then he sternly ordered the disciples not to tell anyone that he was the Messiah. From that time on, Jesus began to show his disciples that he must go to Jerusalem and undergo great suffering at the hands of the elders and chief priests and scribes, and be killed, and on the third day be raised. And Peter took him aside and began to rebuke him, saying, "God forbid it, Lord! This must never happen to you." But he turned and said to Peter, "Get behind me, Satan! You are a stumbling block to me; for you are setting your mind not on divine things but on human things."

- We could be forgiven for being impatient with Peter. He often completely misjudges Jesus. Here he makes an extraordinary confession of faith in the Master. But when Jesus tells his disciples that he must suffer and be killed, it is too much for Peter. And despite the sharp rebuke, Peter consistently makes the same mistake, right up to the Last Supper when he refuses to allow Jesus to wash his feet. He simply cannot accept that the mission of the one whom he has followed will end in failure.

- What strengths of Peter do I see in myself, and what weaknesses?

Friday 9th August
Matthew 16:24–28

Then Jesus told his disciples, "If any want to become my followers, let them deny themselves and take up their cross and follow me. For those who want to save their life will lose it, and those who lose their life for my sake will find it. For what will it profit them if they gain the whole world but forfeit their life? Or what will they give in return for their life? For the Son of Man is to come with his angels in the glory of his Father, and then he will repay everyone for what has been done. Truly I tell you, there are some standing here who will not taste death before they see the Son of Man coming in his kingdom."

- This passage brings us to the heart of the paradox of discipleship. To win, we must lose. To gain, we must give up. To live forever, we must die. We are not called on to go out looking for a cross, simply not to run from it when it comes.

- I pray for the freedom I need to be able to let go, to realize that my life is not mine to save; it comes from God, and its fullness lies in God.

Saturday 10th August
John 12:24–26

[Jesus said,] "Very truly, I tell you, unless a grain of wheat falls into the earth and dies, it remains just a single grain; but if it dies, it bears much fruit. Those who love their life lose it, and those who hate their life in this world will keep it for eternal life. Whoever serves me must follow me, and where I am, there will my servant be also. Whoever serves me, the Father will honor."

- Not every wheat grain will germinate. Without the right conditions, a grain will lie dormant and never bear fruit. The grain needs sun, rain, and nutrients before it can begin to grow. Is my faith life dormant? Or am I nourishing it so that it will yield an abundant harvest?

- What needs to die in me so that I may live more fully? I pray for the grace to see what I have to do and for the grace to do it.

August 11—August 17

Something to think and pray about each day this week:

Imagine is a truly powerful word. If I ask you to read a book, I am asking you to engage your intellect. If I ask you to look at a picture of a bird, you use your faculty of sight. If I ask you to listen to an old David Bowie song, you use your hearing. But if I ask you to imagine a cook preparing your favorite meal, in an instant all of your senses are engaged. You might hear the chopping of celery or the sizzling of butter in a pan. You might smell the aroma of onions. You might feel the heat of the oven and salivate because the scene you are imagining becomes so strong that your body has an involuntary reaction to it. What happens in the end is that a series of imagined sensory events becomes a unique and creative physical experience. Ignatius realized that the imagination could transform the events of Jesus' life into personal and emotional experience. As David Fleming puts it in *What Is Ignatian Spirituality?*, "To follow Jesus we must know him, and we get to know him through our imagination. Imaginative Ignatian prayer teaches us things about Jesus that we would not learn through scripture study or theological reflection. . . . It brings Jesus into our hearts."

—Gary Jansen, *Station to Station*

The Presence of God
I pause for a moment and think of the love and the grace that God showers on me. I am created in the image and likeness of God; I am God's dwelling place.

Freedom
I am free. When I look at these words in writing, they seem to create in me a feeling of awe. Yes, a wonderful feeling of freedom. Thank you, God.

Consciousness
In the presence of my loving Creator, I look honestly at my feelings over the past day: the highs, the lows, and the level ground. Can I see where the Lord has been present?

The Word
I read the word of God slowly, a few times over, and I listen to what God is saying to me. (Please turn to the Scripture on the following pages. Inspiration points are there, should you need them. When you are ready, return here to continue.)

Conversation
Remembering that I am still in God's presence,
I imagine Jesus standing or sitting beside me,
and I say whatever is on my mind, whatever is in my heart,
speaking as one friend to another.

Conclusion
Glory be to the Father, and to the Son, and to the Holy Spirit,
As it was in the beginning, is now and ever shall be,
World without end. Amen.

Sunday 11th August
Luke 12:32–48

[Jesus said,] "Do not be afraid, little flock, for it is your Father's good pleasure to give you the kingdom. Sell your possessions, and give alms. Make purses for yourselves that do not wear out, an unfailing treasure in heaven, where no thief comes near and no moth destroys. For where your treasure is, there your heart will be also. Be dressed for action and have your lamps lit; be like those who are waiting for their master to return from the wedding banquet, so that they may open the door for him as soon as he comes and knocks. Blessed are those slaves whom the master finds alert when he comes; truly I tell you, he will fasten his belt and have them sit down to eat, and he will come and serve them. If he comes during the middle of the night, or near dawn, and finds them so, blessed are those slaves. But know this: if the owner of the house had known at what hour the thief was coming, he would not have let his house be broken into. You also must be ready, for the Son of Man is coming at an unexpected hour." Peter said, "Lord, are you telling this parable for us or for everyone?" And the Lord said, "Who then is the faithful and prudent manager whom his master will put in charge of his slaves, to give them their allowance of food at the proper time? Blessed is that slave whom his master will find at work when he arrives. Truly I tell you, he will put that one in charge of all his possessions. But if that slave says to himself, 'My master is delayed in coming,' and if he begins to beat the other slaves, men and women, and to eat and drink and get drunk, the master of that slave will come on a day when he does not expect him and at an hour that he does not know, and will cut him in pieces, and put him with the unfaithful. That slave who knew what his master wanted, but did not prepare himself or do what was wanted, will receive a severe beating. But one who did not know and did what deserved a beating will receive a light beating. From everyone to whom much has been given, much will be required; and from one to whom much has been entrusted, even more will be demanded."

- Think of moments when you have been most spiritually alert. Times when you were paying attention to things and disposed to welcome people or change. Jesus seems to be getting at this kind of mentality, this kind of heart that stays awake. It's not something for the clever only: it's for everybody. I pray to have alertness and readiness for a new prompting of the Spirit, for God to work some new grace in my life.

- What helps me remain alert to the Spirit? I pray for awareness of habits and distractions that dull my spiritual senses.

Monday 12th August
Matthew 17:22–27

As they were gathering in Galilee, Jesus said to them, "The Son of Man is going to be betrayed into human hands, and they will kill him, and on the third day he will be raised." And they were greatly distressed. When they reached Capernaum, the collectors of the temple tax came to Peter and said, "Does your teacher not pay the temple tax?" He said, "Yes, he does." And when he came home, Jesus spoke of it first, asking, "What do you think, Simon? From whom do kings of the earth take toll or tribute? From their children or from others?" When Peter said, "From others," Jesus said to him, "Then the children are free. However, so that we do not give offense to them, go to the lake and cast a hook; take the first fish that comes up; and when you open its mouth, you will find a coin; take that and give it to them for you and me.

- The matter of Christ's suffering comes up frequently in the Gospels; this is the second prophecy of the Passion. The fact that the disciples became very sad suggests that they understood what he was saying but it did not really sink in. Jesus speaks to each of us and patiently waits for us to hear.

- Suffering disorients us. We cannot understand it fully. Jesus brings meaning from it at a profound level we cannot grasp, except in faith. Pray for a greater appreciation of the sufferings of Christ.

Tuesday 13th August
Matthew 18:1–5, 10, 12–14

At that time the disciples came to Jesus and asked, "Who is the greatest in the kingdom of heaven?" He called a child, whom he put among them, and said, "Truly I tell you, unless you change and become like children, you will never enter the kingdom of heaven. Whoever becomes humble like this child is the greatest in the kingdom of heaven. Whoever welcomes one such child in my name welcomes me. . . . Take care that you do not despise one of these little ones; for, I tell you, in heaven their angels continually see the face of my Father in heaven. . . . What do you think?

If a shepherd has a hundred sheep, and one of them has gone astray, does he not leave the ninety-nine on the mountains and go in search of the one that went astray? And if he finds it, truly I tell you, he rejoices over it more than over the ninety-nine that never went astray. So it is not the will of your Father in heaven that one of these little ones should be lost."

- Jesus cares for us individually through our guardian angels. Do I believe that I am personally cared for by God? To believe this is a great gift of faith. We are asked to trust God like little children, whose nature is to trust.

- I thank God for his care—observing the signs of it in my life—and ask him to help me develop a deeper relationship with him.

Wednesday 14th August

Matthew 18:15–20

[Jesus said to his disciples,] "If another member of the church sins against you, go and point out the fault when the two of you are alone. If the member listens to you, you have regained that one. But if you are not listened to, take one or two others along with you, so that every word may be confirmed by the evidence of two or three witnesses. If the member refuses to listen to them, tell it to the church; and if the offender refuses to listen even to the church, let such a one be to you as a Gentile and a tax collector. Truly I tell you, whatever you bind on earth will be bound in heaven, and whatever you loose on earth will be loosed in heaven. Again, truly I tell you, if two of you agree on earth about anything you ask, it will be done for you by my Father in heaven. For where two or three are gathered in my name, I am there among them."

- Jesus is Emmanuel, "God is with us." He is with us in our church community. His message is one of reconciliation, not retribution. We are asked to "regain" our brother or sister. "Regaining" is more than stopping someone's offensive behavior; it seeks to convert that person, bringing about a true change in attitude and direction. Jesus' openness to sinners is always moving in this direction: "Go, and sin no more."

- Because Jesus shares his own spirit with us, the connection between the community of believers and Jesus is very close: what we bind or loose here is bound or loosed in heaven, and whatever we ask in union will be given to us by the Father. I ask for this insight and for a stronger faith in the presence of Jesus in the midst of the church.

Thursday 15th August
The Assumption of the Blessed Virgin Mary
Luke 11:27–28

While Jesus was speaking, a woman in the crowd raised her voice and said to him, "Blessed is the womb that bore you and the breasts that nursed you!" But he said, "Blessed rather are those who hear the word of God and obey it!"

- In today's culture of social media we have become familiar with the terms "Follow" and "Like."' Could the powerful value of social media sometimes cause us to miss the point? Can we be caught in positive adulation rather than positive action? Does the flood of personalities in the media reporting of events excite my appetite so much that it blunts my perception of what meaningful action is important for me?

- This Gospel passage can, at first reading, seem a slight on Mary. But Jesus came to adopt us into a bigger family, the family of God, where we have God as our Father and Mary our mother. Help me to be grateful for this wonderful belonging.

Friday 16th August
Matthew 19:3–12

Some Pharisees came to him, and to test him they asked, "Is it lawful for a man to divorce his wife for any cause?" He answered, "Have you not read that the one who made them at the beginning 'made them male and female,' and said, 'For this reason a man shall leave his father and mother and be joined to his wife, and the two shall become one flesh'? So they are no longer two, but one flesh. Therefore what God has joined together, let no one separate." They said to him, "Why then did Moses command us to give a certificate of dismissal and to divorce her?" He said to them, "It was because you were so hardhearted that Moses allowed you to divorce your wives, but at the beginning it was not so. And I say to you, whoever divorces his wife, except for unchastity, and marries another commits adultery." His disciples said to him, "If such is the case of a man with his wife, it is better not to marry." But he said to them, "Not everyone can accept this teaching, but only those to whom it is given. For there are eunuchs who have been so from birth, and there are eunuchs who have been made eunuchs by others, and there are eunuchs who have made themselves eunuchs for the sake of the kingdom of heaven. Let anyone accept this who can."

- The Pharisees engage Jesus on the notion of marriage about which there was much controversy. All agreed that a man could divorce his wife. The dispute was about the grounds on which a man could divorce his wife. There was a view that held that he could do so for the most trivial reason; there was an opposing view that proposed that only the most serious reason justified divorce. The Pharisees wished to force Jesus to take sides and so win enemies. Jesus resolved the issue by ruling out divorce and placing men and women on the same level; no longer could a man opt to divorce his wife, except for unchastity. Such an equalization of relationship between the sexes was so revolutionary that it drew the astonished response from his disciples.

- I pray with thanks for all the people I know who have been able to live out their desires and dreams through marriage. I pray for those whose marriages are in difficulty. Keep love burning in their hearts, and in mine.

Saturday 17th August
Matthew 19:13–15

Then little children were being brought to Jesus in order that he might lay his hands on them and pray. The disciples spoke sternly to those who brought them; but Jesus said, "Let the little children come to me, and do not stop them; for it is to such as these that the kingdom of heaven belongs." And he laid his hands on them and went on his way.

- In this passage, children are taken as representing those whom the world considers unimportant; similarly, the parable of the lost sheep (Matthew 18:12–14) teaches that the least of all in the eyes of the world is as important as the greatest of all in the eyes of Jesus. This reminds us that the weaker people are, the more they require our care and concern.

- Lord, I pray today that I may deepen my respect for those whom the world holds in low esteem.

Twentieth Week in Ordinary Time
August 18—August 24

Something to think and pray about each day this week:

Humility gives us the sacred gift of being able to learn from everyone. It gives us the ability to take advice from any person who gives it, not just the brilliant or the holy or the great, but from the simple and the ignorant and from those who may be far below our own position or station in life. It gives us the power to imitate Christ himself, who *learned* from Peter how to catch fish, and from Joseph how to make tables, and from Mary how to eat. It gives us the power to learn, even from those who do not appeal to us at all, whom we may not like very much. The humble person knows he doesn't know all things, knows that good advice, no matter what the source, is a rare gift, a gift that helps develop the wonder of self-knowledge. Very often, it is from people we may not like very much, or from people who are a little nasty and mean, that we learn how deep our pride is in reality and how far we still have to go before we have reached any real degree of humility. For such people will tell us what they think of us, will give us advice without bothering to be nice about it, will show us quite brilliantly and quite cuttingly, too, by the way, how proud we really are. Real humility will give us the power to accept such words, and though they may hurt because we are still human, we will be able to take them and because of them grow even closer to Christ.

—Walter Ciszek, *With God in America*

The Presence of God

I pause for a moment and think of the love and the grace that God showers on me. I am created in the image and likeness of God; I am God's dwelling place.

Freedom

Lord, you granted me the great gift of freedom. In these times, O Lord, grant that I may be free from any form of racism or intolerance. Remind me that we are all equal in your loving eyes.

Consciousness

Knowing that God loves me unconditionally, I can afford to be honest about how I am.

How has the day been, and how do I feel now? I share my feelings openly with the Lord.

The Word

I take my time to read the word of God slowly, a few times, allowing myself to dwell on anything that strikes me. (Please turn to the Scripture on the following pages. Inspiration points are there, should you need them. When you are ready, return here to continue.)

Conversation

Sometimes I wonder what I might say if I were to meet you in person, Lord. I think I might say "Thank you" because you are always there for me.

Conclusion

I thank God for these moments we have spent together and for any insights I have been given concerning the text.

Sunday 18th August

Luke 12:49–53

[Jesus said to his disciples,] "I came to bring fire to the earth, and how I wish it were already kindled! I have a baptism with which to be baptized, and what stress I am under until it is completed! Do you think that I have come to bring peace to the earth? No, I tell you, but rather division! From now on five in one household will be divided, three against two and two against three; they will be divided: father against son and son against father, mother against daughter and daughter against mother, mother-in-law against her daughter-in-law and daughter-in-law against mother-in-law."

- The gospel is a call to conversion, to becoming a new creation (2 Corinthians 5:17). It means shedding the skin of a former way of living. Does my Christian faith make a real difference to the kind of person I am and to the kind of life I lead?

- Jesus is totally involved in his mission to save us. Fire is the image he uses to speak of this great desire in his heart. Not everyone would receive his message, and hence it would bring division at a deep level in many relationships. In what ways do I see Jesus' influence on my life causing conflict?

Monday 19th August

Matthew 19:16–22

Then someone came to him and said, "Teacher, what good deed must I do to have eternal life?" And he said to him, "Why do you ask me about what is good? There is only one who is good. If you wish to enter into life, keep the commandments." He said to him, "Which ones?" And Jesus said, "You shall not murder; You shall not commit adultery; You shall not steal; You shall not bear false witness; Honor your father and mother; also, You shall love your neighbor as yourself." The young man said to him, "I have kept all these; what do I still lack?" Jesus said to him, "If you wish to be perfect, go, sell your possessions, and give the money to the poor, and you will have treasure in heaven; then come, follow me." When the young man heard this word, he went away grieving, for he had many possessions.

- This Gospel story is discussed frequently, and it is found in slightly different forms in the three synoptic Gospels (Matthew, Mark, and Luke).

One could interpret the reaction of the young man as raising the bar higher for himself until he was unable to respond to the invitation of Christ and had to go away sad. However, there is no doubt that the man had many possessions to which he was too attached to follow Jesus.

• I pray for the grace to see more clearly those things that block me from giving myself fully to the service of Christ.

Tuesday 20th August
Matthew 19:23–30

Jesus said to his disciples, "Truly I tell you, it will be hard for a rich person to enter the kingdom of heaven. Again I tell you, it is easier for a camel to go through the eye of a needle than for someone who is rich to enter the kingdom of God." When the disciples heard this, they were greatly astounded and said, "Then who can be saved?" But Jesus looked at them and said, "For mortals it is impossible, but for God all things are possible." Then Peter said in reply, "Look, we have left everything and followed you. What then will we have?" Jesus said to them, "Truly I tell you, at the renewal of all things, when the Son of Man is seated on the throne of his glory, you who have followed me will also sit on twelve thrones, judging the twelve tribes of Israel. And everyone who has left houses or brothers or sisters or father or mother or children or fields, for my name's sake, will receive a hundredfold, and will inherit eternal life. But many who are first will be last, and the last will be first."

• Jesus had failed to separate the rich young man from his wealth. The trouble with possessions is that they can too easily possess us. Jesus calls for radical change in our lives, a change that can seem unattainable. However, he reminds us that, while something may seem impossible for mortals, "for God all things are possible."

• Do I believe that God will ask nothing of me that I am not, with his help, capable of doing?

Wednesday 21st August
Matthew 20:1–16

[Jesus said,] "For the kingdom of heaven is like a landowner who went out early in the morning to hire laborers for his vineyard. After agreeing with the laborers for the usual daily wage, he sent them into his vineyard. When he went out about nine o'clock, he saw others standing idle in the market-place; and he said to them, 'You also go into the vineyard, and I will pay you whatever is right.' So they went. When he went out again about noon and about three o'clock, he did the same. And about five o'clock he went out and found others standing around; and he said to them, 'Why are you standing here idle all day?' They said to him, 'Because no one has hired us.' He said to them, 'You also go into the vineyard.' When evening came, the owner of the vineyard said to his manager, 'Call the laborers and give them their pay, beginning with the last and then going to the first.' When those hired about five o'clock came, each of them received the usual daily wage. Now when the first came, they thought they would receive more; but each of them also received the usual daily wage. And when they received it, they grumbled against the landowner, saying, 'These last worked only one hour, and you have made them equal to us who have borne the burden of the day and the scorching heat.' But he replied to one of them, 'Friend, I am doing you no wrong; did you not agree with me for the usual daily wage? Take what belongs to you and go; I choose to give to this last the same as I give to you. Am I not allowed to do what I choose with what belongs to me? Or are you envious because I am generous?' So the last will be first, and the first will be last."

- We all find something disconcerting in this parable. Perhaps we need to look at it from the perspective of the work in the vineyard. Jesus encouraged us to pray for more workers to be sent to the vineyard, for the harvest is plentiful and the workers few. Being called to work in the Father's vineyard is a privilege, a grace to ask for.

- "Are you envious because I am generous?" I let this question linger in my heart, and I ask for the grace of inner freedom when I look at my gifts and limitations, and at those of the persons around me. True love rejoices at the gifts others have.

Thursday 22nd August
Matthew 22:1–14

Once more Jesus spoke to them in parables, saying: "The kingdom of heaven may be compared to a king who gave a wedding banquet for his son. He sent his slaves to call those who had been invited to the wedding banquet, but they would not come. Again he sent other slaves, saying, 'Tell those who have been invited: Look, I have prepared my dinner, my oxen and my fat calves have been slaughtered, and everything is ready; come to the wedding banquet.' But they made light of it and went away, one to his farm, another to his business, while the rest seized his slaves, mistreated them, and killed them. The king was enraged. He sent his troops, destroyed those murderers, and burned their city. Then he said to his slaves, 'The wedding is ready, but those invited were not worthy. Go therefore into the main streets, and invite everyone you find to the wedding banquet.' Those slaves went out into the streets and gathered all whom they found, both good and bad; so the wedding hall was filled with guests. But when the king came in to see the guests, he noticed a man there who was not wearing a wedding robe, and he said to him, 'Friend, how did you get in here without a wedding robe?' And he was speechless. Then the king said to the attendants, 'Bind him hand and foot, and throw him into the outer darkness, where there will be weeping and gnashing of teeth.' For many are called, but few are chosen."

• The parable of the wedding in today's Gospel was spoken when Jesus saw that his own people were moving to reject him. The story is symbolic. But the invitation to us is a real one. It is an invitation to aim at the good life. The invitation to the kingdom of heaven is cast wide, yet we are free to say yes or no. No matter how low a stature I seem to have in life, I am welcome. I will shake off the rags of my injustice, my less good self, and dress in the clothes of a new, more loving person.

• I ask God to help me to respond as best I can to this real invitation.

Friday 23rd August
Matthew 22:34–40

When the Pharisees heard that Jesus had silenced the Sadducees, they gathered together, and one of them, a lawyer, asked him a question to test him. "Teacher, which commandment in the law is the greatest?" He said to him, "'You shall love the Lord your God with all your heart, and with all your soul, and with all your mind.' This is the greatest and first commandment. And a second is like it: 'You shall love your neighbor as yourself.' On these two commandments hang all the law and the prophets."

• The greatest and first commandment is challenging. Do I really believe in God and love God? God's love shines on me as the sun shines on earth.

Nothing I do could make God love me more. In this continual relationship with the mystery of God's love, I know my doubts. I can only say, "Lord, I believe, help my unbelief."

- The second commandment is easier to grasp and harder to follow: Love your neighbor as yourself. God is visible through my neighbor. I can ponder on my love for others, those close to me. And I ponder on my attitude toward every stranger around the world who is my sister and brother. I pray for them. What, today, are my actions on behalf of my neighbor?

Saturday 24th August
John 1:45–51

Philip found Nathanael and said to him, "We have found him about whom Moses in the law and also the prophets wrote, Jesus son of Joseph from Nazareth." Nathanael said to him, "Can anything good come out of Nazareth?" Philip said to him, "Come and see." When Jesus saw Nathanael coming toward him, he said of him, "Here is truly an Israelite in whom there is no deceit!" Nathanael asked him, "Where did you get to know me?" Jesus answered, "I saw you under the fig tree before Philip called you." Nathanael replied, "Rabbi, you are the Son of God! You are the King of Israel!" Jesus answered, "Do you believe because I told you that I saw you under the fig tree? You will see greater things than these." And he said to him, "Very truly, I tell you, you will see heaven opened and the angels of God ascending and descending upon the Son of Man."

- Philip does not waste time in arguing with Nathaniel. "Come and see," he says. Lord, I pray that I might lead others to you by the way I live my life.

- Jesus saw in Nathaniel a quality that surprised and appealed to him. What quality in me might delight Jesus?

Twenty–First Week in Ordinary Time
August 25—August 31

Something to think and pray about each day this week:

I live in a second-floor apartment in a big old Craftsman bungalow in Pasadena. My balcony overlooks a number of giant, old-growth trees. One recent autumn afternoon, I was studying the graceful design of the branches of one of them (whose name I'm sorry to say I don't know): the small flame-red leaves fluttering intermittently to the ground, the glorious trunk resplendent against the setting sun. I thought, *If this were the only tree in the whole world, people would sell all they had and travel halfway around the world to see it. Look at it! This stupendous, mysterious living thing that grows up out of the ground!* "Counter, original, spare, strange," as the poet Gerard Manley Hopkins put it in "Pied Beauty." I stood there for many minutes, pulsating with wonder. Don't get me wrong. That I could marvel at a tree didn't mean that I wasn't on another level also seething with various kinds of anxiety, resentment, distraction, and dread. Christ never promised that we'd be euphorically happy every second, or permanently free from fear. He promised that he'd be with us until the end of time (Matthew 28:20). He said, "I have told you this so that my joy may be in you and your joy may be complete" (John 15:11, NAB)—whether or not we can "feel" the joy. But just for that moment—I did feel it. The universe was pressing back.

—Heather King, *Holy Desperation*

The Presence of God

I pause for a moment
and reflect on God's life-giving presence
in every part of my body,
in everything around me,
in the whole of my life.

Freedom

Many countries are at this moment suffering the agonies of war. I bow my head in thanksgiving for my freedom. I pray for all prisoners and captives.

Consciousness

Knowing that God loves me unconditionally, I look honestly over the past day, its events, and my feelings. Do I have something to be grateful for? Then I give thanks. Is there something I am sorry for? Then I ask forgiveness.

The Word

Now I turn to the Scripture set out for me this day. I read slowly over the words and see if any sentence or sentiment appeals to me. (Please turn to the Scripture on the following pages. Inspiration points are there, should you need them. When you are ready, return here to continue.)

Conversation

I know with certainty that there were times when you carried me, Lord. There were times when it was through your strength that I got through the dark times in my life.

Conclusion

Glory be to the Father, and to the Son, and to the Holy Spirit,
As it was in the beginning, is now and ever shall be,
World without end. Amen.

Sunday 25th August
Luke 13:22–30

Jesus went through one town and village after another, teaching as he made his way to Jerusalem. Someone asked him, "Lord, will only a few be saved?" He said to them, "Strive to enter through the narrow door; for many, I tell you, will try to enter and will not be able. When once the owner of the house has got up and shut the door, and you begin to stand outside and to knock at the door, saying, 'Lord, open to us,' then in reply he will say to you, 'I do not know where you come from.' Then you will begin to say, 'We ate and drank with you, and you taught in our streets.' But he will say, 'I do not know where you come from; go away from me, all you evildoers!' There will be weeping and gnashing of teeth when you see Abraham and Isaac and Jacob and all the prophets in the kingdom of God, and you yourselves thrown out. Then people will come from east and west, from north and south, and will eat in the kingdom of God. Indeed, some are last who will be first, and some are first who will be last."

- Imagine the gentle preacher entering your town today. People are asking him questions, and he answers using images that immediately strike home. He is meek but not weak. He confronts conflict squarely rather than avoiding it. And his standards are always high. This is no watered-down, easy message. But it is within our reach.

- So old and young, rich and poor, powerful and powerless hear a challenge. This "kingdom of God" is a wholly new concept he puts before them. Everybody appears to be welcome, and some of those who "made it" will surprise us. But entry is not without a struggle. What will that struggle be for you?

Monday 26th August
Matthew 23:13–22

[Jesus said to the people,] "But woe to you, scribes and Pharisees, hypocrites! For you lock people out of the kingdom of heaven. For you do not go in yourselves, and when others are going in, you stop them. Woe to you, scribes and Pharisees, hypocrites! For you cross sea and land to make a single convert, and you make the new convert twice as much a child of hell as yourselves. Woe to you, blind guides, who say, 'Whoever swears by the sanctuary is bound by nothing, but whoever swears by the gold of the sanctuary is bound by the oath.' You blind fools! For which is greater, the gold or the sanctuary that has made the gold sacred? And you say, 'Whoever swears by the altar is bound by nothing, but whoever swears by the gift that is on the altar is bound by the oath.' How blind you are! For which is greater, the gift or the altar that makes the gift sacred? So whoever swears by the altar, swears by it and by everything on it; and whoever swears by the sanctuary, swears by it and by the one who dwells in it; and whoever swears by heaven, swears by the throne of God and by the one who is seated upon it."

- Jesus keeps the strongest language to condemn those who confuse the externals of religion with what might be at its heart. I let God lead me in my time of prayer, prepared to let go of habits, rituals, and externals—all so that I may better hear the voice of God.

- I pray for the community with which I worship; may we never confuse the beautiful things we have or do with their source, but may we grow together in humble service of God.

Tuesday 27th August
Matthew 23:23–26

[Jesus said,] "Woe to you, scribes and Pharisees, hypocrites! For you tithe mint, dill, and cumin, and have neglected the weightier matters of the law: justice and mercy and faith. It is these you ought to have practiced without neglecting the others. You blind guides! You strain out a gnat but swallow a camel! Woe to you, scribes and Pharisees, hypocrites! For you clean the outside of the cup and of the plate, but inside they are full of greed and self-indulgence. You blind Pharisee! First clean the inside of the cup, so that the outside also may become clean."

- Jesus reserves some of his harshest criticism for those who lay heavy burdens on others. The scribes and Pharisees, in their misguided zeal for the letter of the law, have completely lost sight of the two great commandments on which all of the law rests—to love the Lord our God with all our heart and all our soul and all our might, and to love our neighbor as ourself.

- I picture myself standing among the Pharisees as Jesus unleashes his anger on them. Do any of his words resonate uncomfortably with me? Have

I made unreasonable demands of others, demands that I am far from meeting myself?

Wednesday 28th August
Matthew 23:27–32

[Jesus said,] "Woe to you, scribes and Pharisees, hypocrites! For you are like whitewashed tombs, which on the outside look beautiful, but inside they are full of the bones of the dead and of all kinds of filth. So you also on the outside look righteous to others, but inside you are full of hypocrisy and lawlessness. Woe to you, scribes and Pharisees, hypocrites! For you build the tombs of the prophets and decorate the graves of the righteous, and you say, 'If we had lived in the days of our ancestors, we would not have taken part with them in shedding the blood of the prophets.' Thus you testify against yourselves that you are descendants of those who murdered the prophets. Fill up, then, the measure of your ancestors."

- Once again Jesus challenges the scribes and Pharisees to think differently about how they live from day to day. He challenges them to look at what is going on in their inner selves, the part of themselves they hide from one another—and, indeed, from themselves. They are living on the surface of life and cannot see how their way of life has impact on others.

- Are my words and actions, like those of the Pharisees, driven by a preoccupation with truth and orthodoxy or by justice, mercy, and love?

Thursday 29th August
Mark 6:17–29

For Herod himself had sent men who arrested John, bound him, and put him in prison on account of Herodias, his brother Philip's wife, because Herod had married her. For John had been telling Herod, "It is not lawful for you to have your brother's wife." And Herodias had a grudge against him, and wanted to kill him. But she could not, for Herod feared John, knowing that he was a righteous and holy man, and he protected him. When he heard him, he was greatly perplexed; and yet he liked to listen to him. But an opportunity came when Herod on his birthday gave a banquet for his courtiers and officers and for the leaders of Galilee. When his daughter Herodias came in and danced, she pleased Herod and his guests; and the king said to the girl, "Ask me for whatever you wish, and I will give it." And he solemnly swore to her, "Whatever you ask me, I will give you, even half of my kingdom." She went out and said to her mother, "What should I ask for?" She replied, "The head of John the baptizer." Immediately she rushed back to the king and requested, "I want you to give me at once the head of John the Baptist on a platter." The king was deeply grieved; yet out of regard for his oaths and for the guests, he did not want to refuse her. Immediately the king sent a soldier of the guard with orders to bring John's head. He went and beheaded him in the prison, brought his head on a platter, and gave it to the girl. Then the girl gave it to her mother. When his disciples heard about it, they came and took his body, and laid it in a tomb.

• The Gospel does not mince its words or soften its picture of the martyrdom of John the Baptist. It is hard to make this scene the subject of prayer, so gross and depraved is the behavior of the characters. We can take what we read as a representation of sinful humanity, and the depths to which sin can lead us.

• Those who work for justice in the world or witness to their faith today often face difficult and even life-threatening situations. I pause to remember them in prayer.

Friday 30th August
Matthew 25:1–13

[Jesus said,] "Then the kingdom of heaven will be like this. Ten bridesmaids took their lamps and went to meet the bridegroom. Five of them were foolish, and five were wise. When the foolish took their lamps, they took no oil with them; but the wise took flasks of oil with their lamps. As the bridegroom was delayed, all of them became drowsy and slept. But at midnight there was a shout, 'Look! Here is the bridegroom! Come out to meet him.' Then all those bridesmaids got up and trimmed their lamps. The foolish said to the wise, 'Give us some of your oil, for our lamps are going out.' But the wise replied, 'No! there will not be enough for you and for us; you had better go to the dealers and buy some for yourselves.' And while they went to buy it, the bridegroom came, and those who were ready went with him into the wedding banquet; and the door was shut. Later the other bridesmaids came also, saying, 'Lord, lord, open to us.' But he replied, 'Truly I tell you, I do not know you.' Keep awake therefore, for you know neither the day nor the hour."

- "Keep awake": this is the invitation we meet so often in the Gospels; not to be afraid of the Lord's coming in our life, but to be awake so that we can welcome him when he arrives. I pray for the grace of a heart that is not distracted, fully alive to Jesus' presence in my world.

- As Christians we wait in readiness, we wait in hope, and we wait together. I may be alone at the moment, but I am conscious of the thousands of my sisters and brothers who are part of my community at this very moment.

Saturday 31st August
Matthew 25:14–30

[Jesus said,] "For it is as if a man, going on a journey, summoned his slaves and entrusted his property to them; to one he gave five talents, to another two, to another one, to each according to his ability. Then he went away. The one who had received the five talents went off at once and traded with them, and made five more talents. In the same way, the one who had the two talents made two more talents. But the one who had received the one talent went off and dug a hole in the ground and hid his master's money. After a long time the master of those slaves came and settled accounts with them. Then the one who had received the five talents came forward, bringing five more talents, saying, 'Master, you handed over to me five talents; see, I have made five more talents.' His master said to him, 'Well done, good and trustworthy slave; you have been trustworthy in a few things, I will put you in charge of many things; enter into the joy of your master.' And the one with the two talents also came forward, saying, 'Master, you handed over to me two talents; see, I have made two more talents.' His master said to him, 'Well done, good and trustworthy slave; you have been trustworthy in a few things, I will put you in charge of many things; enter into the joy of your master.' Then the one who had received the one talent also came forward, saying, 'Master, I knew that you were a harsh man, reaping where you did not sow, and gathering where you did not scatter seed; so I was afraid, and I went and hid your talent in the ground. Here you have what is yours.' But his master replied, 'You wicked and lazy slave! You knew, did you, that I reap where I did not sow, and gather where I did not scatter? Then you ought to have invested my money with the bankers, and on my return I would have received what was my own with interest. So take the talent from him, and give it to the one with the ten talents. For to all those who have, more will be given, and they will have an abundance; but from those who have nothing, even what they have will be taken away. As for this worthless slave, throw him into the outer darkness, where there will be weeping and gnashing of teeth.'"

- In thanksgiving I dwell on my gifts, first looking at them in wonder: my life, my health, my faith, and especially the persons who fill my life and who have made me who I am. I then reflect on the gratuity of all this and ask God for the grace to know how to be grateful by respecting the gifts of others.

- I ask myself whether I am like the first two slaves, who worked hard to make their talents bear fruit; or like the third one who was more concerned not to lose what he had, and ended up losing everything. Probably I am a bit of both, so I ask for the grace of inner freedom to be able to express my gratitude through the way I live.

Twenty–Second Week in Ordinary Time
September 1—September 7

Something to think and pray about each day this week:

When backpacking in an unfamiliar location, it's important to have some navigational assistance—a map or a compass—and some basic information about the wildlife and plant life in the area. These resources usually prove helpful and sometimes prove life-saving. Similarly, on the catechist's journey, it is crucial that we familiarize ourselves with the "terrain" of this world. The Holy Spirit was poured forth so that we would proclaim the gospel to all nations. The Holy Spirit serves as our map, our compass, and ultimately our "GPSS"—our global positioning spiritual system. Without the Holy Spirit, we would wander aimlessly. Catechists are called to be uniquely in touch with the field in which the seeds of the gospel are to be sown: the world. We are called, however, not simply to immerse ourselves in the world but to survey it thoroughly, engage, and challenge it so that it may be transformed in and through Christ.

—Joe Paprocki and Julianne Stanz, *The Catechist's Backpack*

The Presence of God

I remind myself that I am in the presence of God, who is my strength in times of weakness and my comforter in times of sorrow.

Freedom

Saint Ignatius thought that a thick and shapeless tree trunk would never believe that it could become a statue, admired as a miracle of sculpture, and would never submit itself to the chisel of the sculptor, who sees by her genius what she can make of it. I ask for the grace to let myself be shaped by my loving Creator.

Consciousness

Dear Lord, help me to remember that you gave me life. Teach me to slow down, to be still and enjoy the pleasures created for me. To be aware of the beauty that surrounds me: the marvel of mountains, the calmness of lakes, the fragility of a flower petal. I need to remember that all these things come from you.

The Word

In this expectant state of mind, please read the text for the day with confidence. Believe that the Holy Spirit is present and may reveal whatever the passage has to say to you. Read reflectively, listening with a third ear to what may be going on in your heart. (Please turn to the Scripture on the following pages. Inspiration points are there, should you need them. When you are ready, return here to continue.)

Conversation

What feelings are rising in me as I pray and reflect on God's word? I imagine Jesus himself sitting or standing near me, and I open my heart to him.

Conclusion

I thank God for these moments we have spent together and for any insights I have been given concerning the text.

Sunday 1st September
Luke 14:1, 7–14

On one occasion when Jesus was going to the house of a leader of the Pharisees to eat a meal on the sabbath, they were watching him closely. . . . When he noticed how the guests chose the places of honor, he told them a parable. "When you are invited by someone to a wedding banquet, do not sit down at the place of honor, in case someone more distinguished than you has been invited by your host; and the host who invited both of you may come and say to you, 'Give this person your place,' and then in disgrace you would start to take the lowest place. But when you are invited, go and sit down at the lowest place, so that when your host comes, he may say to you, 'Friend, move up higher'; then you will be honored in the presence of all who sit at the table with you. For all who exalt themselves will be humbled, and those who humble themselves will be exalted." He said also to the one who had invited him, "When you give a luncheon or a dinner, do not invite your friends or your brothers or your relatives or rich neighbors, in case they may invite you in return, and you would be repaid. But when you give a banquet, invite the poor, the crippled, the lame, and the blind. And you will be blessed, because they cannot repay you, for you will be repaid at the resurrection of the righteous."

• When you allow this scene to unfold in your imagination a little bit, when you hear the words that Jesus pronounces aloud in front of his host, the guests, and the servants, it looks more and more like what Nicholas King, SJ, calls it (in his "fresh translation" of the New Testament): a "disastrous dinner party." Somebody is going to end up red in the face as Jesus talks about places of honor and the lowest place. Imagine a guest behaving like this at a party that you have organized.

• How do I relate to this story? What does it have to do with me?

Monday 2nd September
Luke 4:16–30

When he came to Nazareth, where he had been brought up, he went to the synagogue on the sabbath day, as was his custom. He stood up to read, and the scroll of the prophet Isaiah was given to him. He unrolled the scroll and found the place where it was written: "The Spirit of the Lord is upon me, because he has anointed me to bring good news to the poor. He has sent me to proclaim release to the captives and recovery of sight to the blind, to let the oppressed go free, to proclaim the year of the Lord's favor." And he rolled up the scroll, gave it back to the attendant, and sat down. The eyes of all in the synagogue were fixed on him. Then he began to say to them, "Today this scripture has been fulfilled in your hearing." All spoke well of him and were amazed at the gracious words that came from his mouth. They said, "Is not this Joseph's son?" He said to them, "Doubtless you will quote to me this proverb, 'Doctor, cure yourself!' And you will say, 'Do here also in your hometown the things that we have heard you did at Capernaum.'" And he said, "Truly I tell you, no prophet is accepted in the prophet's hometown. But the truth is, there were many widows in Israel in the time of Elijah, when the heaven was shut up three years and six months, and there was a severe famine over all the land; yet Elijah was sent to none of them except to a widow at Zarephath in Sidon. There were also many lepers in Israel in the time of the prophet Elisha, and none of them was cleansed except Naaman the Syrian." When they heard this, all in the synagogue were filled with rage. They got up, drove him out of the town, and led him to the brow of the hill on which their town was built, so that they might hurl him off the cliff. But he passed through the midst of them and went on his way.

- Of all the texts available to him, Jesus chose this ringing description of his mission from Isaiah: to bring good news to the poor, to give sight to the blind, to let the oppressed go free, and so on. As I reflect on Jesus' own understanding of his mission, I look at our world as we struggle with so many social issues: the welcome of refugees and migrants to our countries and communities; the growing inequality between those who have and those who have not; the destruction of the environment. What is the Spirit of the Lord sending me to do, as a follower of Jesus? I ask for the grace not to be deaf to his call but to carry it out with great generosity.

- As Jesus preached about inclusion, he found himself excluded. His listeners were appalled at his message. Is there anyone in my community whom I fail to accept?

Tuesday 3rd September
Luke 4:31–37

He went down to Capernaum, a city in Galilee, and was teaching them on the sabbath. They were astounded at his teaching, because he spoke with authority. In the synagogue there was a man who had the spirit of an unclean demon, and he cried out with a loud voice, "Let us alone! What have you to do with us, Jesus of Nazareth? Have you come to destroy us? I know who you are, the Holy One of God." But Jesus rebuked him, saying, "Be silent, and come out of him!" When the demon had thrown him down before them, he came out of him without having done him any harm. They were all amazed and kept saying to one another, "What kind of utterance is this? For with authority and power he commands the unclean spirits, and out they come!" And a report about him began to reach every place in the region.

- Lord, the people were astounded at hearing you. Let me too be amazed by your words, especially when you reveal the goodness of your Father toward me. Jolt me from my dullness. Let me experience your disturbing freshness, your vision of how we should live. May your promises of eternal life give me energy and joy, no matter how difficult my life may be right now.

- The demons of the possessed man were screaming, "Let us alone!" but I beg you *not* to let me alone! Stay with me so that I may live out my life in love before you.

Wednesday 4th September
Luke 4:38–44

After leaving the synagogue he entered Simon's house. Now Simon's mother-in-law was suffering from a high fever, and they asked him about her. Then he stood over her and rebuked the fever, and it left her. Immediately she got up and began to serve them. As the sun was setting, all those who had any who were sick with various kinds of diseases brought them to him; and he laid his hands on each of them and cured them. Demons also came out of many, shouting, "You are the Son of God!" But he rebuked them and would not allow them to speak, because they knew that he was the Messiah. At daybreak he departed and went into a deserted place. And the crowds were looking for him; and when they reached him, they wanted to prevent him from leaving them. But he said to them, "I must proclaim the good news of the kingdom of God to the other cities also; for I was sent for this purpose." So he continued proclaiming the message in the synagogues of Judea.

• We are always impressed by the amount of space given in the Gospels to the healing ministry of Jesus. Today we see him healing a woman in her home and then continuing to cure all those who were brought to him. The people knew that if you brought a sick person to Jesus, that person would be healed. Let me bring some people I know need healing to Jesus, asking him to cure them, to free them from the sickness or the evils that inhabit them.

• I take some moments to let Jesus visit me where I am now. What do I ask of him? Do I allow him to lay his hands on me, and if I do, how does that feel? Does my encounter with him help me in any way?

Thursday 5th September
Luke 5:1–11

Once while Jesus was standing beside the lake of Gennesaret, and the crowd was pressing in on him to hear the word of God, he saw two boats there at the shore of the lake; the fishermen had gone out of them and were washing their nets. He got into one of the boats, the one belonging to Simon, and asked him to put out a little way from the shore. Then he sat down and taught the crowds from the boat. When he had finished speaking, he said to Simon, "Put out into the deep water and let down your nets for a catch." Simon answered, "Master, we have worked all night long but have caught nothing. Yet if you say so, I will let down the nets." When they had done this, they caught so many fish that their nets were beginning to break. So they signaled to their partners in the other boat to come and help them. And they came and filled both boats, so that they began to sink. But when Simon Peter saw it, he fell down at Jesus' knees, saying, "Go away from me, Lord, for I am a sinful man!" For he and all who were with him were amazed at the catch of fish that they had taken; and so also were James and John, sons of Zebedee, who were partners with Simon. Then Jesus said to Simon, "Do not be afraid; from now on you will be catching people." When they had brought their boats to shore, they left everything and followed him.

- This miracle reveals the power and generosity of God. Jesus knew what would please Simon, who would never forget this catch of fish! God knows what will get my attention too.

- Lord, you tell me, as you told Simon, to "Put out into the deep water." This is a challenge but also an invitation. I ponder how I respond to a challenge—with excitement? Fear? Hope? Help me hear your invitation, Lord, and your encouragement.

Friday 6th September
Luke 5:33–39

Then [the Pharisees and the scribes said to Jesus], "John's disciples, like the disciples of the Pharisees, frequently fast and pray, but your disciples eat and drink. Jesus said to them, "You cannot make wedding guests fast while the bridegroom is with them, can you? The days will come when the bridegroom will be taken away from them, and then they will fast in those days." He also told them a parable: "No one tears a piece from a new garment and sews it on an old garment; otherwise the new will be torn, and the piece from the new will not match the old. And no one puts new wine into old wineskins; otherwise the new wine will burst the skins and will be spilled, and the skins will be destroyed. But new wine must be put into fresh wineskins. And no one after drinking old wine desires new wine, but says, 'The old is good.'"

- The little word *new* comes up seven times in this passage. Jesus is trying to get the Pharisees and scribes to see that, with his coming, everything is now new, different. Newness is a quality that God brings to our lives. Each year is a new year of grace; every day is a new day, different from yesterday.

- The daily bread we ask for in the Lord's Prayer is fresh bread, baked today. The decisions we make today give a new shape to our lives. And this encounter I am now having with God is a new one: it has never taken place before. So let me enjoy it to the full and look forward to the next encounter!

Saturday 7th September
Luke 6:1–5

One sabbath while Jesus was going through the cornfields, his disciples plucked some heads of grain, rubbed them in their hands, and ate them. But some of the Pharisees said, "Why are you doing what is not lawful on the sabbath?" Jesus answered, "Have you not read what David did when he and his companions were hungry? He entered the house of God and took and ate the bread of the Presence, which it is not lawful for any but the priests to eat, and gave some to his companions?" Then he said to them, "The Son of Man is lord of the sabbath."

- It was God who told the Hebrews to observe the Sabbath, so when Jesus says that he is Lord of the Sabbath, he is identifying with God. This claim enraged the Pharisees and ultimately led to his death. What new idea would disturb my comfortable faith?

- God's law is the law of freedom, for our lawgiver describes himself as merciful and compassionate. If we insist on the observance of the letter of the law rather than its spirit, then we may easily end up far from God rather than close to his will. This same discussion is going on in today's church, and I pray that it be enlightened by the spirit of Jesus.

Twenty–Third Week in Ordinary Time
September 8—September 14

Something to think and pray about each day this week:

In his autobiography, Ignatius explains how, toward the end of his life, the thought of his own death filled him with intense joy. The prospect of soon being reunited with his Creator and Lord made him "melt into tears." At the same time, Ignatius was in love with life. He could find God in all things and serve him in every activity and event, just as his spirituality teaches us. There was no need to wait until after death to taste the joy of God's presence. In practice, finding God in all things gives us the opportunity to consider our lives here and now as the precise place where we can already experience the fullness of God's love. Ignatius, with his genuine insight into human nature, warned against two possible pitfalls in the spiritual life: nostalgia for the past and needless dreaming about the future. It makes sense to look back on past experiences, for in doing so we can trace specific moments of God's presence. We recognize his presence in experiences of peace and joy, vitality and trust. Our past can provide a rich source of learning, especially since we can use times of reflection to inspire our choices. Such ongoing reflection gives us the opportunity to adapt our lives now so that they're more closely linked to the ways God is drawing us. But we can also get stuck in our own past and end up watching the same film over and over. . . . we allow ourselves to withdraw from the only time that really exists—the present. Ignatius did not want his novices (candidates for the Society of Jesus) to be told today what they would have to do tomorrow. That would only distract them from the great challenge that every person faces of living fully in the present moment, in the now. We can look at it this way: a good parent has to make plans for the future and do so in good time. But even in this situation, parents can be tempted to spend needless time day-dreaming about a not-yet-existing future at the expense of real life. St. John Berchmans (1599–1621), a Flemish Jesuit who died young, understood this concept of living in the present very well. While playing billiards one day, he was asked what he would do if he were told that he only had a few more minutes to live. He answered: "I would go on playing billiards."

—Nikolaas Sintobin, SJ, *Jesuits Telling Jokes*

The Presence of God

I remind myself that, as I sit here now,
God is gazing on me with love and holding me in being.
I pause for a moment and think of this.

Freedom

"There are very few people who realize what God would make of them
if they abandoned themselves into his hands, and let themselves be formed
by his grace" (Saint Ignatius). I ask for the grace to trust myself totally to
God's love.

Consciousness

Where do I sense hope, encouragement, and growth in my life? By looking back over the past few months, I may be able to see which activities
and occasions have produced rich fruit. If I do notice such areas, I will
determine to give those areas both time and space in the future.

The Word

Lord Jesus, you became human to communicate with me.
You walked and worked on this earth.
You endured the heat and struggled with the cold.
All your time on this earth was spent in caring for humanity.
You healed the sick, you raised the dead.
Most important of all, you saved me from death.
(Please turn to the Scripture on the following pages. Inspiration points
are there, should you need them. When you are ready, return here to
continue.)

Conversation

What is stirring in me as I pray? Am I consoled, troubled, left cold? I
imagine Jesus standing or sitting at my side, and I share my feelings with
him.

Conclusion

Glory be to the Father, and to the Son, and to the Holy Spirit,
As it was in the beginning, is now and ever shall be,
World without end. Amen.

Sunday 8th September
Luke 14:25–33

Now large crowds were traveling with him; and he turned and said to them, "Whoever comes to me and does not hate father and mother, wife and children, brothers and sisters, yes, and even life itself, cannot be my disciple. Whoever does not carry the cross and follow me cannot be my disciple. For which of you, intending to build a tower, does not first sit down and estimate the cost, to see whether he has enough to complete it? Otherwise, when he has laid a foundation and is not able to finish, all who see it will begin to ridicule him, saying, 'This fellow began to build and was not able to finish.' Or what king, going out to wage war against another king, will not sit down first and consider whether he is able with ten thousand to oppose the one who comes against him with twenty thousand? If he cannot, then, while the other is still far away, he sends a delegation and asks for the terms of peace. So therefore, none of you can become my disciple if you do not give up all your possessions."

- This passage about the cost of discipleship presumes that following Christ is demanding; do I find it demanding? If so, in what ways? Is giving up "all your possessions" realistic, and, if not, what does the passage mean for me? I speak to the Lord about the points of difficulty in this passage.

- *Carry the cross* reminds us of Good Friday and Jesus stumbling under the weight of his cross. For most of us, the cross is not inflicted from outside us but is part of our makeup: the body's and mind's infirmities, the addictions, temptations, and recurrent desires that rob us of our freedom. *Carrying my cross* means not so much solving these problems as learning to live with them, humble and not easily thrown off the path.

Monday 9th September
Luke 6:6–11

On another sabbath Jesus entered the synagogue and taught, and there was a man there whose right hand was withered. The scribes and the Pharisees watched him to see whether he would cure on the sabbath, so that they might find an accusation against him. Even though he knew what they were thinking, he said to the man who had the withered hand, "Come and stand here." He got up and stood there. Then Jesus said to them, "I ask you, is it lawful to do good or to do harm on the sabbath, to save life or to destroy it?" After looking around at all of them, he said to him, "Stretch out your hand." He did so, and his hand was restored. But they were filled with fury and discussed with one another what they might do to Jesus.

- The authorities were furious at the man's cure and immediately started to discuss how they could stop Jesus. I pray for the pope and for all religious leaders, that they may always know how to respond in an evangelical way to whatever is new and may appear shocking.

- God is a God who is attracted to people in their need. He focuses on my needs too and invites me in turn to give space in my heart to the needs of others. By doing this I become a true disciple.

Tuesday 10th September
Luke 6:12–19

Now during those days he went out to the mountain to pray; and he spent the night in prayer to God. And when day came, he called his disciples and chose twelve of them, whom he also named apostles: Simon, whom he named Peter, and his brother Andrew, and James, and John, and Philip, and Bartholomew, and Matthew, and Thomas, and James son of Alphaeus, and Simon, who was called the Zealot, and Judas son of James, and Judas Iscariot, who became a traitor. He came down with them and stood on a level place, with a great crowd of his disciples and a great multitude of people from all Judea, Jerusalem, and the coast of Tyre and Sidon. They had come to hear him and to be healed of their diseases; and those who were troubled with unclean spirits were cured. And all in the crowd were trying to touch him, for power came out from him and healed all of them.

- Luke's Gospel highlights the centrality of prayer in the life and mission of Jesus. His decisions and choices emerge from lengthy periods of communion with the one he calls "Abba." He chooses twelve very ordinary people and entrusts to them the task of making his values known to the world.

- Lord, I come to you in this time of prayer to feel your presence. Let me hear again your call to me. Let me sense your power at work in and through me.

Wednesday 11th September

Luke 6:20–26

[Jesus] looked up at his disciples and said: "Blessed are you who are poor, for yours is the kingdom of God. Blessed are you who are hungry now, for you will be filled. Blessed are you who weep now, for you will laugh. Blessed are you when people hate you, and when they exclude you, revile you, and defame you on account of the Son of Man. Rejoice on that day and leap for joy, for surely your reward is great in heaven; for that is what their ancestors did to the prophets. But woe to you who are rich, for you have received your consolation. Woe to you who are full now, for you will be hungry. Woe to you who are laughing now, for you will mourn and weep. Woe to you when all speak well of you, for that is what their ancestors did to the false prophets."

• The kingdom of God is mysterious, because it is God's project working out silently in human history. But from this text we know some of those who will be in it. The poor and the hungry will be there. So will those who weep, and also the dominated, the persecuted, the outcasts of the earth. What an extraordinary group! Those who are at the bottom of the human pyramid will be rejoicing and leaping for joy at God's goodness to them.

• When my heart is breaking because of the misery of so many today, I must not think that God has forgotten them. Instead I thank God that for them the best is yet to come, and I ask to be included among them, at least as someone who cares about them.

Thursday 12th September

Luke 6:27–38

[Jesus looked up at his disciples and said,] "But I say to you that listen, Love your enemies, do good to those who hate you, bless those who curse you, pray for those who abuse you. If anyone strikes you on the cheek, offer the other also; and from anyone who takes away your coat do not withhold even your shirt. Give to everyone who begs from you; and if anyone takes away your goods, do not ask for them again. Do to others as you would have them do to you. If you love those who love you, what credit is that to you? For even sinners love those who love them. If you do good to those who do good to you, what credit is that to you? For even sinners do the same. If you lend to those from whom you hope to receive, what credit is that to you? Even sinners lend to sinners, to receive as much again. But love your enemies, do good, and lend, expecting nothing in return. Your reward will be great, and you will be children of the Most High; for he is kind to the ungrateful and the wicked. Be merciful, just as your Father is merciful. Do not judge, and you will not be judged; do not condemn, and you will not be condemned. Forgive, and you will be forgiven; give, and it will be given to you. A good measure, pressed down, shaken together, running over, will be put into your lap; for the measure you give will be the measure you get back."

- I try to see which beatitude touches me today, whether because it helps me rejoice in God's gifts to me or because I feel a resistance in my heart. I pray for a listening heart.

- I ask myself to what extent I understand and live the Christian life in the perspective of the beatitudes, as the seeking of blessedness and happiness, and beyond a mere living according to the rules.

Friday 13th September
Luke 6:39–42

He also told them a parable: "Can a blind person guide a blind person? Will not both fall into a pit? A disciple is not above the teacher, but everyone who is fully qualified will be like the teacher. Why do you see the speck in your neighbor's eye, but do not notice the log in your own eye? Or how can you say to your neighbor, 'Friend, let me take out the speck in your eye,' when you yourself do not see the log in your own eye? You hypocrite, first take the log out of your own eye, and then you will see clearly to take the speck out of your neighbor's eye."

- We like to guide and correct people. It gives us a bit of status. This means of course that we are quick to see the flaws in others. I wonder how much of our conversation is focused on the failings of public figures and of those close to us.

- Jesus doesn't deny that people have failings, but he invites me to look to my own blind spots first. If the just person falls seven times, how often do I fall? Jesus uses humor to make his point. He invites me to imagine how many people I would be hurting if I had a log attached to my eye!

Saturday 14th September

John 3:13–17

[Jesus said,] "No one has ascended into heaven except the one who descended from heaven, the Son of Man. And just as Moses lifted up the serpent in the wilderness, so must the Son of Man be lifted up, that whoever believes in him may have eternal life. For God so loved the world that he gave his only Son, so that everyone who believes in him may not perish but may have eternal life. Indeed, God did not send the Son into the world to condemn the world, but in order that the world might be saved through him."

- The cross is the icon of great faith, hope, and love. As I gaze and contemplate Christ on the cross, I ask the Lord for his redemptive and healing love that embraces the whole world.

- If all the Gospels had been lost except the verse given here, "God so loved the world . . ." (John 3:16), that alone would be enough to give hope to humankind! Here we have the heart of the good news: the limitless love of God for us all, proved by his sending his Son to bring us home into eternal life. The rest of the New Testament is a commentary on this truth.

Twenty–Fourth Week in Ordinary Time
September 15—September 21

Something to think and pray about each day this week:

Q. Where is God?
A. Everywhere!

—The Baltimore Catechism

A tattered copy of this standard text sat on the desk of every girl and boy in Catholic schools from 1885 till the late 1960s. You will not find a Catholic adult who cannot repeat that remarkable Q and A. It's a simple expression of faith that points to the chosen part of *everything*. I was surprised not to find anything like it in the new *Catechism of the Catholic Church*, but that may just be me. *The Baltimore Catechism* was a sixty-two-page booklet, and the Vatican catechism has 928 pages and weighs more than my brain. I did find the word *omnipotence* five times in the index but no mention of the word *omnipresence*. I thought, *Gee, this is like having a classic songbook of the Beatles that doesn't include "Here, There, and Everywhere."* On the other hand, *The Baltimore Catechism* doesn't tell us what Easter is about. It's helpful to have more than one catechism in the house. That's because we can never hear enough of this wonderful Catholic idea: God is everywhere. We know from the movie, *The Big Lebowski*, that the Dude abides but we know from Scripture and tradition that Grace abounds. Grace runs through everything because God is "here, there, and everywhere." What could be more comforting? At the end of the novel *Diary of a Country Priest* a young priest lies dying, waiting for an old pastor to arrive and administer last rites. The friend at his bedside worries that the pastor won't get there on time and the priest will not receive the church's last blessing. The dying priest senses his concern and, in a halting but clear voice, says, "Does it matter? Grace is everywhere." The church may not always be there for us, but Catholicism teaches that God is everywhere for us. That's all that matters.

—Michael Leach, *Positively Catholic*

The Presence of God

Lord, help me to be fully alive to your holy presence. Enfold me in your love. Let my heart become one with yours.

My soul longs for your presence, Lord. When I turn my thoughts to You, I find peace and contentment.

Freedom

Your death on the cross has set me free. I can live joyously and freely without fear of death. Your mercy knows no bounds.

Consciousness

At this moment, Lord, I turn my thoughts to you.

I will leave aside my chores and preoccupations.

I will take rest and refreshment in your presence.

The Word

The word of God comes down to us through the Scriptures.

May the Holy Spirit enlighten my mind and my heart

to respond to the gospel teachings:

to love my neighbor as myself,

to care for my sisters and brothers in Christ.

(Please turn to the Scripture on the following pages. Inspiration points are there, should you need them. When you are ready, return here to continue.)

Conversation

Begin to talk to Jesus about the Scripture you have just read. What part of it strikes a chord in you? Perhaps the words of a friend—or some story you have heard recently—will slowly rise to the surface of your consciousness. If so, does the story throw light on what the Scripture passage may be saying to you?

Conclusion

I thank God for these moments we have spent together and for any insights I have been given concerning the text.

Sunday 15th September
Luke 15:1–10

Now all the tax collectors and sinners were coming near to listen to him. And the Pharisees and the scribes were grumbling and saying, "This fellow welcomes sinners and eats with them." So he told them this parable: "Which one of you, having a hundred sheep and losing one of them, does not leave the ninety-nine in the wilderness and go after the one that is lost until he finds it? When he has found it, he lays it on his shoulders and rejoices. And when he comes home, he calls together his friends and neighbors, saying to them, 'Rejoice with me, for I have found my sheep that was lost.' Just so, I tell you, there will be more joy in heaven over one sinner who repents than over ninety-nine righteous people who need no repentance. Or what woman having ten silver coins, if she loses one of them, does not light a lamp, sweep the house, and search carefully until she finds it? When she has found it, she calls together her friends and neighbors, saying, 'Rejoice with me, for I have found the coin that I had lost.' Just so, I tell you, there is joy in the presence of the angels of God over one sinner who repents."

- The parables of the lost sheep and the lost coin illustrate the constant, faithful, unrelenting love of God for each of us, but especially for sinners. God never gives up on anyone. God never gives up on *me*.

- This is not the sort of doctrine you learn in business schools. It sounds outlandish, to abandon the well-behaved and spend your energies on the outside chance of rescuing the delinquent 1 percent. Yet over the centuries these words have inspired good Christians to plug the gaps in social systems and reach out to those who have drifted into isolation and despair. Common sense urges us to spend ourselves on those who reward our efforts. Jesus worked in another direction: "The healthy have no need of a doctor." Lord, remind me of this attitude as I go about my day.

Monday 16th September
Luke 7:1–10

After Jesus had finished all his sayings in the hearing of the people, he entered Capernaum. A centurion there had a slave whom he valued highly, and who was ill and close to death. When he heard about Jesus, he sent some Jewish elders to him, asking him to come and heal his slave. When they came to Jesus, they appealed to him earnestly, saying, "He is worthy of having you do this for him, for he loves our people, and it is he who built our synagogue for us." And Jesus went with them, but when he was not far from the house, the centurion sent friends to say to him, "Lord, do not trouble yourself, for I am not worthy to have you come under my roof; therefore I did not presume to come to you. But only speak the word, and let my servant be healed. For I also am a man set under authority, with soldiers under me; and I say to one, 'Go,' and he goes, and to another, 'Come,' and he comes, and to my slave, 'Do this,' and the slave does it." When Jesus heard this he was amazed at him, and turning to the crowd that followed him, he said, "I tell you, not even in Israel have I found such faith." When those who had been sent returned to the house, they found the slave in good health.

- Like the centurion, I ask Jesus to come and heal someone I know who is seriously ill. I try to do it with the same humility and grace as the Roman officer, entrusting myself and my friend as fully as I can to Jesus.

- Jesus' words praising the faith of the pagan centurion cannot but impress us as we struggle to find the best Christian way of understanding people who are inspired by different religious traditions. I ask for the grace, for myself and for the whole church, to grow in this Christlike attitude to such peoples and groups.

Tuesday 17th September
Luke 7:11–17

Soon afterwards he went to a town called Nain, and his disciples and a large crowd went with him. As he approached the gate of the town, a man who had died was being carried out. He was his mother's only son, and she was a widow; and with her was a large crowd from the town. When the Lord saw her, he had compassion for her and said to her, "Do not weep." Then he came forward and touched the bier, and the bearers stood still. And he said, "Young man, I say to you, rise!" The dead man sat up and began to speak, and Jesus gave him to his mother. Fear seized all of them; and they glorified God, saying, "A great prophet has risen among us!" and "God has looked favorably on his people!" This word about him spread throughout Judea and all the surrounding country.

- I look at the scene and imagine myself present at Nain, witnessing this miracle. I see Jesus, who has compassion on the widow and performs the miracle without being asked to. Is there someone I would like to pray for today, someone who has been through a serious loss, is grieving or feeling lost? Jesus, teach me to be compassionate like you.

- I may be like the young man, not feeling anything, just carried by others. Or I may be the one carrying someone who seems dead. Or like the heartbroken mother. I pray to meet Jesus—who in his compassion can change my life for the better, giving me life and joy.

Wednesday 18th September

Luke 7:31–35

[Jesus said,] "To what then will I compare the people of this generation, and what are they like? They are like children sitting in the marketplace and calling to one another, 'We played the flute for you, and you did not dance; we wailed, and you did not weep.' For John the Baptist has come eating no bread and drinking no wine, and you say, 'He has a demon'; the Son of Man has come eating and drinking, and you say, 'Look, a glutton and a drunkard, a friend of tax collectors and sinners!' Nevertheless, wisdom is vindicated by all her children."

- It can be very easy to find excuses in a given situation, to remain sitting on the fence, finding fault with all the available alternatives without getting involved. I ask for wisdom, which is always related to concrete action, notwithstanding all the limitations of real situations.

- I wonder who are the children who vindicate wisdom. Probably those who are wise enough to accept their lot and see possibilities of good action, those who struggle to bring up their families silently but faithfully, those who do their duty without fear or favor, those who strive to live with integrity even when they feel alone and isolated in doing this. I ask to be counted among these blessed children of wisdom.

Thursday 19th September

Luke 7:36–50

One of the Pharisees asked Jesus to eat with him, and he went into the Pharisee's house and took his place at the table. And a woman in the city, who was a sinner, having learned that he was eating in the Pharisee's house, brought an alabaster jar of ointment. She stood behind him at his feet, weeping, and began to bathe his feet with her tears and to dry them with her hair. Then she continued kissing his feet and anointing them with the ointment. Now when the Pharisee who had invited him saw it, he said to himself, "If this man were a prophet, he would have known who and what kind of woman this is who is touching him—that she is a sinner." Jesus spoke up and said to him, "Simon, I have something to say to you." "Teacher," he replied, "speak." "A certain creditor had two debtors; one owed five hundred denarii, and the other fifty. When they could not pay, he canceled the debts for both of them. Now which of them will love him more?" Simon answered, "I suppose the one for whom he canceled the greater debt." And Jesus said to him, "You have judged rightly." Then turning toward the woman, he said to Simon, "Do you see this woman? I entered your house; you gave me no water for my feet, but she has bathed my feet with her tears and dried them with her hair. You gave me no kiss, but from the time I came in she has not stopped kissing my feet. You did not anoint my head with oil, but she has anointed my feet with ointment. Therefore, I tell you, her sins, which were many, have been forgiven; hence she has shown great love. But the one to whom little is forgiven, loves little." Then he said to her, "Your sins are forgiven." But those who were at the table with him began to say among themselves, "Who is this who even forgives sins?" And he said to the woman, "Your faith has saved you; go in peace."

- Like this anonymous woman, I am searching for Jesus, and I bring my sinfulness with me. In some way, that sinfulness is my gift to him. I observe his respect for her: he could have recoiled from her touch and demanded that she be thrown out. Instead he has all the time in the world for her, and he has endless time for me, too. He notices small gestures: the tiny touches of love shown in water, oil, tears, kisses.

- What small gestures of love can I show him? This woman is simple, extravagant, humble, trusting. Let me learn from her and so come closer to Jesus.

Friday 20th September

Luke 8:1–3

Soon afterwards he went on through cities and villages, proclaiming and bringing the good news of the kingdom of God. The twelve were with him, as well as some women who had been cured of evil spirits and infirmities:

Mary, called Magdalene, from whom seven demons had gone out, and Joanna, the wife of Herod's steward Chuza, and Susanna, and many others, who provided for them out of their resources.

- This passage illustrates the call of the women who followed Jesus. It shows how people of means supported the Lord's mission; Jesus and the Christian community depended on the generosity of people to sustain its mission. In what ways do I support the mission of the church?

- We see here Jesus, the man with a mission that he felt passionately about. It is described here as "proclaiming and bringing the good news of the kingdom of God." I pray that I too understand my mission in these terms. I pray the same grace for the church.

Saturday 21st September
Matthew 9:9–13

As Jesus was walking along, he saw a man called Matthew sitting at the tax booth; and he said to him, "Follow me." And he got up and followed him. And as he sat at dinner in the house, many tax collectors and sinners came and were sitting with him and his disciples. When the Pharisees saw this, they said to his disciples, "Why does your teacher eat with tax collectors and sinners?" But when he heard this, he said, "Those who are well have no need of a physician, but those who are sick. Go and learn what this means, 'I desire mercy, not sacrifice.' For I have come to call not the righteous but sinners."

- At this dinner, Jesus was surrounded by the kind of people no "good" Jew would come near or talk with. Have I seen any version of this scene in my own time and place? What would it look like? Who would be in Jesus' position as teacher, healer, and bringer of good news? What sort of people would surround that person? And what sort of people would be appalled at this?

- I pray in gratitude for the evangelist Matthew, through whose Gospel we know so much about Jesus and his message: the Beatitudes, the Our Father, his preaching of the kingdom of heaven, and so much else in the longest Gospel of the four.

September 22—September 28

Something to think and pray about each day this week:

Let the risen Jesus enter your life—welcome him as a friend, with trust: he is life! If up till now you have kept him at a distance, step forward. He will receive you with open arms. If you have been indifferent, take a risk; you won't be disappointed. If following him seems difficult, don't be afraid. Trust him, be confident that he is close to you, he is with you, and he will give you the peace you are looking for and the strength to live as he would have you do.

—Pope Francis, *The Church of Mercy*

The Presence of God
The more we call on God the more we can feel God's presence. Day by day we are drawn closer to the loving heart of God.

Freedom
I am free. When I look at these words in writing, they seem to create in me a feeling of awe. Yes, a wonderful feeling of freedom. Thank you, God.

Consciousness
Help me, Lord, become more conscious of your presence. Teach me to recognize your presence in others. Fill my heart with gratitude for the times your love has been shown to me through the care of others.

The Word
The word of God comes down to us through the Scriptures. May the Holy Spirit enlighten my mind and my heart to respond to the gospel teachings. (Please turn to the Scripture on the following pages. Inspiration points are there, should you need them. When you are ready, return here to continue.)

Conversation
Conversation requires talking and listening.
As I talk to Jesus, may I also learn to pause and listen.
I picture the gentleness in his eyes and the love in his smile.
I can be totally honest with Jesus as I tell him my worries and cares.
I will open my heart to Jesus as I tell him my fears and doubts.
I will ask him to help me place myself fully in his care, knowing that he always desires good for me.

Conclusion
Glory be to the Father, and to the Son, and to the Holy Spirit,
As it was in the beginning, is now and ever shall be,
World without end. Amen.

Sunday 22nd September

Luke 16:1–13

Then Jesus said to the disciples, "There was a rich man who had a manager, and charges were brought to him that this man was squandering his property. So he summoned him and said to him, 'What is this that I hear about you? Give me an account of your management, because you cannot be my manager any longer.' Then the manager said to himself, 'What will I do, now that my master is taking the position away from me? I am not strong enough to dig, and I am ashamed to beg. I have decided what to do so that, when I am dismissed as manager, people may welcome me into their homes.' So, summoning his master's debtors one by one, he asked the first, 'How much do you owe my master?' He answered, 'A hundred jugs of olive oil.' He said to him, 'Take your bill, sit down quickly, and make it fifty.' Then he asked another, 'And how much do you owe?' He replied, 'A hundred containers of wheat.' He said to him, 'Take your bill and make it eighty.' And his master commended the dishonest manager because he had acted shrewdly; for the children of this age are more shrewd in dealing with their own generation than are the children of light. And I tell you, make friends for yourselves by means of dishonest wealth so that when it is gone, they may welcome you into the eternal homes. Whoever is faithful in a very little is faithful also in much; and whoever is dishonest in a very little is dishonest also in much. If then you have not been faithful with the dishonest wealth, who will entrust to you the true riches? And if you have not been faithful with what belongs to another, who will give you what is your own? No slave can serve two masters; for a slave will either hate the one and love the other, or be devoted to the one and despise the other. You cannot serve God and wealth."

- The point of this passage is in the commendation of the dishonest steward, not for the moral quality of his behavior, but for his worldly prudence in using the things of this life to ensure his future in this life. Believers should behave with prudence to ensure their eternal future. One might reflect on how diligently people work for the goods that pass away while neglecting the goods that are eternal.

- I ask for the courage to be shrewd with my resources and to not be afraid to use my reason and influence for the good.

Monday 23rd September
Luke 8:16–18

[Jesus said to his disciples,] "No one after lighting a lamp hides it under a jar, or puts it under a bed, but puts it on a lampstand, so that those who enter may see the light. For nothing is hidden that will not be disclosed, nor is anything secret that will not become known and come to light. Then pay attention to how you listen; for to those who have, more will be given; and from those who do not have, even what they seem to have will be taken away."

- The lamp is lit for a purpose; the light it gives shows it at its fullest potential. When loving others, we express our love of God. Our acts of kindness, thoughtfulness, or thanks are ways in which we can be lamps that are lit.

- Jesus asks me to pay attention to how I listen, to notice how I notice. If my prayer is full of distraction or if my mind is always racing, I need to do as Jesus asks and pay attention. If I see only deficiency, I will lose everything; if I am able to see, appreciate, and receive blessing, I can trust in God's goodness and love.

Tuesday 24th September
Luke 8:19–21

Then [Jesus'] mother and his brothers came to him, but they could not reach him because of the crowd. And he was told, "Your mother and your brothers are standing outside, wanting to see you." But he said to them, "My mother and my brothers are those who hear the word of God and do it."

- People naturally assumed that Jesus would give first place to his family. But with one sentence he reveals that every human being can become a member of his family. Closeness to Jesus does not depend on social standing or academic achievement or affluence. It depends instead on "hearing the word and doing it."

- But what is the word, and how do we "do" it? The primary word told us by Jesus is that the love of his Father for us is infinite; we are to trust this word and live by it. As Pope Francis says: "When everything is said and done, we are infinitely loved." When we know how well we are loved and how well our neighbors are loved, our attitude to others is transformed and the world becomes a warmer place.

Wednesday 25th September
Luke 9:1–6

Then Jesus called the twelve together and gave them power and authority over all demons and to cure diseases, and he sent them out to proclaim the kingdom of God and to heal. He said to them, "Take nothing for your journey, no staff, nor bag, nor bread, nor money—not even an extra tunic. Whatever house you enter, stay there, and leave from there. Wherever they do not welcome you, as you are leaving that town shake the dust off your feet as a testimony against them." They departed and went through the villages, bringing the good news and curing diseases everywhere.

- I notice how Jesus sends the twelve to do the same things he is doing: to expel demons, to heal, and to proclaim the kingdom of God. After his resurrection, he told the apostles, "As the Father has sent me, so I send you" (John 20:21). I dwell in wonder at the trust Jesus places in us, by sharing his own mission and his own powers with us in all our frailty.

- Even in our super-rational world that seeks efficiency above all else, the option of preaching in poverty is still very effective and always touches people's hearts powerfully. We can recall the example of Mother Teresa, Pope Francis, Taizé. I pray for today's church as she strives to be faithful to her calling by Jesus.

Thursday 26th September
Luke 9:7–9

Now Herod the ruler heard about all that had taken place, and he was perplexed, because it was said by some that John had been raised from the dead, by some that Elijah had appeared, and by others that one of the ancient prophets had arisen. Herod said, "John I beheaded; but who is this about whom I hear such things?" And he tried to see Jesus.

- This time it is King Herod who is intrigued by Jesus and asks himself if he is actually John the Baptist raised from the dead. We too can find it difficult to accept the novelty of Jesus, and sometimes we end up reducing him to an imitation of someone we know or have heard about. I pray to be open always to the newness and mystery of Jesus, letting him enable me to know him.

- Herod tried to see Jesus, and he managed to do so only during Jesus' trial. There Herod showed he was not really interested in having a personal encounter with Jesus, but rather in meeting a celebrity. Jesus once thanked the Father for showing the little ones who he really was and hiding it from the wise and the proud. I pray to be small enough to desire a personal encounter with Jesus.

Friday 27th September
Luke 9:18–22

Once when Jesus was praying alone, with only the disciples near him, he asked them, "Who do the crowds say that I am?" They answered, "John the Baptist; but others, Elijah; and still others, that one of the ancient prophets has arisen." He said to them, "But who do you say that I am?" Peter answered, "The Messiah of God." He sternly ordered and commanded them not to tell anyone, saying, "The Son of Man must undergo great suffering, and be rejected by the elders, chief priests, and scribes, and be killed, and on the third day be raised."

- In my prayer, I imagine Jesus asking me, "Who do you say that I am?" What do I say? Do I believe that this mysterious Messiah of God will be with me even if, like him, I must suffer greatly, and that in his own good time he will raise me up?

- Today Jesus still asks this central question: Who do people say that I am? Who do you say that I am? I let myself hear this question, and I listen to my answer, asking for the grace to know Jesus better so that I accept him lovingly as the Messiah of God for me.

Saturday 28th September
Luke 9:43–45

And all were astounded at the greatness of God. While everyone was amazed at all that he was doing, he said to his disciples, "Let these words sink into your ears: The Son of Man is going to be betrayed into human hands." But they did not understand this saying; its meaning was concealed from them, so that they could not perceive it. And they were afraid to ask him about this saying.

- The disciples need some inspiration points here! They cannot take in the fact that Jesus will be betrayed. Why would anyone betray him when he is doing so much good, and is at the height of his powers and so popular? But when I feel myself betrayed, then I am glad that his life took this form. So many people experience betrayal, and the lives of others are cut short, as his was, by the malice of evil people. I am strengthened by the fact that the Son of God knows the anguish from personal experience and that he has grappled with it and brought great good out of it by his love.

- Lord, when things go badly wrong and I am discouraged, remind me of your Passion. Then I will be able to continue in the belief that you have radically defeated the evil of the world from the inside.

September 29—October 5

Something to think and pray about each day this week:

It can be the hardest thing when intuitively it should be the easiest—to let go of the pain, to truly and completely entrust it to Jesus, to place it at the foot of the Cross, and never pick it up again. Our pain is precious to us, like the tears in Magdalene's vial. It defines us and marks us and tells us what matters. And to let it go can feel like saying, "This doesn't matter to me anymore." But that's not what Jesus is asking. He is not asking us to let go of our identity or to deny what is precious to us or to say that our pain is unimportant. Letting go is a much more nuanced and liberating maneuver of heart than that. Instead, he is asking us to give him this most precious pain so he may put comfort in its place. He is asking us to anchor our identity in him, he who is able to redeem all pain, make it worthy, powerful, transformative, a force for good in the world and in us, to give it a proper and eternal horizon. He does this because he receives it perfectly, knows it completely, carries it entirely—easily—for us. He does this because he loves us so mightily.

—Elizabeth Kelly, *Jesus Approaches*

The Presence of God

"Be still and know that I am God!" Lord, your words lead us to the calmness and greatness of your presence.

Freedom

"In these days, God taught me as a schoolteacher teaches a pupil" (Saint Ignatius). I remind myself that there are things God has to teach me yet, and I ask for the grace to hear them and let them change me.

Consciousness

How am I really feeling? Lighthearted? Heavyhearted? I may be very much at peace, happy to be here.

Equally, I may be frustrated, worried or angry.

I acknowledge how I really am. It is the real me whom the Lord loves.

The Word

God speaks to each of us individually. I listen attentively to hear what he is saying to me. Read the text a few times; then listen. (Please turn to the Scripture on the following pages. Inspiration points are there, should you need them. When you are ready, return here to continue.)

Conversation

Do I notice myself reacting as I pray with the word of God? Do I feel challenged, comforted, angry? Imagining Jesus sitting or standing by me, I speak out my feelings, as one trusted friend to another.

Conclusion

I thank God for these moments we have spent together and for any insights I have been given concerning the text.

Sunday 29th September

Luke 16:19–31

[Jesus said to the Pharisees,] "There was a rich man who was dressed in purple and fine linen and who feasted sumptuously every day. And at his gate lay a poor man named Lazarus, covered with sores, who longed to satisfy his hunger with what fell from the rich man's table; even the dogs would come and lick his sores. The poor man died and was carried away by the angels to be with Abraham. The rich man also died and was buried. In Hades, where he was being tormented, he looked up and saw Abraham far away with Lazarus by his side. He called out, 'Father Abraham, have mercy on me, and send Lazarus to dip the tip of his finger in water and cool my tongue; for I am in agony in these flames.' But Abraham said, 'Child, remember that during your lifetime you received your good things, and Lazarus in like manner evil things; but now he is comforted here, and you are in agony. Besides all this, between you and us a great chasm has been fixed, so that those who might want to pass from here to you cannot do so, and no one can cross from there to us.' He said, 'Then, father, I beg you to send him to my father's house—for I have five brothers—that he may warn them, so that they will not also come into this place of torment.' Abraham replied, 'They have Moses and the prophets; they should listen to them.' He said, 'No, father Abraham; but if someone goes to them from the dead, they will repent.' He said to him, 'If they do not listen to Moses and the prophets, neither will they be convinced even if someone rises from the dead.'"

- Note that the rich man is not presented as being cruel to Lazarus or mistreating him. He was condemned for doing nothing, for seeing the miserable state of Lazarus and doing nothing about it. Ask the Lord to help you see the extent that you do something about the misery you see about you and to help you see what more you could do.

- "If they do not listen to Moses and the prophets . . ." We are tempted to think that if only God were revealed to humans in more obvious and powerful ways, people would believe. But Jesus' story of Lazarus and the rich man tells us flatly that belief involves an open heart, not merely a convinced mind. I pray for help in appealing to people's hearts—their soul needs—rather than trying to argue them into faith.

Monday 30th September
Luke 9:46–50

An argument arose among them as to which one of them was the greatest. But Jesus, aware of their inner thoughts, took a little child and put it by his side, and said to them, "Whoever welcomes this child in my name welcomes me, and whoever welcomes me welcomes the one who sent me; for the least among all of you is the greatest." John answered, "Master, we saw someone casting out demons in your name, and we tried to stop him, because he does not follow with us." But Jesus said to him, "Do not stop him; for whoever is not against you is for you."

- Over and over Jesus tries to get his disciples to see that they are called to serve, not to dominate. In the kingdom of God everyone is equal: there are no positions of power. Everyone is a daughter or son of God; all are fully loved by God.

- In prayer we must grapple with these extraordinary truths and try to let them sink in, so that we emerge from our time with God with a more inclusive and respectful attitude toward others. Prayer stretches our imagination, and prayer is real only when we begin to see and love the world as God does.

Tuesday 1st October
Luke 9:51–56

When the days drew near for him to be taken up, he set his face to go to Jerusalem. And he sent messengers ahead of him. On their way they entered a village of the Samaritans to make ready for him; but they did not receive him, because his face was set toward Jerusalem. When his disciples James and John saw it, they said, "Lord, do you want us to command fire to come down from heaven and consume them?" But he turned and rebuked them. Then they went on to another village.

- The Scripture shows Jesus refusing revenge and violence. Violence is forever on our daily newscasts, but it solves nothing.

- What causes feelings of revenge to enter me? Do I sometimes feel a desire for revenge on some person, or some group, with whom I cannot resolve my differences? Could I place those feelings before the Lord in silence and pray to become more like Christ in my attitudes?

Wednesday 2nd October
Matthew 18:1–5, 10

At that time the disciples came to Jesus and asked, "Who is the greatest in the kingdom of heaven?" He called a child, whom he put among them, and said, "Truly I tell you, unless you change and become like children, you will never enter the kingdom of heaven. Whoever becomes humble like this child is the greatest in the kingdom of heaven. Whoever welcomes one such child in my name welcomes me. . . . Take care that you do not despise one of these little ones; for, I tell you, in heaven their angels continually see the face of my Father in heaven."

- Am I free to challenge my friends, my family, or my work colleagues with a childlike fearlessness when my heart tells me that something is not right?

- The clear heart and the simple honesty of a child make us sit up and pay attention and smile in admiration. I might pause in silence to reflect on the true greatness to be found in a child. I also pray for those who have children in their care.

Thursday 3rd October
Luke 10:1–12

After this the Lord appointed seventy others and sent them on ahead of him in pairs to every town and place where he himself intended to go. He said to them, "The harvest is plentiful, but the laborers are few; therefore ask the Lord of the harvest to send out laborers into his harvest. Go on your way. See, I am sending you out like lambs into the midst of wolves. Carry no purse, no bag, no sandals; and greet no one on the road. Whatever house you enter, first say, 'Peace to this house!' And if anyone is there who shares in peace, your peace will rest on that person; but if not, it will return to you. Remain in the same house, eating and drinking whatever they provide, for the laborer deserves to be paid. Do not move about from house to house. Whenever you enter a town and its people welcome you, eat what is set before you; cure the sick who are there, and say to them, 'The kingdom of God has come near to you.' But whenever you enter a town and they do not welcome you, go out into its streets and say, 'Even the dust of your town that clings to our feet, we wipe off in protest against you. Yet know this:

the kingdom of God has come near.' I tell you, on that day it will be more tolerable for Sodom than for that town."

- One of the great gifts that Jesus wishes to share with us is peace, and that we should share it with one another. Perhaps I can recall those whom I have the ability to share peace with. How do I feel when my goodwill is rejected? I can ask the Lord to strengthen me in my resolve to be a peace-bearer and for the grace to be able to "fight nice" when I meet opposition.

- Looking around the globe today we see many examples of hostility, injustice, and lack of love. The gospel challenges us to be messengers of peace. Maybe by entering the chaos of someone within your own radius you will discover that "the kingdom of God has come near" and that you are one of the "seventy others" bringing the good news of the kingdom. Perhaps, quietly bring to mind one person you know who is suffering and who needs "the good news" of human support.

Friday 4th October
Luke 10:13–16

[Jesus said,] "Woe to you, Chorazin! Woe to you, Bethsaida! For if the deeds of power done in you had been done in Tyre and Sidon, they would have repented long ago, sitting in sackcloth and ashes. But at the judgment it will be more tolerable for Tyre and Sidon than for you. And you, Capernaum, will you be exalted to heaven? No, you will be brought down to Hades. Whoever listens to you listens to me, and whoever rejects you rejects me, and whoever rejects me rejects the one who sent me."

- Jesus berates the people for not recognizing him and listening to him, poising retribution to those who do not listen to those sent by Jesus. He singles out especially those who were privileged to observe his deeds.

- Could this Gospel reading be asking me to review my moral compass? Could it be asking us: *Who* sets the boundaries between what is a good and what is a bad way to live? Where do I look to find the boundaries that can truly free me?

Saturday 5th October

Luke 10:17–24

The seventy returned with joy, saying, "Lord, in your name even the demons submit to us!" He said to them, "I watched Satan fall from heaven like a flash of lightning. See, I have given you authority to tread on snakes and scorpions, and over all the power of the enemy; and nothing will hurt you. Nevertheless, do not rejoice at this, that the spirits submit to you, but rejoice that your names are written in heaven." At that same hour Jesus rejoiced in the Holy Spirit and said, "I thank you, Father, Lord of heaven and earth, because you have hidden these things from the wise and the intelligent and have revealed them to infants; yes, Father, for such was your gracious will. All things have been handed over to me by my Father; and no one knows who the Son is except the Father, or who the Father is except the Son and anyone to whom the Son chooses to reveal him." Then turning to the disciples, Jesus said to them privately, "Blessed are the eyes that see what you see! For I tell you that many prophets and kings desired to see what you see, but did not see it, and to hear what you hear, but did not hear it."

- Jesus reminds us that valuing ourselves only according to our successes can cause us to miss the essential. God values us more deeply, simply because of who we are. Inner contentment, which comes from knowing and loving God, makes us indeed blessed.

- As I talk to the Lord, I can ask for a growth in friendship with him.

October 6—October 12

Something to think and pray about each day this week:

We can begin to understand the bigger story we are a part of when we engage with the unique Christian sense of time, process, and journey. This perception is presented beautifully in the Grail quest; it's the story of a young man searching for God and himself. Through ongoing trials and temptations, the young man pushes toward God, almost without knowing it. God leads him forward through family, failure, violence, visitors, betrayal, sexuality, nature, shadow, and vision. God comes to him "disguised as his life." The story is told in language most men can relate to, not in "churchy" language. It's a tale told with muscle, merit, and meaning. Everything on this journey is necessary and grace filled. For the man on the quest, the universe becomes enchanting—an effect that good religion accomplishes. There are no dead ends, no wasted time, no useless characters or meaningless happenings. All has meaning, and God is in all things waiting to speak and to bless. Everything belongs once a man is on his real quest and asking the right questions.

—Richard Rohr, *On the Threshold of Transformation*

The Presence of God
To be present is to arrive as one is and open up to the other.
At this instant, as I arrive here, God is present waiting for me.
God always arrives before me, desiring to connect with me
even more than my most intimate friend.
I take a moment and greet my loving God.

Freedom
Leave me here / freely all alone / In cell where never sunlight shone / Should
no one ever speak to me. / This golden silence makes me free!
   —Part of a poem by Bl. Titus Brandsma, written while he was a prisoner
                                        at Dachau concentration camp

Consciousness
Where am I with God? With others?
Do I have something to be grateful for? Then I give thanks.
Is there something I am sorry for? Then I ask forgiveness.

The Word
I take my time to read the word of God slowly, a few times, allowing myself
to dwell on anything that strikes me. (Please turn to the Scripture on the
following pages. Inspiration points are there, should you need them. When
you are ready, return here to continue.)

Conversation
How has God's word moved me? Has it left me cold?
Has it consoled me or moved me to act in a new way?
I imagine Jesus standing or sitting beside me;
I turn and share my feelings with him.

Conclusion
Glory be to the Father, and to the Son, and to the Holy Spirit,
As it was in the beginning, is now and ever shall be,
World without end. Amen.

Sunday 6th October
Luke 17:5–10

The apostles said to the Lord, "Increase our faith!" The Lord replied, "If you had faith the size of a mustard seed, you could say to this mulberry tree, 'Be uprooted and planted in the sea,' and it would obey you. Who among you would say to your slave who has just come in from ploughing or tending sheep in the field, 'Come here at once and take your place at the table?' Would you not rather say to him, 'Prepare supper for me, put on your apron and serve me while I eat and drink; later you may eat and drink'? Do you thank the slave for doing what was commanded? So you also, when you have done all that you were ordered to do, say, 'We are worthless slaves; we have done only what we ought to have done!'"

* I join the apostles and pray insistently, "Increase my faith." I listen with the same openness and wonder to Jesus' encouraging reply as I look at the quality of my faith: it's enough for my faith to be as small as a mustard seed!

* While it seems obvious that the servant eats only once the master has been served, at the Last Supper Jesus did just the opposite: he insisted on washing the feet of his disciples. Then he called them his friends. I ask for the grace to have the freedom to see myself as the humble servant not seeking to be superior to his master.

Monday 7th October
Luke 10:25–37

A lawyer stood up to test Jesus. "Teacher," he said, "what must I do to inherit eternal life?" He said to him, "What is written in the law? What do you read there?" He answered, "You shall love the Lord your God with all your heart, and with all your soul, and with all your strength, and with all your mind; and your neighbor as yourself." And he said to him, "You have given the right answer; do this, and you will live." But wanting to justify himself, he asked Jesus, "And who is my neighbor?" Jesus replied, "A man was going down from Jerusalem to Jericho, and fell into the hands of robbers, who stripped him, beat him, and went away, leaving him half dead. Now by chance a priest was going down that road; and when he saw him, he passed by on the other side. So likewise a Levite, when he came to the place and saw him, passed by on the other side. But a Samaritan while traveling came near him; and when he saw him, he was moved with pity. He went to him and bandaged his wounds, having poured oil and wine on them. Then he put him on his own animal, brought him to an inn, and took care of him. The next day he took out two denarii, gave them to the innkeeper, and said, 'Take care of him; and when I come back, I will repay you whatever more you spend.' Which of these three, do you think, was a neighbor to the man who fell into the hands of the robbers?" He said, "The one who showed him mercy." Jesus said to him, "Go and do likewise."

- Does this story touch me? Could I spend some time reflecting on this parable as if it were addressed personally to me? I may love the Lord with all my heart and all my soul, but who in my life is my neighbor? And to whom am I a good neighbor?

- Jesus often told stories to make his point. What stories—in novels, children's books, movies, songs, poems—have touched me deeply and helped me gain wisdom? I linger with one of those stories now, enjoying again the grace of God I received through it.

Tuesday 8th October
Luke 10:38–42

Now as they went on their way, Jesus entered a certain village, where a woman named Martha welcomed him into her home. She had a sister named Mary, who sat at the Lord's feet and listened to what he was saying. But Martha was distracted by her many tasks; so she came to him and asked, "Lord, do you not care that my sister has left me to do all the work by myself? Tell her then to help me." But the Lord answered her, "Martha, Martha, you are worried and distracted by many things; there is need of only one thing. Mary has chosen the better part, which will not be taken away from her."

- I notice that Jesus does not condemn Martha for trying to be a good hostess. Rather, he tells her that she has become anxious and troubled over catering issues! She has lost her perspective of why she is serving in the first place.

- Have I lost sight of what is most important in life? Am I so busy doing many things that I do not have any time for God? Is my work for the Lord causing me to be anxious and troubled? Has love disappeared? Lord, please help me put things in perspective and not to lose sight of my mission in life, which is "to love and serve in all things."

Wednesday 9th October
Luke 11:1–4

[Jesus] was praying in a certain place, and after he had finished, one of his disciples said to him, "Lord, teach us to pray, as John taught his disciples." He said to them, "When you pray, say: Father, hallowed be your name. Your kingdom come. Give us each day our daily bread. And forgive us our sins, for we ourselves forgive everyone indebted to us. And do not bring us to the time of trial."

• I call you Father; Jesus taught me to use this metaphor. I know that you, Lord, are beyond gender and surpass our imagination. But I relish the overtones of Father, one who knows and loves me, and whose often mysterious providence is there in everything that befalls me.

• Have I found a word in postmodern culture for that eternally dependable figure—a personal word for God? We might pray before the Holy One that peace and love will prevail. We might pray that the earth will continue to sustain us. We might ask to be forgiven. When fraught and distraught, we might pray to be saved from doing wrong or being subjected to evil action. To whom do we pray?

Thursday 10th October
Luke 11:5–13

[Jesus said to the people,] "Suppose one of you has a friend, and you go to him at midnight and say to him, 'Friend, lend me three loaves of bread; for a friend of mine has arrived, and I have nothing to set before him.' And he answers from within, 'Do not bother me; the door has already been locked, and my children are with me in bed; I cannot get up and give you anything.' I tell you, even though he will not get up and give him anything because he is his friend, at least because of his persistence he will get up and give him whatever he needs. So I say to you, Ask, and it will be given to you; search, and you will find; knock, and the door will be opened for you. For everyone who asks receives, and everyone who searches finds, and for everyone who knocks, the door will be opened. Is there anyone among you who, if your child asks for a fish, will give a snake instead of a fish? Or if the child asks for an egg, will give a scorpion? If you then, who are evil, know how to give good gifts to your children, how much more will the heavenly Father give the Holy Spirit to those who ask him!"

- Asking, searching, and knocking are the actions of someone in need. The theme of prayer continues in today's Gospel reading. The question Jesus raises is faith. Do you believe that God the Father will give if you ask?

- Human generosity and care, especially for our own children, is evident. If we can be generous, surely God can too. But do I believe that God listens?

Friday 11th October
Luke 11:15–26

]Some of the crowd said of Jesus], "He casts out demons by Beelzebul, the ruler of the demons." Others, to test him, kept demanding from him a sign from heaven. But he knew what they were thinking and said to them, "Every kingdom divided against itself becomes a desert, and house falls on house. If Satan also is divided against himself, how will his kingdom stand?—for you say that I cast out the demons by Beelzebul. Now if I cast out the demons by Beelzebul, by whom do your exorcists cast them out? Therefore they will be your judges. But if it is by the finger of God that I cast out the demons, then the kingdom of God has come to you. When a strong man, fully armed, guards his castle, his property is safe. But when one stronger than he attacks him and overpowers him, he takes away his armor in which he trusted and divides his plunder. Whoever is not with me is against me, and whoever does not gather with me scatters. When the unclean spirit has gone out of a person, it wanders through waterless regions looking for a resting place, but not finding any, it says, 'I will return to my house from which I came.' When it comes, it finds it swept and put in order. Then it goes and brings seven other spirits more evil than itself, and they enter and live there; and the last state of that person is worse than the first."

- The Gospel text today gives the story of some people who refused to accept the great good that Jesus was doing and instead accused him of doing this good work as an agent of evil. The logic of this baffles us, but people can go to extremes rather than change their convictions. Likewise, Jesus reminds us that when we have been helped to make progress under his guidance, we should be careful to stay in his company lest we are tempted to revert to our old ways.

• I can speak to the Lord and ask him to help me be open to goodness and to avoid being overcritical of others.

Saturday 12th October
Luke 11:27–28

While Jesus was speaking, a woman in the crowd raised her voice and said to him, "Blessed is the womb that bore you and the breasts that nursed you!" But he said, "Blessed rather are those who hear the word of God and obey it!"

• It seems that God always takes our good impulses and desires and expands them. In this short exchange, Jesus takes the woman's worthy praise and invites her to enlarge her view of what it means to be blessed. When has Jesus challenged my vision to grow?

• Sometimes we feel more kinship with people who share our beliefs than with those who share our bloodline and family ties. I pause to thank God for my vast family in the faith.

Twenty–Eighth Week in Ordinary Time
October 13—October 19

Something to think and pray about each day this week:

Listening to another person might be the greatest act of compassion you can perform. It is the easiest way to welcome someone into your heart. When I listen, I am accepting an invitation to become part of another person's story. I am saying, "Yes, your story is important and needs to be heard. I want to make your story part of my own." But all too often, I find myself dismissive of other people. I might be too busy. I might not like what I hear; their story offends my sensibilities. When I dismiss another person's story, I am dismissing them. I rob people of their dignity by ignoring them. Imagine how St. Scholastica must have felt. She had been enjoying her conversation with her brother Benedict—whom she only saw once a year—and she asked him to stay the night so they could continue their conversation. He refused, saying that his rule forbade it. Benedict ignored her story, which was really his own story, a story about how much he meant to her. But God did not ignore her. A furious thunderstorm erupted that night that prevented Benedict from leaving. God never ignores us. And since we are made in the image and likeness of God—if we are to imitate Christ—then we are called to listen to others.

—Bob Burnham, *Little Lessons from the Saints*

The Presence of God
What is present to me is what has a hold on my becoming.
I reflect on the presence of God always there in love,
amid the many things that have a hold on me.
I pause and pray that I may let God
affect my becoming in this precise moment.

Freedom
By God's grace I was born to live in freedom. Free to enjoy the pleasures
he created for me. Dear Lord, grant that I may live as you intended, with
complete confidence in your loving care.

Consciousness
To be conscious about something is to be aware of it.
Dear Lord, help me to remember that you gave me life.
Thank you for the gift of life.
Teach me to slow down, to be still and enjoy the pleasures created for me.
To be aware of the beauty that surrounds me: the marvel of mountains, the
calmness of lakes, the fragility of a flower petal. I need to remember that all
these things come from you.

The Word
God speaks to each of us individually. I listen attentively to hear what he
is saying to me. Read the text a few times; then listen. (Please turn to the
Scripture on the following pages. Inspiration points are there, should you
need them. When you are ready, return here to continue.)

Conversation
I begin to talk with Jesus about the Scripture I have just read. What part of
it strikes a chord in me? Perhaps the words of a friend—or some story I have
heard recently—will rise to the surface in my consciousness. If so, does the
story throw light on what the Scripture passage may be saying to me?

Conclusion
Glory be to the Father, and to the Son, and to the Holy Spirit,
As it was in the beginning, is now and ever shall be,
World without end. Amen.

Sunday 13th October

Luke 17:11–19

On the way to Jerusalem Jesus was going through the region between Samaria and Galilee. As he entered a village, ten lepers approached him. Keeping their distance, they called out, saying, "Jesus, Master, have mercy on us!" When he saw them, he said to them, "Go and show yourselves to the priests." And as they went, they were made clean. Then one of them, when he saw that he was healed, turned back, praising God with a loud voice. He prostrated himself at Jesus' feet and thanked him. And he was a Samaritan. Then Jesus asked, "Were not ten made clean? But the other nine, where are they? Was none of them found to return and give praise to God except this foreigner?" Then he said to him, "Get up and go on your way; your faith has made you well."

• The Jesuit writer Tony de Mello used to say that you cannot be grateful and unhappy. There is so much to be grateful for, and we need to remind ourselves of this from time to time. In the great joy at their cure, the other nine lepers forgot the greater joy that they were the recipients of this wonderful yet unearned gift. Let me spend some time counting my blessings and being grateful for them.

• Jesus tells the Samaritan, "Your faith has made you well." I thank God for the gift of faith, which makes me more capable of facing life with all its suffering and contradictions. I ask the Lord Jesus to strengthen my faith.

Monday 14th October

Luke 11:29–32

When the crowds were increasing, Jesus began to say, "This generation is an evil generation; it asks for a sign, but no sign will be given to it except the sign of Jonah. For just as Jonah became a sign to the people of Nineveh, so the Son of Man will be to this generation. The queen of the South will rise at the judgment with the people of this generation and condemn them, because she came from the ends of the earth to listen to the wisdom of Solomon, and see, something greater than Solomon is here! The people of Nineveh will rise up at the judgment with this generation and condemn it, because they repented at the proclamation of Jonah, and see, something greater than Jonah is here!"

- Jesus uses imagination trying to help his audience catch on to the mystery of who he is. He reminds them of famous characters in stories they already know well. He then tries to open their minds further by saying twice that "something greater" is here in his person.

- This is a mysterious assertion. But God is mysterious, so coming closer to the truth about God means being led along the path of mystery. Do I cultivate my capacity for mystery, or do I live on the surface of life? Do I reduce the wonders of nature and of the cosmos to mere facts, or do I let myself be drawn to wonder what their author must be like? Everything is a divine mystery because all comes from God. Let me sit with Jesus and ask him to enliven the mystical dimension that may be dormant in me.

Tuesday 15th October
Luke 11:37–41

While [Jesus] was speaking, a Pharisee invited him to dine with him; so he went in and took his place at the table. The Pharisee was amazed to see that he did not first wash before dinner. Then the Lord said to him, "Now you Pharisees clean the outside of the cup and of the dish, but inside you are full of greed and wickedness. You fools! Did not the one who made the outside make the inside also? So give for alms those things that are within; and see, everything will be clean for you."

- What is my focus? Do I need help, honest feedback from a friend to clarify my heart? You know my heart, Lord. You know the movements and thoughts under the surface of my behavior. Teach me to live first of all in your presence, free from seeking human respect.

- True freedom is a marvelous gift. It can be all too easy to fall into the trap of conforming to the expectations of others. We miss out then by not developing our own inner life, which helps us to live other than through mere conformity to outside show. I ask Jesus for the gift of inner freedom from which good judgment comes.

Wednesday 16th October
Luke 11:42–46

[Jesus said,] "But woe to you Pharisees! For you tithe mint and rue and herbs of all kinds, and neglect justice and the love of God; it is these you ought to have practiced, without neglecting the others. Woe to you Pharisees! For you love to have the seat of honor in the synagogues and to be greeted with respect in the marketplaces. Woe to you! For you are like unmarked graves, and people walk over them without realizing it." One of the lawyers answered him, "Teacher, when you say these things, you insult us too." And he said, "Woe also to you lawyers! For you load people with burdens hard to bear, and you yourselves do not lift a finger to ease them."

- It is clear that Jesus is unafraid of offending people. While, so often, his words were gentle and inviting, on this occasion he chose a harsher tone. He sounds angry, doesn't he? In what situations today can you imagine Jesus delivering such a scathing message? And how would you respond?

- "You load people with burdens hard to bear"; these are the words of Jesus, who also said, "Come to me, all who are heavy laden." Even in Jesus' anger, his focus is on God's mercy; he speaks so sternly to the religious leaders because they have used their influence to make people's lives harder. I pray for people who are overburdened.

Thursday 17th October
Luke 11:47–54

Jesus said to the lawyers, "Woe to you! For you build the tombs of the prophets whom your ancestors killed. So you are witnesses and approve of the deeds of your ancestors; for they killed them, and you build their tombs. Therefore also the Wisdom of God said, 'I will send them prophets and apostles, some of whom they will kill and persecute,' so that this generation may be charged with the blood of all the prophets shed since the foundation of the world, from the blood of Abel to the blood of Zechariah, who perished between the altar and the sanctuary. Yes, I tell you, it will be charged against this generation. Woe to you lawyers! For you have taken away the key of knowledge; you did not enter yourselves, and you hindered those who were entering." When he went outside, the scribes and the Pharisees began to be very hostile toward him and to cross-examine him about many things, lying in wait for him, to catch him in something he might say.

- As the Gospel of Luke moves along, Jesus can be seen to be on a collision course with the religious and political Jewish leaders. He becomes more and more outspoken. The lawyers, the scribes, and the Pharisees become more and more angry and intent on taking him down. Jesus points out that their legality, applied to religious observance, is far removed from the love of God. They lie in wait looking for a legal reason to arrest him. How can I relate this scene to the world I live in today?

- Today I pray for the Christian communities who are suffering persecution in so many parts of the world. I pray especially for the Christians in the Middle East where Christianity first appeared and where it is running the real risk of disappearing.

Friday 18th October
Luke 10:1–9

After this the Lord appointed seventy others and sent them on ahead of him in pairs to every town and place where he himself intended to go. He said to them, "The harvest is plentiful, but the laborers are few; therefore ask the Lord of the harvest to send out laborers into his harvest. Go on your way. See, I am sending you out like lambs into the midst of wolves. Carry no purse, no bag, no sandals; and greet no one on the road. Whatever house you enter, first say, 'Peace to this house!' And if anyone is there who shares in peace, your peace will rest on that person; but if not, it will return to you. Remain in the same house, eating and drinking whatever they provide, for the laborer deserves to be paid. Do not move about from house to house. Whenever you enter a town and its people welcome you, eat what is set before you; cure the sick who are there, and say to them, 'The kingdom of God has come near to you.'"

- If I can place myself in this Gospel passage I may find that I am one of those "seventy others." I am a follower of Jesus. I listen and look as I enter the challenge of this Gospel scene. And I am sent out. I carry with me no resources, only a clear vision, my unique interior gifts, and an open heart.

- Jesus sent the disciples in pairs, and he sent them where he himself intended to go. In a way, he sent them to prepare the people for his arrival.

We can see ourselves as people who prepare others for an encounter with Christ. We can minister to others, but only Christ can bring them fullness of life. How will I act as his ambassador this day?

Saturday 19th October

Luke 12:8–12

[Jesus said to the disciples,] "And I tell you, everyone who acknowledges me before others, the Son of Man also will acknowledge before the angels of God; but whoever denies me before others will be denied before the angels of God. And everyone who speaks a word against the Son of Man will be forgiven; but whoever blasphemes against the Holy Spirit will not be forgiven. When they bring you before the synagogues, the rulers, and the authorities, do not worry about how you are to defend yourselves or what you are to say; for the Holy Spirit will teach you at that very hour what you ought to say."

• I acknowledge each human person I meet and offer each one dignity. In that way I acknowledge Jesus. When I spend time adoring God in a church, I am challenged to find him in the pulse of humanity when I walk back out on the street.

• Jesus speaks here of the different ways that a relationship with him affects our lives. In prayer, we approach him in our own hearts as our friend and Lord, and this prayer encourages us to be strong as we live our Christian values in today's world. In moments of special difficulty, the Holy Spirit helps us according to our need at the time.

Twenty–Ninth Week in Ordinary Time
October 20—October 26

Something to think and pray about each day this week:

In a community we are each gifts to one another. The rich, with their resources, are a gift to the poor. And the poor, with their hard-earned wisdom,
are a gift to the rich. The priests and bishops are a gift to the faithful, but
if the faithful did not exist, there would be no need for priests and bishops.
We are all pilgrims from many places climbing a rocky hill together. And
this jumble of a community is the greatest gift of all. But only if the gift is
accepted. This is our choice, and sometimes it is not a clear choice at all.
Sometimes the community looks oddly fuzzy, multicolored, and useless to
us, and we hesitate to open the lid. And if we take the chance, we may
discover that we are all pieces of string too small to save. But God saves us
anyway.

—Jane Knuth, *Thrift Store Graces*

The Presence of God
"Be still and know that I am God!" Lord, your words lead us to the calmness and greatness of your presence.

Freedom
Everything has the potential to draw forth from me a fuller love and life. Yet my desires are often fixed, caught, on illusions of fulfillment. I ask that God, through my freedom, may orchestrate my desires in a vibrant, loving melody rich in harmony.

Consciousness
I exist in a web of relationships: links to nature, people, God.
I trace out these links, giving thanks for the life that flows through them.
Some links are twisted or broken; I may feel regret, anger, disappointment.
I pray for the gift of acceptance and forgiveness.

The Word
I read the word of God slowly, a few times over, and I listen to what God is saying to me. (Please turn to the Scripture on the following pages. Inspiration points are there, should you need them. When you are ready, return here to continue.)

Conversation
Jesus, you speak to me through the words of the Gospels. May I respond to your call today. Teach me to recognize your hand at work in my daily living.

Conclusion
I thank God for these moments we have spent together and for any insights I have been given concerning the text.

Sunday 20th October
Luke 18:1–8

Then Jesus told them a parable about their need to pray always and not to lose heart. He said, "In a certain city there was a judge who neither feared God nor had respect for people. In that city there was a widow who kept coming to him and saying, 'Grant me justice against my opponent.' For a while he refused; but later he said to himself, 'Though I have no fear of God and no respect for anyone, yet because this widow keeps bothering me, I will grant her justice, so that she may not wear me out by continually coming.'" And the Lord said, "Listen to what the unjust judge says. And will not God grant justice to his chosen ones who cry to him day and night? Will he delay long in helping them? I tell you, he will quickly grant justice to them. And yet, when the Son of Man comes, will he find faith on earth?"

- "Will not God grant justice to his chosen ones who cry to him day and night?" I join those crying for justice, bringing to my prayer some situation of deep-seated conflict or injustice I know well.

- The persistence of my prayer indicates the depth of my need. Even if I find myself asking for what I need or desire, I take time to see how God may already be offering me some answer.

Monday 21st October
Luke 12:13–21

Someone in the crowd said to Jesus, "Teacher, tell my brother to divide the family inheritance with me." But he said to him, "Friend, who set me to be a judge or arbitrator over you?" And he said to them, "Take care! Be on your guard against all kinds of greed; for one's life does not consist in the abundance of possessions." Then he told them a parable: "The land of a rich man produced abundantly. And he thought to himself, 'What should I do, for I have no place to store my crops?' Then he said, 'I will do this: I will pull down my barns and build larger ones, and there I will store all my grain and my goods. And I will say to my soul, Soul, you have ample goods laid up for many years; relax, eat, drink, be merry.' But God said to him, 'You fool! This very night your life is being demanded of you. And the things you have prepared, whose will they be?' So it is with those who store up treasures for themselves but are not rich toward God."

- Many people struggle to manage financially. Have I reached a balance in my desire for wealth? Am I driven by an unhealthy level of consumerism? Am I convinced that money is not the answer to finding happiness and a peaceful heart?

- Saint Ignatius was a mystic who had very enriching ideas about God and about ourselves. He saw God as the great lover and ourselves as God's beloveds. He saw too that God gives us everything and even wants to give his very self to us, so far as he can. Lord, make me grounded enough to want only to love and humbly serve others as best I can. Help me do everything for the greater glory of God.

Tuesday 22nd October
Luke 12:35–38

[Jesus said to his disciples,] "Be dressed for action and have your lamps lit; be like those who are waiting for their master to return from the wedding banquet, so that they may open the door for him as soon as he comes and knocks. Blessed are those slaves whom the master finds alert when he comes; truly I tell you, he will fasten his belt and have them sit down to eat, and he will come and serve them. If he comes during the middle of the night, or near dawn, and finds them so, blessed are those slaves."

- Life is a challenging journey, and we can never be ready for every event along the way. The Gospel says: "Be dressed for action," and blessed are those who are ready and alert. It takes a deep breath of faith to be ready for any event that may come upon us. We know that on some level within us we must be always ready for death. Do I make a habit of considering my own death and my readiness for it?

- "Be dressed for action." What does this mean for me? What prepares me for surprises, unpleasant or otherwise? Today, I consider what my clothing for action might include.

Wednesday 23rd October
Luke 12:39–48

[Jesus said to the people,] "But know this: if the owner of the house had known at what hour the thief was coming, he would not have let his house be broken into. You also must be ready, for the Son of Man is coming at an unexpected hour." Peter said, "Lord, are you telling this parable for us or for everyone?" And the Lord said, "Who then is the faithful and prudent manager whom his master will put in charge of his slaves, to give them their allowance of food at the proper time? Blessed is that slave whom his master will find at work when he arrives. Truly I tell you, he will put that one in charge of all his possessions. But if that slave says to himself, 'My master is delayed in coming,' and if he begins to beat the other slaves, men and women, and to eat and drink and get drunk, the master of that slave will come on a day when he does not expect him and at an hour that he does not know, and will cut him in pieces, and put him with the unfaithful. That slave who knew what his master wanted, but did not prepare himself or do what was wanted, will receive a severe beating. But one who did not know and did what deserved a beating will receive a light beating. From everyone to whom much has been given, much will be required; and from one to whom much has been entrusted, even more will be demanded."

• The disciples still haven't understood Jesus' message about being ready. The drama of Jesus' parable is perhaps a bit exaggerated to stress its importance. When it comes to leadership and those who are in authority in the community of believers, the parable points out how much more they have to account for because of their trusted positions of power. I pray for religious leaders in my community and beyond.

• Today we are reminded to pay attention to what is important. We don't want to wake up and discover we are too late to receive a gift or opportunity. I ask Jesus how I might develop my paying-attention powers.

Thursday 24th October
Luke 12:49–53

[Jesus said to his disciples,] "I came to bring fire to the earth, and how I wish it were already kindled! I have a baptism with which to be baptized, and what stress I am under until it is completed! Do you think that I have come to bring peace to the earth? No, I tell you, but rather division! From now on five in one household will be divided, three against two and two against three; they will be divided: father against son and son against father, mother against daughter and daughter against mother, mother-in-law against her daughter-in-law and daughter-in-law against mother-in-law."

- It is interesting that Jesus uses the example of family members to point out that his message will divide people. He describes division in families as a fact, not a rare possibility. I ask the Holy Spirit to help me examine my heart and my loyalties. When am I the most tempted to sacrifice Jesus' mission to family pressure or tradition?

- Jesus is under stress in awaiting his own suffering and crucifixion. And though his message is peace, it is such a hard-won peace that it is more like division because he is fighting off the corruption of the world. He knows that the radical purity of his message will cause people to waver and doubt and oppose his message. He is like the prophet Micah, whom Luke quotes here, who, while seeing the divisions in families, puts his trust in God alone (Micah 7:6). I consider how processes toward peace can also include conflict and discomfort.

Friday 25th October
Luke 12:54–59

[Jesus] also said to the crowds, "When you see a cloud rising in the west, you immediately say, 'It is going to rain'; and so it happens. And when you see the south wind blowing, you say, 'There will be scorching heat'; and it happens. You hypocrites! You know how to interpret the appearance of earth and sky, but why do you not know how to interpret the present time? And why do you not judge for yourselves what is right? Thus, when you go with your accuser before a magistrate, on the way make an effort to settle the case, or you may be dragged before the judge, and the judge hand you over to the officer, and the officer throw you in prison. I tell you, you will never get out until you have paid the very last penny."

- It is good to apply this text to our own situations. How often people can refuse to see what is obvious. How easy it is to pass responsibility or blame to someone else and to refuse to speak or take action when I am capable of making the call. I pray for light and guidance.

- When I am honest with myself, it helps me to interpret my inner life more accurately. In my prayer I ask the Lord for the gift of interior sensitivity.

Saturday 26th October
Luke 13:1–9

At that very time there were some present who told him about the Galileans whose blood Pilate had mingled with their sacrifices. He asked them, "Do you think that because these Galileans suffered in this way they were worse sinners than all other Galileans? No, I tell you; but unless you repent, you will all perish as they did. Or those eighteen who were killed when the tower of Siloam fell on them—do you think that they were worse offenders than all the others living in Jerusalem? No, I tell you; but unless you repent, you will all perish just as they did." Then he told this parable: "A man had a fig tree planted in his vineyard; and he came looking for fruit on it and found none. So he said to the gardener, 'See here! For three years I have come looking for fruit on this fig tree, and still I find none. Cut it down! Why should it be wasting the soil?' He replied, 'Sir, let it alone for one more year, until I dig round it and put manure on it. If it bears fruit next year, well and good; but if not, you can cut it down.'"

- As with so many of Jesus' words, these must be set in context. He is speaking to his own people, using an image from the prophets: Israel as the Lord's vineyard. He is begging his people to wake up to their opportunity, to bear fruit.

- You speak to me, too, Lord. You look to me for fruit, for signs of love in my life. I do not want to be wasting my opportunities, but I rely on you to have patience and help me. Dig around me and cultivate me, even if it hurts. You alone know how to make something good of my life.

October 27—November 2

Something to think and pray about each day this week:

Early on I was struck by the boldness of Ignatian spirituality. The question posed in the Spiritual Exercises is "What ought I *do* for Christ?" and we're not to be shy about seeking an answer. Ignatius repeatedly counsels those making the Exercises to ask God for what they want. When obstacles appear, you're to confront them, following the principle of *agere contra*—do the opposite. If you don't feel like praying, pray more; if you're drawn to riches, give some money away; if you can't stand your annoying coworker, spend some more time with them. Ignatius wasn't much inclined to sit around and wait for things to happen. He told a Jesuit complaining about dryness of soul that "it may easily come from a lack of confidence, or faintheartedness and, consequently, can be cured by the contrary." He wrote to Jesuits in Portugal: "No commonplace achievement will satisfy the great obligations you have of excelling." Boldness is a big part of the way the Jesuits see themselves. "A holy boldness, 'a certain apostolic aggressivity,' is typical of our way of proceeding," the Thirty-Fourth General Congregation said in 1995.

—Jim Manney, *Ignatian Spirituality A to Z*

The Presence of God

"Come to me, all you who are weary and are carrying heavy burdens, and I will give you rest." Here I am, Lord. I come to seek your presence. I long for your healing power.

Freedom

God is not foreign to my freedom. The Spirit breathes life into my most intimate desires, gently nudging me toward all that is good. I ask for the grace to let myself be enfolded by the Spirit.

Consciousness

I remind myself that I am in the presence of the Lord. I will take refuge in his loving heart. He is my strength in times of weakness. He is my comforter in times of sorrow.

The Word

I take my time to read the word of God slowly, a few times, allowing myself to dwell on anything that strikes me. (Please turn to the Scripture on the following pages. Inspiration points are there, should you need them. When you are ready, return here to continue.)

Conversation

Jesus, you always welcomed little children when you walked on this earth. Teach me to have a childlike trust in you. Teach me to live in the knowledge that you will never abandon me.

Conclusion

Glory be to the Father, and to the Son, and to the Holy Spirit,
As it was in the beginning, is now and ever shall be,
World without end. Amen.

Sunday 27th October
Luke 18:9–14

He also told this parable to some who trusted in themselves that they were righteous and regarded others with contempt: "Two men went up to the temple to pray, one a Pharisee and the other a tax collector. The Pharisee, standing by himself, was praying thus, 'God, I thank you that I am not like other people: thieves, rogues, adulterers, or even like this tax collector. I fast twice a week; I give a tenth of all my income.' But the tax collector, standing far off, would not even look up to heaven, but was beating his breast and saying, 'God, be merciful to me, a sinner!' I tell you, this man went down to his home justified rather than the other; for all who exalt themselves will be humbled, but all who humble themselves will be exalted."

- In what ways am I tempted to "regard others with contempt"? Sharing gossip about someone I don't like? Posting criticism or sarcasm about individuals or groups of people on social media? I pray for wisdom to see my own heart and its deceptions.

- How easy it is to measure our goodness by the things we do and not by what fills our heart. I ask for the grace of a pure heart.

Monday 28th October
Luke 6:12–16

Now during those days he went out to the mountain to pray; and he spent the night in prayer to God. And when day came, he called his disciples and chose twelve of them, whom he also named apostles: Simon, whom he named Peter, and his brother Andrew, and James, and John, and Philip, and Bartholomew, and Matthew, and Thomas, and James son of Alphaeus, and Simon, who was called the Zealot, and Judas son of James, and Judas Iscariot, who became a traitor.

- It seems that Jesus and his Father spent the whole night in conversation about the choosing of the twelve apostles. Can I imagine how the conversation went?

- Do I ever consult God about the decisions I have to make, especially those that will have a long-term effect? It is worth the trouble to look for his advice, even if it takes all night.

Tuesday 29th October

Luke 13:18–21

Jesus said to the crowds, "What is the kingdom of God like? And to what should I compare it? It is like a mustard seed that someone took and sowed in the garden; it grew and became a tree, and the birds of the air made nests in its branches." And again he said, "To what should I compare the kingdom of God? It is like yeast that a woman took and mixed in with three measures of flour until all of it was leavened."

• The secret of the kingdom of God is to allow Jesus to grow in us. As we do so, we come to love him and depend on him as our traveling companion. Like the birds making their nests in the branches of the trees, we nestle in the heart of Jesus and find nourishment in his care.

• I think of the second image of the kingdom of God. "It is like the yeast that a woman took and mixed in with three measures of flour until it was all leavened." How does that connect with me?

Wednesday 30th October

Luke 13:22–30

Jesus went through one town and village after another, teaching as he made his way to Jerusalem. Someone asked him, "Lord, will only a few be saved?" He said to them, "Strive to enter through the narrow door; for many, I tell you, will try to enter and will not be able. When once the owner of the house has got up and shut the door, and you begin to stand outside and to knock at the door, saying, 'Lord, open to us,' then in reply he will say to you, 'I do not know where you come from.' Then you will begin to say, 'We ate and drank with you, and you taught in our streets.' But he will say, 'I do not know where you come from; go away from me, all you evildoers!' There will be weeping and gnashing of teeth when you see Abraham and Isaac and Jacob and all the prophets in the kingdom of God, and you yourselves thrown out. Then people will come from east and west, from north and south, and will eat in the kingdom of God. Indeed, some are last who will be first, and some are first who will be last."

• Lord, these are frightening words! Were you trying to scare people? Wake them up? Jar them out of complacency? And what work do you desire these words to do in me today?

- The first will be last, and the last will be first. Jesus turns conventional wisdom on its head. He warns us not to be so sure of ourselves and our position. He warns that God's way is a narrow way, one not well-known or well-traveled. I ask for guidance to keep my life on that path.

Thursday 31st October
Luke 13:31–35

At that very hour some Pharisees came and said to him, "Get away from here, for Herod wants to kill you." He said to them, "Go and tell that fox for me, 'Listen, I am casting out demons and performing cures today and tomorrow, and on the third day I finish my work. Yet today, tomorrow, and the next day I must be on my way, because it is impossible for a prophet to be killed away from Jerusalem.' Jerusalem, Jerusalem, the city that kills the prophets and stones those who are sent to it! How often have I desired to gather your children together as a hen gathers her brood under her wings, and you were not willing! See, your house is left to you. And I tell you, you will not see me until the time comes when you say, 'Blessed is the one who comes in the name of the Lord.'"

- Jesus is free before all threats of suffering and persecution. The source of this freedom is his passionate awareness of who he is and what he is called to. I pray for the freedom to stay on my course this day.
- There is no doubt that Jesus had a special love for Jerusalem. Even nowadays it is a city that is so symbolic of many of the tensions that rile our world. Today I pray that Jerusalem can become a city of peace, one that accepts its mission to bring people together as a hen gathers her chicks under her wings.

Friday 1st November
All Saints
Matthew 5:1–12

When Jesus saw the crowds, he went up the mountain; and after he sat down, his disciples came to him. Then he began to speak, and taught them, saying: "Blessed are the poor in spirit, for theirs is the kingdom of heaven. Blessed are those who mourn, for they will be comforted. Blessed are the meek, for they will inherit the earth. Blessed are those who hunger and thirst for righteousness, for they will be filled. Blessed are the merciful, for they will receive mercy. Blessed are the pure in heart, for they will see God. Blessed are the peacemakers, for they will be called children of God. Blessed are those who are persecuted for righteousness' sake, for theirs is the kingdom of heaven. Blessed are you when people revile you and persecute you and utter all kinds of evil against you falsely on my account. Rejoice and be glad, for your reward is great in heaven, for in the same way they persecuted the prophets who were before you."

- On this feast of All Saints, I call to mind those—whether famous canonized saints or "ordinary" people who have been saints to me—who have demonstrated the blessed happiness found in a life of humility, mercy, purity, and hunger for righteousness.

- Each of the saints I remember today brings an aspect of the Beatitudes to life; I give thanks to God for what I learn from these many examples and for their encouragement in living as they did.

Saturday 2nd November
The Commemoration of All the Faithful Departed (All Souls' Day)
John 6:37–40

[Jesus said,] "Everything that the Father gives me will come to me, and anyone who comes to me I will never drive away; for I have come down from heaven, not to do my own will, but the will of him who sent me. And this is the will of him who sent me, that I should lose nothing of all that he has given me, but raise it up on the last day. This is indeed the will of my Father, that all who see the Son and believe in him may have eternal life; and I will raise them up on the last day."

- It is the will of God that nothing should be lost; may I look on everything that is good as a gift from God and an invitation to embrace the life that God offers. I thank God that, even though we die, we are not lost and our days on earth are not wasted.

- Jesus welcomes everyone who comes to him. I pray to become a constant expression to others of God's welcoming embrace.

November 3—November 9

Something to think and pray about each day this week:

"Pick up your cross daily." To many of us, this phrase sounds perfectly pious: We must do as Jesus did. To Jesus' followers, who had yet to see him die on the cross, it must have sounded insane. In contemporary terms, it might have sounded like this: "if anyone wishes to follow me, he must pick up a syringe filled with a lethal injection." In essence, Jesus is telling us that each day we must embrace the very instrument that leads to our death so that we might be reborn. Rather than run away from whatever is "killing us"— whatever is wearing us down, making us angry, or making us sick in mind, body, or spirit—we must turn and face it so that both it and our old self may be defeated—not with bigger, badder weapons, but with acceptance and love. This is why, in Twelve-Step programs, hitting rock bottom is an occasion for hope: only when one comes face to face with defeat is recovery truly possible. Likewise, to "pick up your cross" is *not* to be confused with patiently bearing up under a burden that life has dealt you: sickness, the loss of a job, the death of a loved one, and so on. While we can and should unite our sufferings to the suffering of Jesus, he doesn't want us to passively endure. Instead, he wants us to open ourselves to the transformation that suffering can bring, knowing that "death" to an old way of life or to an old attachment is necessary if we are truly to be born again. To bear your cross is to embrace any instrument that will crucify your human tendency to respond with anything less than total, selfless love. Indeed, the "way of the cross" is not simply a devotional prayer practiced by many Christians, especially Catholics. It is a way of life—a way of entering the kingdom of God.

—Joe Paprocki, *Under the Influence of Jesus*

The Presence of God

"I am standing at the door, knocking" says the Lord. What a wonderful privilege that the Lord of all creation desires to come to me. I welcome his presence.

Freedom

I will ask God's help
to be free from my own preoccupations,
to be open to God in this time of prayer,
to come to know, love, and serve God more.

Consciousness

In God's loving presence I unwind the past day,
starting from now and looking back, moment by moment.
I gather in all the goodness and light, in gratitude.
I attend to the shadows and what they say to me,
seeking healing, courage, forgiveness.

The Word

Now I turn to the Scripture set out for me this day. I read slowly over the words and see if any sentence or sentiment appeals to me. (Please turn to the Scripture on the following pages. Inspiration points are there, should you need them. When you are ready, return here to continue.)

Conversation

Sometimes I wonder what I might say if I were to meet you in person, Lord. I think I might say "Thank you" because you are always there for me.

Conclusion

I thank God for these moments we have spent together and for any insights I have been given concerning the text.

Sunday 3rd November
Luke 19:1–10

He entered Jericho and was passing through it. A man was there named Zacchaeus; he was a chief tax collector and was rich. He was trying to see who Jesus was, but on account of the crowd he could not, because he was short in stature. So he ran ahead and climbed a sycamore tree to see him, because he was going to pass that way. When Jesus came to the place, he looked up and said to him, "Zacchaeus, hurry and come down; for I must stay at your house today." So he hurried down and was happy to welcome him. All who saw it began to grumble and said, "He has gone to be the guest of one who is a sinner." Zacchaeus stood there and said to the Lord, "Look, half of my possessions, Lord, I will give to the poor; and if I have defrauded anyone of anything, I will pay back four times as much." Then Jesus said to him, "Today salvation has come to this house, because he too is a son of Abraham. For the Son of Man came to seek out and to save the lost."

- Prayer helps us to strike up a deep relationship with Jesus, and he calls us by name. Life is never the same again after Jesus enters your house and builds up a friendship that is far more valuable than you could ever ask or imagine. Today, will you welcome his presence?

- Jesus accepts and praises Zacchaeus's efforts to repair the damage he has done. He seems happy enough that he was giving one half of his money to the poor and did not ask him to give it all up. I ask Jesus to help me believe he accepts my poor efforts, as he proclaims that I too am a child of Abraham.

Monday 4th November
Luke 14:12–14

Jesus said also to the one who had invited him, "When you give a luncheon or a dinner, do not invite your friends or your brothers or your relatives or rich neighbors, in case they may invite you in return, and you would be repaid. But when you give a banquet, invite the poor, the crippled, the lame, and the blind. And you will be blessed, because they cannot repay you, for you will be repaid at the resurrection of the righteous."

- Jesus invites me to freedom—not to look for anything for myself because this invitation may seem too much! But then I remember that everything I have comes from God, who blesses me freely and generously.

- I consider those who are on Jesus' guest list. How do I find myself among them? Do I notice similar people being on my list of those I would really like to invite?

Tuesday 5th November
Luke 14:15–24

One of the dinner guests, on hearing this, said to him, "Blessed is anyone who will eat bread in the kingdom of God!" Then Jesus said to him, "Someone gave a great dinner and invited many. At the time for the dinner he sent his slave to say to those who had been invited, 'Come; for everything is ready now.' But they all alike began to make excuses. The first said to him, 'I have bought a piece of land, and I must go out and see it; please accept my regrets.' Another said, 'I have bought five yoke of oxen, and I am going to try them out; please accept my regrets.' Another said, 'I have just been married, and therefore I cannot come.' So the slave returned and reported this to his master. Then the owner of the house became angry and said to his slave, 'Go out at once into the streets and lanes of the town and bring in the poor, the crippled, the blind, and the lame.' And the slave said, 'Sir, what you ordered has been done, and there is still room.' Then the master said to the slave, 'Go out into the roads and lanes, and compel people to come in, so that my house may be filled. For I tell you, none of those who were invited will taste my dinner.'"

- Property, power, and relationships are good reasons for staying away from the banquet; what would it be for me? What would be the reason for my saying, "Just one more minute and I'll be with you?"

- The abounding generosity of God can be matched only by our ability to grow in humility and to trust as we ask again and again.

Wednesday 6th November
Luke 14:25–33

Now large crowds were traveling with him; and he turned and said to them, "Whoever comes to me and does not hate father and mother, wife and children, brothers and sisters, yes, and even life itself, cannot be my disciple. Whoever does not carry the cross and follow me cannot be my disciple. For which of you, intending to build a tower, does not first sit down and estimate the cost, to see whether he has enough to complete it? Otherwise, when he has laid a foundation and is not able to finish, all who see it will begin to ridicule him, saying, 'This fellow began to build and was not able to finish.' Or what king, going out to wage war against another king, will not sit down first and consider whether he is able with ten thousand to oppose the one who comes against him with twenty thousand? If he cannot, then, while the other is still far away, he sends a delegation and asks for the terms of peace. So therefore, none of you can become my disciple if you do not give up all your possessions."

- In prayer it is just me and God; for a while all else is given up. I need nothing to pray except myself. This is how I came into the world and how I will go: naked of all I possess and own. This can be an experience of great freedom. Prayer is the moment of offering the self to God, the true and real self without the possessions that can sometimes block God's invitation and grace.

- There is a cost to discipleship. Jesus wants to be accompanied by friends, not by complaining conscripts. He paints a stark picture, asking if we are ready to accept difficulty with him. If we are, we know that he will not leave us alone but will carry our burdens with us and show us what love and courage mean.

Thursday 7th November
Luke 15:1–10

Now all the tax collectors and sinners were coming near to listen to him. And the Pharisees and the scribes were grumbling and saying, "This fellow welcomes sinners and eats with them." So he told them this parable: "Which one of you, having a hundred sheep and losing one of them, does not leave the ninety-nine in the wilderness and go after the one that is lost until he finds it? When he has found it, he lays it on his shoulders and rejoices. And when he comes home, he calls together his friends and neighbors, saying to them, 'Rejoice with me, for I have found my sheep that was lost.' Just so, I tell you, there will be more joy in heaven over one sinner who repents than over ninety-nine righteous persons who need no repentance. Or what woman having ten silver coins, if she loses one of them, does not light a lamp, sweep the house, and search carefully until she finds it? When she has found it, she calls together her friends and neighbors, saying, 'Rejoice with me, for I have found the coin that I had lost.' Just so, I tell you, there is joy in the presence of the angels of God over one sinner who repents."

• Think of the trouble you go to in searching for something you have lost. The search is more thorough when what we have lost is valuable. Jesus gives us two examples of people searching for what is precious to them. And we hear of the joy that comes when they find it. He uses these examples to explain to us the sense of how God seeks us, and his joy when our friendship with him is renewed. His searching for us cost him more than just the search: it cost him his life.

• What does this Scripture verse tell me about God? Is it not foolish to go after a lost sheep and neglect the ninety-nine? Who are sinners in my eyes? How do I cope with my disapproval of sinners?

Friday 8th November
Luke 16:1–8

Then Jesus said to the disciples, "There was a rich man who had a manager, and charges were brought to him that this man was squandering his property. So he summoned him and said to him, 'What is this that I hear about you? Give me an account of your management, because you cannot be my manager any longer.' Then the manager said to himself, 'What will I do, now that my master is taking the position away from me? I am not strong enough to dig, and I am ashamed to beg. I have decided what to do so that, when I am dismissed as manager, people may welcome me into their homes.' So, summoning his master's debtors one by one, he asked the first, 'How much do you owe my master?' He answered, 'A hundred jugs of olive oil.' He said to him, 'Take your bill, sit down quickly, and make it fifty.' Then he asked another, 'And how much do you owe?' He replied, 'A hundred containers of wheat.' He said to him, 'Take your bill and make it eighty.' And his master commended the dishonest manager because he had acted shrewdly; for the children of this age are more shrewd in dealing with their own generation than are the children of light."

• Jesus makes the point that we should take stock of how we stand with God. We have our weaknesses, perhaps, at times, squandering our

God-given gifts. In the end, our God is a God of compassion on whom we depend for forgiveness.

- There was nothing that couldn't speak to Jesus about the kingdom of God! I ask the Holy Spirit to help me look at my life and to help me, rather than being put off by what seems scandalous, to be encouraged to use my energies assiduously in the service of the gospel.

Saturday 9th November
John 2:13–22

The Passover of the Jews was near, and Jesus went up to Jerusalem. In the temple he found people selling cattle, sheep, and doves, and the money changers seated at their tables. Making a whip of cords, he drove all of them out of the temple, both the sheep and the cattle. He also poured out the coins of the money changers and overturned their tables. He told those who were selling the doves, "Take these things out of here! Stop making my Father's house a marketplace!" His disciples remembered that it was written, "Zeal for your house will consume me." The Jews then said to him, "What sign can you show us for doing this?" Jesus answered them, "Destroy this temple, and in three days I will raise it up." The Jews then said, "This temple has been under construction for forty-six years, and will you raise it up in three days?" But he was speaking of the temple of his body. After he was raised from the dead, his disciples remembered that he had said this; and they believed the scripture and the word that Jesus had spoken.

- Jesus cautions us against being careless or blasé. I think again about how I need to take him seriously, reviewing my life with the help of the Holy Spirit so I may see how I honor what is really important.

- In imagination I stand in the temple courtyard as the young rabbi from Galilee enters. I notice the courtyard, the sounds, the smells, the rattle of coins on the tables, the reek and cries of the animals. I watch Jesus, see the blood rush to his face. He has come to reverence the temple and to pray. Instead he finds all the focus is on business. Suddenly I sense a whirlwind of anger as he whips the hucksters and scatters their money. This is a new side of Jesus and it shakes me. I stay with it.

November 10—November 16

Something to think and pray about each day this week:

Nature's resilience to harsh conditions and extremes of weather is quite amazing. Different creatures adapt in different ways. Some dig themselves into burrows to ride out the winter storms, while those with wings take off to warmer climes, risking hazardous migratory journeys. What about us? How do we react when things get tough? Perhaps nature's wintering can teach us something. Will we dig in and hide until the troubles have passed? Will we try to fly away in the hope of escaping them? Maybe wisdom invites us to do neither, and both. Not to hide away, but to go deeper into our hearts and draw on resources we perhaps never knew we possessed. Not to flee, but to rise above the immediate situation, and see it from a higher perspective. What difficulties or trouble do you face now? What's your instinct? Burrow? Fly? How might you modify your way of reacting?

—Margaret Silf in *Daily Inspiration for Women*

The Presence of God

"Be still and know that I am God!" Lord, your words lead us to the calmness and greatness of your presence.

Freedom

If God were trying to tell me something, would I know?
If God were reassuring me or challenging me, would I notice?
I ask for the grace to be free of my own preoccupations
and open to what God may be saying to me.

Consciousness

In the presence of my loving Creator, I look honestly at my feelings over the past day: the highs, the lows, and the level ground. Can I see where the Lord has been present?

The Word

In this expectant state of mind, please read the text for the day with confidence. Believe that the Holy Spirit is present and may reveal whatever the passage has to say to you. Read reflectively, listening with a third ear to what may be going on in your heart. (Please turn to the Scripture on the following pages. Inspiration points are there, should you need them. When you are ready, return here to continue.)

Conversation

Remembering that I am still in God's presence,
I imagine Jesus standing or sitting beside me,
and I say whatever is on my mind, whatever is in my heart,
speaking as one friend to another.

Conclusion

Glory be to the Father, and to the Son, and to the Holy Spirit,
As it was in the beginning, is now and ever shall be,
World without end. Amen.

Sunday 10th November
Luke 20:27–38

Some Sadducees, those who say there is no resurrection, came to Jesus and asked him a question, "Teacher, Moses wrote for us that if a man's brother dies, leaving a wife but no children, the man shall marry the widow and raise up children for his brother. Now there were seven brothers; the first married, and died childless; then the second and the third married her, and so in the same way all seven died childless. Finally the woman also died. In the resurrection, therefore, whose wife will the woman be? For the seven had married her." Jesus said to them, "Those who belong to this age marry and are given in marriage; but those who are considered worthy of a place in that age and in the resurrection from the dead neither marry nor are given in marriage. Indeed they cannot die anymore, because they are like angels and are children of God, being children of the resurrection. And the fact that the dead are raised Moses himself showed, in the story about the bush, where he speaks of the Lord as the God of Abraham, the God of Isaac, and the God of Jacob. Now he is God not of the dead, but of the living; for to him all of them are alive."

- By answering the exaggerated story of the Sadducees, who did not believe in the resurrection, Jesus points out that the resurrected state is a new creation by which we are sharing in the divine life of God. It is different from our present life but a continuation nonetheless of our personalities, as molded by our present life.

- To believe in your own personal resurrection is a wonderful gift in this life. It gives meaning to all that makes up your life. It is expressed also in our prayers that we offer for the repose of the souls of all those who have gone before us, which we emphasize during this month of November.

Monday 11th November
Luke 17:1–6

Jesus said to his disciples, "Occasions for stumbling are bound to come, but woe to anyone by whom they come! It would be better for you if a millstone were hung around your neck and you were thrown into the sea than for you to cause one of these little ones to stumble. Be on your guard! If another disciple sins, you must rebuke the offender, and if there is repentance, you must forgive. And if the same person sins against you seven times a day, and turns back to you seven times and says, 'I repent,' you must forgive." The apostles said to the Lord, "Increase our faith!" The Lord replied, "If you had faith the size of a mustard seed, you could say to this mulberry tree, 'Be uprooted and planted in the sea,' and it would obey you."

- "Forgive us our trespasses," we say repeatedly to God—and we need to repeat it as we trespass again and again. You tell me, Lord, to be as patient with others' repentance as you are with mine. Thank you, Lord. I needed this reminder. Forgiveness is not a cover-all blanket but a reaching out toward the one who repents. You bid me be discerning, not foolish; but when I forgive, I must bury the hatchet without marking the spot.

- Living among others calls for care and attention to how I am in my relationships; I ask God to help me to see how I help others to growth by how I give attention and by how I forgive.

Tuesday 12th November

Luke 17:7–10

[Jesus said,] "Who among you would say to your slave who has just come in from ploughing or tending sheep in the field, 'Come here at once and take your place at the table'? Would you not rather say to him, 'Prepare supper for me, put on your apron and serve me while I eat and drink; later you may eat and drink'? Do you thank the slave for doing what was commanded? So you also, when you have done all that you were ordered to do, say, 'We are worthless slaves; we have done only what we ought to have done!'"

- It is not easy to think of myself as a slave or servant. While I may want to serve generously, I admit that I also want appreciation in return. Perhaps I need to pray for greater freedom—freedom to serve without needing reward or recognition.

- A servant has a role, competence, and limits to her work and considers the will of another. Jesus does not want to enslave me but asks me to consider where I notice the limits of my service.

Wednesday 13th November
Luke 17:11–19

On the way to Jerusalem Jesus was going through the region between Samaria and Galilee. As he entered a village, ten lepers approached him. Keeping their distance, they called out, saying, "Jesus, Master, have mercy on us!" When he saw them, he said to them, "Go and show yourselves to the priests." And as they went, they were made clean. Then one of them, when he saw that he was healed, turned back, praising God with a loud voice. He prostrated himself at Jesus' feet and thanked him. And he was a Samaritan. Then Jesus asked, "Were not ten made clean? But the other nine, where are they? Was none of them found to return and give praise to God except this foreigner?" Then he said to him, "Get up and go on your way; your faith has made you well."

• In returning to Jesus, the Samaritan heard Jesus bless and encourage him. Taking time to be grateful and addressing myself to God allows me to receive a deeper blessing in hearing God's response.

• Saint Ignatius prized gratitude highly; it is an attitude that keeps us aware of how we are blessed and of who blesses us. If I can graciously receive the gratitude of others, I allow what God does in my life to be seen and appreciated.

Thursday 14th November
Luke 17:20–25

Once Jesus was asked by the Pharisees when the kingdom of God was coming, and he answered, "The kingdom of God is not coming with things that can be observed; nor will they say, 'Look, here it is!' or 'There it is!' For, in fact, the kingdom of God is among you." Then he said to the disciples, "The days are coming when you will long to see one of the days of the Son of Man, and you will not see it. They will say to you, 'Look there!' or 'Look here!' Do not go, do not set off in pursuit. For as the lightning flashes and lights up the sky from one side to the other, so will the Son of Man be in his day. But first he must endure much suffering and be rejected by this generation."

• The kingdom of God is beyond the sight of many; I ask God to bless me that I may see how God's Spirit is already at work in the world around me. I might look again at where I feel most challenged, in the hope of seeing how God might be working for good.

- This is the tension of every Christian: to hope that God will intervene and bring about a better world, and at the same time to work and act, knowing that it all depends on us. Lord, you are warning me not to be distracted by scaremongers and prophets who claim private revelations about the end of the world. It is our world; we must shape it and care for it with patience and courage.

Friday 15th November
Luke 17:26–37

[Jesus said,] "Just as it was in the days of Noah, so too it will be in the days of the Son of Man. They were eating and drinking, and marrying and being given in marriage, until the day Noah entered the ark, and the flood came and destroyed all of them. Likewise, just as it was in the days of Lot: they were eating and drinking, buying and selling, planting and building, but on the day that Lot left Sodom, it rained fire and sulphur from heaven and destroyed all of them—it will be like that on the day that the Son of Man is revealed. On that day, anyone on the housetop who has belongings in the house must not come down to take them away; and likewise anyone in the field must not turn back. Remember Lot's wife. Those who try to make their life secure will lose it, but those who lose their life will keep it. I tell you, on that night there will be two in one bed; one will be taken and the other left. There will be two women grinding meal together; one will be taken and the other left." Then they asked him, "Where, Lord?" He said to them, "Where the corpse is, there the vultures will gather."

- In this month of November, church tradition suggests that we recall those who have gone before us and that we think of our own passing from this life and also, as this text reminds us, of the eventual ending of the world.

- As we know from experience, many overwhelming events catch us by surprise, just when we think that ordinary life will continue as usual. These moments often cause us to stop and think: What is it all about and what are we really living for? God, please help me live in the confidence of your love, knowing that all sorts of events will catch me by surprise but that you have made a way for your people.

Saturday 16th November
Luke 18:1–8

Then Jesus told them a parable about their need to pray always and not to lose heart. He said, "In a certain city there was a judge who neither feared God nor had respect for people. In that city there was a widow who kept coming to him and saying, 'Grant me justice against my opponent.' For a while he refused; but later he said to himself, 'Though I have no fear of God and no respect for anyone, yet because this widow keeps bothering me, I will grant her justice, so that she may not wear me out by continually coming.'" And the Lord said, "Listen to what the unjust judge says. And will not God grant justice to his chosen ones who cry to him day and night? Will he delay long in helping them? I tell you, he will quickly grant justice to them. And yet, when the Son of Man comes, will he find faith on earth?"

• Our prayers become an exercise in pure faith. But our prayer is also a conversation with a very close friend who knows best what we need and frequently answers us in a surprising way.

• Do I find it easy to persist in praying for what I need? I might be surprised to discover that prolonged prayer opens my heart even more to God's provident care in my life, so that I find myself growing in trust.

November 17—November 23

Something to think and pray about each day this week:

Through concrete action, Jesus shows us how God loves. In the Gospels we see Jesus showing us how God loves through healing, forgiveness, mercy, and compassion. Jesus sees and responds to the deepest needs of human hearts. To a blind person he gives sight; to a paralyzed person he gives the ability to stand up and walk; to a leper and social outcast he gives cleansing and restoration to community; to a woman isolated by her illness he gives healing in both body and soul; to a person with a sinful history he gives mercy and hope for a better future. Jesus shows us how God looks at us with eyes of compassion and love, accepting us where we are and loving us as we are. Jesus doesn't wait for people to be perfect or have their lives in order or for them to sin no more. Rather, Jesus enters the messiness of humanity and encounters people along the way in their brokenness, hurt, and mess.

—Becky Eldredge, *Busy Lives & Restless Souls*

The Presence of God

As I sit here, the beating of my heart,
the ebb and flow of my breathing, the movements of my mind
are all signs of God's ongoing creation of me.
I pause for a moment and become aware
of this presence of God within me.

Freedom

It is so easy to get caught up
with the trappings of wealth in this life.
Grant, O Lord, that I may be free
from greed and selfishness.
Remind me that the best things in life are free:
Love, laughter, caring, and sharing.

Consciousness

Knowing that God loves me unconditionally, I can afford to be honest about how I am.
How has the day been, and how do I feel now? I share my feelings openly with the Lord.

The Word

Lord Jesus, you became human to communicate with me.
You walked and worked on this earth.
You endured the heat and struggled with the cold.
All your time on this earth was spent in caring for humanity.
You healed the sick, you raised the dead.
Most important of all, you saved me from death.
(Please turn to the Scripture on the following pages. Inspiration points are there, should you need them. When you are ready, return here to continue.)

Conversation

Sometimes I wonder what I might say if I were to meet you in person, Lord.
I think I might say "Thank you" because you are always there for me.

Conclusion

I thank God for these moments we have spent together and for any insights I have been given concerning the text.

Sunday 17th November

Luke 21:5–19

When some were speaking about the temple, how it was adorned with beautiful stones and gifts dedicated to God, he said, "As for these things that you see, the days will come when not one stone will be left upon another; all will be thrown down." They asked him, "Teacher, when will this be, and what will be the sign that this is about to take place?" And he said, "Beware that you are not led astray; for many will come in my name and say, 'I am he!' and, 'The time is near!' Do not go after them. When you hear of wars and insurrections, do not be terrified; for these things must take place first, but the end will not follow immediately." Then he said to them, "Nation will rise against nation, and kingdom against kingdom; there will be great earthquakes, and in various places famines and plagues; and there will be dreadful portents and great signs from heaven. But before all this occurs, they will arrest you and persecute you; they will hand you over to synagogues and prisons, and you will be brought before kings and governors because of my name. This will give you an opportunity to testify. So make up your minds not to prepare your defense in advance; for I will give you words and a wisdom that none of your opponents will be able to withstand or contradict. You will be betrayed even by parents and brothers, by relatives and friends; and they will put some of you to death. You will be hated by all because of my name. But not a hair of your head will perish. By your endurance you will gain your souls."

- It is remarkable that Jesus' prophecy is being fulfilled in our own time. The level of unrest among people and even in nature itself is frightening. The Christian message of "love your neighbor as yourself" stands out in complete contrast to this scene. The little we can do is not in vain.

- Pope Francis has highlighted the need for compassion in our dealings with one another. We can see this intervention by Pope Francis as coming from Jesus, when he said in the text above, "I will give you words and wisdom that none of your opponents can withstand or contradict."

Monday 18th November
Luke 18:35–43

As he approached Jericho, a blind man was sitting by the roadside begging. When he heard a crowd going by, he asked what was happening. They told him, "Jesus of Nazareth is passing by." Then he shouted, "Jesus, Son of David, have mercy on me!" Those who were in front sternly ordered him to be quiet; but he shouted even more loudly, "Son of David, have mercy on me!" Jesus stood still and ordered the man to be brought to him; and when he came near, he asked him, "What do you want me to do for you?" He said, "Lord, let me see again." Jesus said to him, "Receive your sight; your faith has saved you." Immediately he regained his sight and followed him, glorifying God; and all the people, when they saw it, praised God.

- How is life going for you? Did you ever feel that you have lost something that once was precious to you? Often we are afraid to turn to the Lord to ask him to restore or compensate us in some way that would give us life again. To turn to God when we are suffering loss is a great act of faith and trust.

- The crowd could not relate to the depth of the blind man's need and tried to hush him. His insistence brought Jesus to a standstill and saw his desire acknowledged and answered. I make my prayer with the same confidence and trust that my faith will be seen and rewarded.

Tuesday 19th November
Luke 19:1–10

He entered Jericho and was passing through it. A man was there named Zacchaeus; he was a chief tax collector and was rich. He was trying to see who Jesus was, but on account of the crowd he could not, because he was short in stature. So he ran ahead and climbed a sycamore tree to see him, because he was going to pass that way. When Jesus came to the place, he looked up and said to him, "Zacchaeus, hurry and come down; for I must stay at your house today." So he hurried down and was happy to welcome him. All who saw it began to grumble and said, "He has gone to be the guest of one who is a sinner." Zacchaeus stood there and said to the Lord, "Look, half of my possessions, Lord, I will give to the poor; and if I have defrauded anyone of anything, I will pay back four times as much." Then Jesus said to him, "Today salvation has come to this house, because he too is a son of Abraham. For the Son of Man came to seek out and to save the lost."

- We have to admire Zacchaeus. He risked ridicule to see Jesus, but his good will was more than rewarded by Jesus, who invited himself to Zacchaeus's house. The onlookers grumbled that Jesus would go to the house of a sinner. What would my reaction have been had I been there? I ask for real repentance for my sins and to have a strong faith in the surprising mercy of God as we see it in Jesus. Do I really believe that the Son of Man came primarily to seek out and save what is lost?

- Zacchaeus wanted to see who Jesus was by looking at him from a *safe position*. But you cannot know anyone just by looking at them; something else has to happen. Jesus struck up a relationship with Zacchaeus, and this caused a great change in his future way of living. When am I tempted to observe Jesus rather than walk with him?

Wednesday 20th November
Luke 19:11–28

As they were listening to this, he went on to tell a parable, because he was near Jerusalem, and because they supposed that the kingdom of God was to appear immediately. So he said, "A nobleman went to a distant country to get royal power for himself and then return. He summoned ten of his slaves, and gave them ten pounds, and said to them, 'Do business with these until I come back.' But the citizens of his country hated him and sent a delegation after him, saying, 'We do not want this man to rule over us.' When he returned, having received royal power, he ordered these slaves, to whom he had given the money, to be summoned so that he might find out what they had gained by trading. The first came forward and said, 'Lord, your pound has made ten more pounds.' He said to him, 'Well done, good slave! Because you have been trustworthy in a very small thing, take charge of ten cities.' Then the second came, saying, 'Lord, your pound has made five pounds.' He said to him, 'And you, rule over five cities.' Then the other came, saying, 'Lord, here is your pound. I wrapped it up in a piece of cloth, for I was afraid of you, because you are a harsh man; you take what you did not deposit, and reap what you did not sow.' He said to him, 'I will judge you by your own words, you wicked slave! You knew, did you, that I was a harsh man, taking what I did not deposit and reaping what I did not sow? Why then did you not put my money into the bank? Then when I returned, I could have collected it with interest.' He said to the bystanders, 'Take the pound from him and give it to the one who has ten pounds.' (And they said to him, 'Lord, he has ten pounds!') 'I tell you, to all those who have, more will be given; but from those who have nothing, even what they have will be taken away. But as for these enemies of mine who did not want me to be king over them—bring them here and slaughter them in my presence.'"

• Two of the servants took the risk in investing the money of the unpopular nobleman. I can easily find reasons for keeping quiet about my faith and practice, my talents and abilities. I pray that I might learn to use my opportunities well.

• One servant in the story was paralyzed by his fear. I can recognize such fear and hesitation in myself. I ask God for the courage I need.

Thursday 21st November
Luke 19:41–44

As he came near and saw the city, he wept over it, saying, "If you, even you, had only recognized on this day the things that make for peace! But now they are hidden from your eyes. Indeed, the days will come upon you, when your enemies will set up ramparts around you and surround you, and hem you in on every side. They will crush you to the ground, you and your children within you, and they will not leave within you one stone upon another; because you did not recognize the time of your visitation from God."

• Peace and contentment are two blessings that we desire, and when we lack them, we are greatly disturbed. Jesus, too, was disturbed and wept at the future destruction of his beloved Jerusalem. He offers us a peace that the world cannot give and that can only be found in friendship with him. Stand quietly beside Jesus and allow yourself to be drawn into his lament.

• Jesus wept over his city. The Semites who live there, some Arab, some Jew, still weep over it. We who live far away cannot forget Jesus' city. "If I forget you, O Jerusalem, let my right hand wither! Let my tongue cling to the roof of my mouth, if I do not remember you, if I do not set Jerusalem above my highest joy" (Psalm 137:5-6). Lord God of Jews, Muslims, and Christians, look with pity on Jerusalem, so that she may cease to be a sign of contradiction and become a mother to all the children of Abraham.

Friday 22nd November

Luke 19:45–48

Then he entered the temple and began to drive out those who were selling things there; and he said, "It is written, 'My house shall be a house of prayer'; but you have made it a den of robbers." Every day he was teaching in the temple. The chief priests, the scribes, and the leaders of the people kept looking for a way to kill him; but they did not find anything they could do, for all the people were spellbound by what they heard.

• The contrast between the ideal and the reality struck Jesus forcibly: the holy house had become a commercial opportunity; the needs of the hungry people were ignored by the scheming authorities. If I am confronted by everyday tensions between ideals and experience, I pray that I may not become cynical but stand with Jesus, keeping in mind what God desires.

• Although he saw the contradictions there, Jesus chose the temple as the place to which he went to teach. I ask Jesus to help me witness to his good news wherever I am, even if the place doesn't seem ideal to me.

Saturday 23rd November

Luke 20:27–40

Some Sadducees, those who say there is no resurrection, came to him and asked him a question, "Teacher, Moses wrote for us that if a man's brother dies, leaving a wife but no children, the man shall marry the widow and raise up children for his brother. Now there were seven brothers; the first married, and died childless; then the second and the third married her, and so in the same way all seven died childless. Finally the woman also died. In the resurrection, therefore, whose wife will the woman be? For the seven had married her." Jesus said to them, "Those who belong to this age marry and are given in marriage; but those who are considered worthy of a place in that age and in the resurrection from the dead neither marry nor are given in marriage. Indeed they cannot die anymore, because they are like angels and are children of God, being children of the resurrection. And the fact that the dead are raised Moses himself showed, in the story about the bush, where he speaks of the Lord as the God of Abraham, the God of Isaac, and the God of Jacob. Now he is God not of the dead, but of the living; for to him all of them are alive." Then some of the scribes answered, "Teacher, you have spoken well." For they no longer dared to ask him another question.

- The question asked by the Sadducees is somewhat contrived, intended not to seek clarity but to present a conundrum. It sometimes happens that people we encounter present us with big imponderables, sure that the answer will elude us too. I pray for the wisdom I need not to be drawn into traps of pride or intelligence and for the courage to live in the simplicity to which Jesus calls me.

- Jesus often shows the poor and simple as being exemplars of God's kingdom; I pray for the kind of intelligence that Jesus values, careful not to get caught up in clever distractions.

November 24—November 30

Something to think and pray about each day this week:

Transition is the bridge that leads from the no longer to the not yet. Nobody can predict what that bridge is going to look like. It may be obvious and sturdy, and we may find it easily through the fogs of our bewilderment. Or it may be rickety and clearly unsafe, and we hardly dare entrust our weight to it. The point is, however, that we have to cross the bridge, and as we risk that crossing, we will discover that the bridge itself is our guide and mentor, and it has everything to teach us about the path that lies ahead, beyond the transition. In fact, we will learn much more on that bridge, about ourselves, about life, and about God, in our transitions than on all the smoother pathways that we journey.

—Margaret Silf, *The Other Side of Chaos*

The Presence of God
At any time of the day or night we can call on Jesus.
He is always waiting, listening for our call.
What a wonderful blessing.
No phone needed, no emails, just a whisper.

Freedom
Lord grant me the grace to have freedom of the spirit. Cleanse my heart and soul so that I may live joyously in your love.

Consciousness
Knowing that God loves me unconditionally, I look honestly over the past day, its events, and my feelings. Do I have something to be grateful for? Then I give thanks. Is there something I am sorry for? Then I ask forgiveness.

The Word
The word of God comes down to us through the Scriptures.
May the Holy Spirit enlighten my mind and my heart
to respond to the gospel teachings:
to love my neighbor as myself,
to care for my sisters and brothers in Christ.
(Please turn to the Scripture on the following pages. Inspiration points are there, should you need them. When you are ready, return here to continue.)

Conversation
I know with certainty that there were times when you carried me, Lord. There were times when it was through your strength that I got through the dark times in my life.

Conclusion
Glory be to the Father, and to the Son, and to the Holy Spirit,
As it was in the beginning, is now and ever shall be,
World without end. Amen.

Sunday 24th November
Our Lord Jesus Christ, King of the Universe
Luke 23:35–43

And the people stood by, watching; but the leaders scoffed at Jesus, saying, "He saved others; let him save himself if he is the Messiah of God, his chosen one!" The soldiers also mocked him, coming up and offering him sour wine, and saying, "If you are the King of the Jews, save yourself!" There was also an inscription over him, "This is the King of the Jews." One of the criminals who were hanged there kept deriding him and saying, "Are you not the Messiah? Save yourself and us!" But the other rebuked him, saying, "Do you not fear God, since you are under the same sentence of condemnation? And we indeed have been condemned justly, for we are getting what we deserve for our deeds, but this man has done nothing wrong." Then he said, "Jesus, remember me when you come into your kingdom." He replied, "Truly I tell you, today you will be with me in Paradise."

- This is one of the most striking passages in Scripture. I meditate on this conversation between Jesus and the two thieves. What stands out for me? What challenges me or gives me hope?

- The central message of Jesus, eager to free us from our sins and grant us the gift of everlasting life, brings out the deep meaning of the feast of Our Lord Jesus Christ, King of the Universe, which we celebrate today.

Monday 25th November
Luke 21:1–4

He looked up and saw rich people putting their gifts into the treasury; he also saw a poor widow put in two small copper coins. He said, "Truly I tell you, this poor widow has put in more than all of them; for all of them have contributed out of their abundance, but she out of her poverty has put in all she had to live on."

- Being poor, the widow knew the value of what she gave. If I am aware of how little I have to offer, may it not stop me from improving the situation of those who have even less.

- The poor woman's simple act stirred in Jesus appreciation; he saw the woman's action as an invitation to live with trust. I ask God to help me observe what is going on around me, to see and to appreciate even small actions of love and care.

Tuesday 26th November
Luke 21:5–11

When some were speaking about the temple, how it was adorned with beautiful stones and gifts dedicated to God, Jesus said, "As for these things that you see, the days will come when not one stone will be left upon another; all will be thrown down." They asked him, "Teacher, when will this be, and what will be the sign that this is about to take place?" And he said, "Beware that you are not led astray; for many will come in my name and say, 'I am he!' and, 'The time is near!' Do not go after them. When you hear of wars and insurrections, do not be terrified; for these things must take place first, but the end will not follow immediately." Then he said to them, "Nation will rise against nation, and kingdom against kingdom; there will be great earthquakes, and in various places famines and plagues; and there will be dreadful portents and great signs from heaven."

- Many of the happenings spoken by Jesus in today's Gospel have been taking place over the centuries, such as dreadful wars and natural catastrophes. These are continuing in our time. At a personal level, I can remind myself how tenuous life is and how all things in this world are passing. This helps me reflect on what has true value.

- Jesus knew that there would be many claims on our attention, many distractions that might lead us astray. My time of prayer may help me see who Jesus is to me and remind me to value how I receive his word. I ask God to help me not to be led astray by persuasive voices.

Wednesday 27th November
Luke 21:12–19

[Jesus said,] "But before all this occurs, they will arrest you and persecute you; they will hand you over to synagogues and prisons, and you will be brought before kings and governors because of my name. This will give you an opportunity to testify. So make up your minds not to prepare your defense in advance; for I will give you words and a wisdom that none of your opponents will be able to withstand or contradict. You will be betrayed even by parents and brothers, by relatives and friends; and they will put some of you to death. You will be hated by all because of my name. But not a hair of your head will perish. By your endurance you will gain your souls."

- Many people today are suffering because of lack of freedom to live their beliefs. For many it can be difficult to openly profess their faith. It is important to pray for the church and also for those who find it difficult to believe in a God of love.

- The preparation you need to make: don't make any preparation! The call to trust challenges our habits of anxiety and worry, and it's an invitation to live in the present moment, where Jesus meets us and says, "Peace be with you!"

Thursday 28th November
Luke 21:20–28

Jesus said to his disciples, "When you see Jerusalem surrounded by armies, then know that its desolation has come near. Then those in Judea must flee to the mountains, and those inside the city must leave it, and those out in the country must not enter it; for these are days of vengeance, as a fulfillment of all that is written. Woe to those who are pregnant and to those who are nursing infants in those days! For there will be great distress on the earth and wrath against this people; they will fall by the edge of the sword and be taken away as captives among all nations; and Jerusalem will be trampled on by the Gentiles, until the times of the Gentiles are fulfilled. There will be signs in the sun, the moon, and the stars, and on the earth distress among nations confused by the roaring of the sea and the waves. People will faint from fear and foreboding of what is coming upon the world, for the powers of the heavens will be shaken. Then they will see 'the Son of Man coming in a cloud' with power and great glory. Now when these things begin to take place, stand up and raise your heads, because your redemption is drawing near."

- This text describes the terrible destruction of Jerusalem and the events that will signal the end of the world. The final sentence sounds strange in the light of the signs mentioned. What is Christ saying to us here?

- Despite these happenings, the thought of Christ's second coming gives us the hope of redemption. I ponder that my Savior and friend, Jesus, is also the one who will arrive in great power and glory. What does this mean to me?

Friday 29th November
Luke 21:29–33

Then Jesus told them a parable: "Look at the fig tree and all the trees; as soon as they sprout leaves you can see for yourselves and know that summer is already near. So also, when you see these things taking place, you know that the kingdom of God is near. Truly I tell you, this generation will not pass away until all things have taken place. Heaven and earth will pass away, but my words will not pass away."

• This parable could be used to illustrate part of what we mean today by *discernment*. The word is applied to a process of searching for God's will and deciding how to respond to it. Through Gospel contemplation we allow ourselves to absorb the attitudes and values of Jesus. These then become the criteria by which we evaluate our situation and the particular issue calling for a decision. In a way we are looking for signs. These will not be cosmic disturbances in the heavens but inner movements of spiritual consolation or desolation.

• As the liturgical year ends, is there anything in my life that I need to discern? If so, I pray that I may see the signs and interpret them correctly.

Saturday 30th November
Matthew 4:18–22

As he walked by the Sea of Galilee, he saw two brothers, Simon, who is called Peter, and Andrew his brother, casting a net into the sea—for they were fishermen. And he said to them, "Follow me, and I will make you fish for people." Immediately they left their nets and followed him. As he went from there, he saw two other brothers, James son of Zebedee and his brother John, in the boat with their father Zebedee, mending their nets, and he called them. Immediately they left the boat and their father, and followed him.

• Can you recall events or occasions when you changed direction? For example, falling in love, being guided by a teacher or friend, a hurt or loss, great or small? These calls come to us throughout our lives, and they can have a great effect on us. We are the product of our decisions, and we have a friend in the Lord who wishes to guide us.

- Simon Peter and Andrew heard the voice of Jesus as he walked by; James and John, while at their work, heeded and responded. Jesus speaks to them, not in a time of retreat, meeting them at their work. What does it mean for me to work in a way that keeps me tuned in to a message that is for my salvation?

THE IRISH JESUITS ✳ Sacred Space

A Little Book of Encouragement

SACRED SPACE